AN AMATEUR
AT THE KEYBOARD

An
AMATEUR
at the
KEYBOARD

being
an Invitation to the Keyboard
and its Pleasures, a Discussion and Brief History
of its Literature, and Advice how
one may serve the Community as Accompanist,
Maker of Programs, Critic,
or by encouraging the Public Music,

written for the Amateur, *or* Lover of Music

by

PETER YATES

London
GEORGE ALLEN & UNWIN LTD

PRINTED IN GREAT BRITAIN BY
JOHN DICKENS AND CO LTD, NORTHAMPTON

DEDICATION

My friend Wesley Kuhnle died before the final draft of this book was written. He had read and approved the substance of the first draft; the two Appendixes were written in collaboration with and revised by him. He knew that this book was dedicated in admiration of him.

Wesley Kuhnle had devoted more than thirty years to the study of musical keyboard practice in every aspect: the uses of the keyboard, the correct reading, elaboration, and embellishment of notation, the building and registration of instruments, and the practical consequences of the historic European tunings.

He continued the revolt, begun in the 1890s by Arnold Dolmetsch, against the decline of variety in musical intonation and in keyboard playing. He recognized the great authority of Wanda Landowska, even while he deplored the frequent waste of that authority in displays of alternating virtuosity and pedantry. In his own playing he forsook the virtuosity that is no more than the extra horsepower of a car that does not need it. He forbade himself pedantry by following the practice of earlier centuries that each repetition of a movement should be played with some difference. In this belief he said to me earnestly at our last meeting: "I make one stipulation: nobody should ever imitate what I have done or my solutions." He meant that no one should imitate an embellishment or a phrase or movement as he had played it; to do so was to evade understanding and to perpetuate merely one of the many possible readings. That is why the Appendix on embellishment in this book contains no notated examples.

He practised alone in the evenings during his last years, and when the street was empty would tape a reading that he felt to be in shape, repeating it several times, perhaps, or coming back to it another night. From these recordings he chose the best single reading and abided by it, though one might hear flaws, because the best was that which revealed as much of the possibility within a composition as he could at one time read from it.

Before his death he had completed his *History of Tuning* on tape, with the tuning orders described so that one could tune from the keyboard in the old fashion, and the first part of his *Historical Survey of Keyboard Music*—his studies in keyboard practice: both with spoken text and many performed examples. His work, when known and appreciated and put to use, should help to revive the personal enjoyment of the keyboard instruments and their literature which is the purpose of this book, replacing the habits of reproductive note-reading and memorization which are nearly all that remains of a great art.

He was unappreciated in his musical community but would not leave it; he retired from public playing and devoted his time to perfecting his instruments and to the studies which came to fruition in his recorded tapes. One can learn more about the five centuries of keyboard music from his taped examples than by reading books. Nothing among the present developments in new composition reaches towards the future of music more consequently than his exposition of its recent past.

the mute
string
unbroken
speaks
the mind
that forsook
money
amusement
leaving
to the un-
forgiving
gift
that all
he had learned

PREFACE

Music exists as it is somehow performed, and each performance should be fresh. Any recorded performance is a single instance; it is not the composition itself but an example.

When did you last hear someone play an instrument for his own pleasure?

The nineteenth century brought into existence one entirely new situation: the absolute division between performer and audience. Our century has added another: the distinction between professional and amateur, which holds that no amateur, unless a student, should perform alone in public.

It isn't a conscious rule; it's a state of mind. But I can say with assurance, as one who has insisted on mingling amateur soloists with professionals in public recital, that the rule exists because plenty of people in the audience, and professional musicians, are determined to enforce it.

Every year in this country thousands of fine young musicians, discovering that there is no place for them in the professional concert business, not only cease their study of music but actually give up music. They don't keep up their skill and widen their knowledge of musical literature for their pleasure. Nobody has taught them to think of music as pleasure, except in listening to it, or that art is for maturity, or that it involves taste, judgement, and the use of the mind, except as somebody applies these critically to musical performance. No one seems to believe that exploring the literature of music for oneself can give a lifelong pleasure. Nor have these lost talents been educated to enjoy music as immediately and naturally as their neighbors enjoy playing golf or a good game of cards.

In our society we encourage children to make music; we expect any musical adolescent to become a prodigy; yet we regard as peculiar any adult who continues playing serious music for the fun of doing so—unless he teaches or earns money by it or performs as a member of a group.

If young musicians, for lack of another skill, grow up to become teachers, they take their satisfaction from their pupils; they teach but seldom play, as if they were unworthy, as if they had suffered a fatal, public condemnation. This is damnable nonsense, and the purpose of this book is to persuade many readers to think otherwise.

I have written a book directed to the *Amateur* in the original and live meaning of that word, the lover of his art. I hope to encourage tastes, knowledge, habits, and those uses of music that will serve the literate sight-reader, like myself, as well as the trained student who has been left shoaled at the end of his musical education, without musical career or purpose.

I speak to a new attitude, not now widely encouraged or cultivated, though quietly gaining ground among us, that looks to the arts not to be entertained by them but for enjoyment. That regards enjoyment as a discipline instead of an indulgence; a giving of ourselves in some measure to the art, instead of taking from it. That does not need audience or reward, because the enjoyment we achieve is the best measure of success. That leads us to open our minds to the whole art and know it as completely as opportunity and skill allow us, so that the commitments of taste are balanced by an uncommitted exploration, not always far upstream in musicological jungles but in the woods over the next ridge. That induces us to welcome, instead of keeping out, whatever is unknown to us.

In every generation the majority believe that music ended as an art something beyond fifty years ago. Such are the critics who wrote of Igor Stravinsky in his eightieth year that he had composed his best music before he was thirty. Their judgement had stood still, but his creation had not.

Let us be among those who communicate throughout society the strange information that music is not dead; music is still being created. So doing, we become ourselves companions of the living artist. And if from our understanding of music we draw right inference, we can welcome as if we were already posterity the unknown composer who is preparing the future in our midst.

This book is directed to three groups of readers.

There are, first, those readers who know little or nothing about music but have decided that they want to have some share in it for themselves.

I recall my own first failures in listening to music. Every gain in my capacity to hear music has been a rejection followed by an overcoming. Let no one who reads this book put it aside saying that he is incapable of it. He cannot be more incapable than I have been.

For this first type of reader I have begun every exposition in the most simple terms, hoping to assist him in becoming a more active and knowledgeable participant in music. Learning to read notes at the keyboard should be the least of his troubles; to do so is no more difficult than learning the typewriter keyboard.

The second group for whom I have written is the largest. They are all those who have learned to listen at ease and with some share of information to music of the standard repertoire, and those also who have learned to read notes and reproduce passages at the keyboard. I would stimulate them to change their passive appreciation into an actively participative enjoyment, to widen their reach of musical literature and extend their critical vocabulary. I urge them above all to make music for themselves.

For the third group, the musically skilled, their ability to make music, their presence in any audience can be used to the benefit of the community. I urge them not to let their skill and equipment rust, not to confine their enjoyment but to spread it abroad. They are or can be the true Amateurs.

In this book, as in my past writing about music, I have tried to avoid all but the most necessary language of the insider, and I have done without examples of notated music. Those who can interpret examples will know how to find them.

I pay proud tribute, as an Amateur, to the friends who have contributed to me of their enthusiasm, learning, and genius:

To Gerald Gross, who commissioned this book and found for

it the one title that made the writing of it necessary; to Wolfgang Sauerlander, who, acting for the publisher, endured the early stages of the manuscript, and Paula Van Doren who helped bring it to completion; and to her anonymous friend, an Amateur, who gave caustic and pertinent criticism;

to the composer-scholars Gerald Strang, Ingolf Dahl, and Lou Harrison, who read the manuscript to criticize it out of knowledge greater than my own;

to Sol Babitz, rediscoverer of the pre-Tourte violin and bow, for many discussions of rhythm and embellishment, and his examples;

to the late Charles Ives, Arnold Schoenberg, and pianist Richard Buhlig, to Igor Stravinsky, John Cage, Harry Partch, Lawrence Morton, and John Edmunds, who helped and glorified my musical self-education;

to Sister Magdalene Mary IHM, Rudolf Kolisch, and George Tremblay, for quotations;

to Eileen Strang, and Mary Jeanette and Bill Selwyn, for reading and commenting on the manuscript; to Gertrud Schoenberg, and to Veda and Paul Kuhnle, for practical help;

to my longtime friends Peyton Houston and Melissa Blake (Mrs. Charles Levitzky), in whose growing record libraries I began and sustained my musical education, for many years of encouragement;

to the music librarians of the Los Angeles Public Library, for many helpful courtesies; and to John DeKeyser, dealer in sheet music in Los Angeles, who for more than thirty years has granted, to poor and provident alike, immediate access to his shelves, stocked with early and contemporary music;

to my wife, Frances Mullen, whose playing opened to me, as it has to many others, a wider comprehension of the keyboard literature; whose gift made possible the formation of Evenings on the Roof;

and to the more than a hundred musicians who, sharing in the fifteen-year adventure of Evenings on the Roof, broadened and elevated my understanding of their art.

The list could go on extending, for I have come to music through my friends.

I owe a special statement of gratitude in memory of my favorite Amateur, the Honourable Roger North, Esq., for the several quotations in these pages from his Essays written during the years *c.* 1695–1728, transcribed and edited by John Wilson in his book *Roger North on Music* (London, Novello and Company Ltd., 1959). No writing about music at any period has given me more delight.

The author wishes to thank the following authors, or their representatives, and publishers for their kind permission to quote from copyright material:

Lou Harrison and Mercury Records for a selection from record-cover notes by Mr. Harrison for *Charles Ives, Sonata No. 1 for Violin and Piano,* Mercury Records MG50097.

Zoltán Kodály and Boosey & Hawkes for excerpt from Zoltán Kodály, "Folk Music and Art Music in Hungary," from *Tempo, A Quarterly Review of Modern Music,* Winter 1962–63.

G. & C. Merriam Company, by permission, for excerpt from *Webster's New Collegiate Dictionary,* copyright 1961 by G. & C. Merriam Co., Publishers of the Merriam-Webster Dictionaries. London: Hall.

W. W. Norton & Company, Inc., for excerpts from *Essay on the True Art of Playing Keyboard Instruments* by Carl Philipp Emanuel Bach, trans. and ed. William J. Mitchell; also for excerpts from J. N. Forkel, *On Johann Sebastian Bach's Life, Genius and Works,* from *The Bach Reader,* eds. Hans T. David and Arthur Mendel.

Novello & Company Ltd. for excerpt from *Roger North on Music,* ed. John Wilson.

Oxford University Press, Inc., for excerpts from *The Oxford Companion to Music,* 9th ed., by Percy Scholes.

Penguin Books Ltd. for excerpts from *Musical Instruments Through the Ages* by Cecil Clutton, ed. Anthony Baines.

Mrs. Gertrud Schoenberg and The Free Press of Glencoe for excerpts from *The Works of Arnold Schoenberg, a catalogue of his compositions, writings & paintings* by Josef Rufer, trans. Dika Newlin. London: Calder.

Mrs. Gertrud Schoenberg and The League of Composers for excerpts from Arnold Schoenberg, "Problems of Harmony," trans. Adolph Weiss, from *Modern Music, A Quarterly Review,* Vol. XI, No. 4.

Igor Stravinsky, Robert Craft, and Doubleday & Company, Inc., for excerpt from *Conversations with Igor Stravinsky* by Igor Stravinsky and Robert Craft. London: Faber.

CONTENTS

The Literature
of Keyboard
Music

MUSIC FOR
ONESELF

Suppose I were on a desert island. And I had with me only my Steinway—or a Bechstein had washed up on the beach. Precisely the situation of a person who, after looking at his piano as ornamental furniture for a dozen years or having put it out of mind as an instrument of forgotten learning, suddenly sits down at it and exposes the keys to his fingers.

If I could do no better, I should let my fingers play sound as a child fingerpaints, a good discipline for any adult. This is therapy; it may bring you release or to a relevation. Forget yourself and listen to the beauty of unharmonized sound. Then you will wish to learn how to read music.

If you read music, sit at the piano and let music come out. Forget about performance. Forget to be self-conscious. Forget the neighbors. Don't listen to yourself to criticize; listen for enjoyment.

Read—and let the message of the notation communicate directly to your fingers. Hands and eyes will work together, if you don't force them. As in all enterprises, it's the willing that inhibits. Willing sets up false goals by anticipation, cramps ease, knots muscles, erases naturalness. The professional performer, too, must overcome these problems.

When I sit at the keyboard and start playing myself back into music, time ceases. The masters of the keyboard are my companions, politely silent, not interfering, though they must deplore my clumsiness. I am my own explorer, my own interpreter, my own false absolute.

Learn to know, to play and share if you can, the greater part of musical literature that is never heard in public concert. Learn to read at the keyboard according to the style of each period. The information is there; all you need do is apply it. You cannot be more wrong than the ordinary recitalist who has never learned to use that information.

Mature in music as you wish to mature in wisdom. Bring your knowledge of music to the use of the community you live in. This does not mean hiring a hall and expecting your neighbors to buy tickets to hear you perform in public. Show your imagination, not your ego. Share music with your friends; be sensible, be modest, don't crave their attention.

I was invited to a home where my young hostess, having put the children to bed, first served us an unusual and well-prepared dinner, then before an invited audience of twenty friends sat at the harpsichord to read an exquisite recital—Bach, Couperin, Handel, Scarlatti. Afterwards she brought out an expertly home-baked, strawberry-covered cheesecake. Remembering her multiple skills, I bow to her.

Formerly she had hidden her musical gift in privacy and silence.

Music will not survive in the concert hall, if we do not keep it living in our homes.

Too many of the piano recitals of our childhood used to be—often they still are—made up of sweet tunes lethargically harmonized, undifferentiated strumming as emotion, flimsy decorative passage-work, skipping and swirling in arabesques instead of rhythm. Mothers and daughters dutifully endured such recitals; sons rebelled at practising for them; and fathers, when unable to escape these periodic rites, saw in them good proof that music is not for adult males.

Up to the full stretch of the individual span of attention, the ordinary human mind can respond to the challenge of first-rate art as willingly and capably as the mind of a professional, often with a more open expressiveness because it has not been committed in advance to any limiting prejudice. My experience in presenting concerts has proved to me that the male rises to the challenge of great or unusual music at least as actively as the female. He is more likely than his wife to be the record-collector, the devotee of Byrd, Berlioz, Bartók, or recondite jazz. When art or music has recaptured or awakened his fresh interest, he brings to it the full resources of his attention and will waste no time or thought on less than what he believes to be the best.

His belief may be no more than fashionable misinformation.

Do you have any music—I mean any printed music—in the house?

If you look under the top of the piano bench, you may find that copy of Mendelssohn's *Songs Without Words* which belonged to Grandmother when she was a girl. Or perhaps a copy of the Chopin *Nocturnes*. These will last you to struggle with a few days. Don't be discouraged by them.

Or you may come instead on an album of the type called *Piano Pieces Everybody Likes To Play*. These pieces, many of them the no longer popular grist of an earlier generation's piano recitals, will supply good mash for feeding. You should make the most of the opportunity they give you, trying to apply to this music whatever skill and taste you have. Some of these well-known melodies deserve careful reading. You can satisfy your wished-for virtuosity with them. They were composed for that purpose.

Or play hymns. Indeed, that's not a bad idea. Much hymn-writing may be stodgy and complacent in broken-down vertical harmonies, but it does preserve in harmonic narrowness the older habit of voices singing individual parts. One can learn from it.

From hymns one can move to Bach. That means going to Bach backwards, in the wrong direction, carrying all the wrong information from the wrong century. This is the backward path trodden by the organist, who tries to keep a balance between what he knows of music and what he has to do in church. Our musical taste, musical judgement, musical theory, and accepted rituals of performance look backwards in the same way, causing a mess of technical misunderstandings and false appreciation.

Anyone with some patience and a good amount of determination can begin playing Bach, the simple music the home-loving Cantor wrote for the education of his wife and children. Here is a complete musical education written out in music.

The patient and determined reader may also, if he has his heart set on self-improvement, go buy *The First Term at the*

Piano, the collections called *For Children*, and the first two or three books of *Mikrokosmos* by Béla Bartók. In the presence of music of this quality we are all able to be children; no composer since Bach has written self-teaching music of the quality of *Mikrokosmos*. The opening five-finger exercises are as pure as plainsong.

Bach and Bartók are the two great teachers at the keyboard, who composed all their teaching as music to be read. Other composers, for example Muzio Clementi and Carl Czerny, wrote out their teaching as formal practice exercises. Still others, among them Domenico Scarlatti and Frédéric Chopin, composed *exercises* or *études* (studies), in the same way that a designer of golf courses lays out his eighteen or thirty-six holes, a few easier and a few more difficult but none easy enough for a beginner.

There are also many well-made series of up-to-the-minute instruction books that will help you as much as any instruction book ever helped a beginner at bridge, badminton, swimming, or chess. Myself, I have always gone to the originals.

Meanwhile, don't give up reading everything you can manage in *Piano Pieces Everybody Likes To Play*. Read any printed music you can find around the house. If you are able to sing, as I am not, read songs. When you visit a friend who has a piano, sit down and play. Your friend, though surprised, even astonished, should feel complimented, whatever he may think of your performance. You are reading for your own pleasure, as you might pick up one of his books, so you don't care what he thinks. You'll play better, anyway, if you practise being unembarrassed.

Don't be afraid of Bartók, though your ear may at first resent his wonderfully individual harmonies, which we think of as *modern*. They are not modern at all, really, but the product of Bartók's deep study of disappearing Hungarian, Slavic, and Arabic folk melodies. Only the skill in setting these melodies to make keyboard music of them is modern. You will find written into each composition all the instruction you will need to play it correctly.

Bach's music presents difficulties of another sort. In Bach's century the fine performer was not one who memorized a piece of music and repeatedly performed it in the same way he had learned it; he was the one who could without hesitating improvise at the keyboard a new composition (not often a very good

one) or read at sight with good taste and musical expressiveness
any piece of music placed before him.

Bach expected his pupils to add to the written notation, when
playing, certain "additional notes of taste" or ornaments. Sometimes he wrote these into the music as examples, or he indicated
the playing of them by conventional signs. Players of good taste
were accustomed to adding these expressive ornaments, even
where not indicated or written.

The one sure guide to the proper playing of such music is a
book by the great revivalist of earlier instruments and playing
styles, Arnold Dolmetsch: *The Interpretation of the Music of the
17th and 18th Centuries.*

No one can learn easily from fellow enthusiast Dolmetsch. If
ever a book was confused with a superabundance, it is that book.
But there it is, no true Amateur ever expects to reach the end of
anything. What he has and knows, is his; he is ever at a start.
Wisdom, he is aware, cannot be arrived at by an underestimate.
The amateur of amateurs is the amateur of gardening. Every
year, every season, every weekend he has to go to work again.
Weeds, bugs, slugs, the small mindless viciousness of these ani-
mate stomachs must be overcome at every planting. But he
doesn't quit. And when the tiny chewed leaves push above
ground and unfold, he has his reward.

In the eighteenth century, knowledge of musical convention
took priority over what we call originality. In our own time
originality is all-important, and many conventions, once highly
valued, are misunderstood or forgotten. The rational ordering of
conventional idiom is the method by which we convey meaning
as language; originality uncontrolled by convention resembles
the irrational, symbolic messages of dreams. We know that composers and poets of the Age of Reason transcended their conventions by figurative and visionary metaphor. We know that composers today are anchoring their originality to a substantial
foundation of newly conceived styles and methods.

By keeping our attention open and receptive to the experimentation in means, methods, forms, and conventions which is
going on around us, we shall be better able to appreciate the
great diversity of styles, experiments, and conventions out of
which grew what we think of as the musical classics. We may

learn to hear them as intricate, risky, diverse, as the composers heard them.

These are a few of the experiences and particularities we shall be looking for as we find our way into music. There are those who believe that one should learn to read music from the score silently, as we read poetry without speaking it. That is of course one of the things that has gone wrong with poetry: too many have forgotten how to read and speak it. In music as in poetry silent reading places the emphasis where it does not belong, on the visual instead of the auditory experience. Since neither art is visual, the experience ceases to be esthetic and is instead interpretative, analytical, and explanatory, or like reading a foreign language which one does not speak. Music is a language of sound, without the equivalence of words; not an idiom of sounds or sound combinations each having like a word its distinct meaning. Nor can one see musical pictures, though artful suggestion of familiar sounds can convey musical landscape.

Architecture may be "frozen music," but music is not melted architecture. Sometimes we shall be hearing or reading music as lyric poetry; sometimes as drama or a kind of mobile sculpture; sometimes as spoken prose, unmetrical if not arhythmic; as speaking sound or speaking silence; as narrative or philosophy, or parable or theological message, as in the chorale preludes and cantatas of Bach, the oratorios of Handel—and these include some of the most beautiful music ever written.

IMPROVISING,
READING,
AND PERFORMING

The history of keyboard music covers about five hundred years. For more than three hundred years, beginning early in the seventeenth century, the greater part of musical composition originated at or from the keyboard.

The *clavier* (meaning any keyboard instrument: organ, clavichord, harpsichord, piano) was the familiar instrument of nearly all composers after the year 1600. At the keyboard they conceived form and enlarged upon it. They thought spontaneously in the idiomatic habits of the keyboard. The greater part even of their orchestral music, and as time went on their choral music, resembled keyboard writing in the distribution of parts, and can usually be reduced without violating its character to a keyboard version for four hands.

Igor Stravinsky has said: "Composing begins for me as the feeling of intervals in my fingers." And again: "I do not hear my composition until it has been sounded at the keyboard."

Johann Sebastian Bach taught his pupils to think at the keyboard but disdained composing at it; he called composers who did so "keyboard hussars"—keyboard riders. Hector Berlioz was perhaps the first and certainly the most influential of modern composers to compose without reference to the keyboard; the originator of modern orchestration, he seems to have thought almost entirely in the language of orchestral instruments.

From the compositional result, we have no reason to think either practice the better.

We are poor today, who can load our shelves with printed replicas of the five centuries of keyboard music. The mechanical player for which Haydn, Mozart, and Beethoven composed with disdainful curiosity has become the monarch of our musical experience: first the clockwork and then the player piano, then phonograph and radio, and today tape. A performing art, once the privilege of a few great cities and their country neighborhoods, has become the anonymous possession of the entire world. Kalmucks and aborigines, jaded Western sophisticates and new Oriental devotees, can hear, regardless of their own or any other tradition, the finished surfaces of an art rapidly becoming all too finished. In the momentary excitement are seeds of rapid dissolution.

There are two main divisions of the keyboard literature: music to perform and music to read.

Awareness of the larger repertoire of music to read has been closed off by the habit, developed during the nineteenth century, of preparing all keyboard music as if for the concert stage, memorizing it and smoothing away its difficulties—difficulties which the composer may have relied on to control the flow, shape, rhythm, or harmonic functioning of his music. Grooved performances of this sort make things easier for the player and win audience applause; they can be very memorable when they are the resultant of long, concentrated musical thought and recital experience. They become then unique collaborations of performer and composer, involving changes in technique and instrument which the composer could not anticipate, and which, like changes in esthetic attitude, are not always for the better.

The habit of memorizing music has replaced the ability to read it with fluency and expressiveness. The tendency to accept music as secondhand experience, to think of music as existing only in the presence of an audience, has driven out the pleasure of reading it for oneself or for others, as one reads books.

Musicians of the harpsichord period, as far back as the fifteenth century, placed improvising first among keyboard skills, reading at sight second, and playing pieces from memory a poor third, more suitable for pupils. During the fifteenth century, keyboard music seems to have been almost entirely improvised and only a small part written down—enough to convince us, however, that the ability to conceive music at the keyboard was already skilled.

The tradition of improvising vanished towards the middle of the nineteenth century; reading at sight has deteriorated to a convenience.

The one composer-pianist of my acquaintance who improvises with fluency and grace, George Tremblay, has told me that he does not consciously plan an improvisation before starting to play, nor does his conscious intention run ahead of his hands. The sound-patterns are translated through images in his mind into further developments of mood and image. Organists and the majority of jazz musicians improvise around a predetermined fixed pattern.

These habits differ markedly from that of J. S. Bach, who after hearing the subject of an improvisation would say at once what might be done with it, or at a wrong turning remark, "There he went wrong," before the consequence was evident. For Bach the hearing of a theme exposed its entire potentiality to become an individual composition.

Mozart when a boy customarily improvised in public performance. "I preluded and then played a sonata," he would write home after such an occasion, the prelude being a free fantasia in scalewise or arpeggiated movement on whatever subject came to hand, and the sonata a rather lightly organized piece, perhaps on the same theme, in the manner of his early sonatas with obbligato violin.

When Mozart traveled he would visit in every city where he stopped the church or monastery which had the best organ and improvise at that instrument for two or three hours, to the astonishment and gratification of the resident organist—and the weariness of the organ-pumper.

As he matured, Mozart seems to have preferred to improvise, as Beethoven did later, by varying a theme: one dated example being the 8 Variations on a March from Grétry's *Les Mariages samnites*. Although we have no sure evidence, I think it likely that all of Mozart's published keyboard variations may have originated in improvising. Around well-known operatic tunes he would develop elaborate obbligato passages, often of much feeling, according to a strict but flexible pattern. Students have too often put aside these variations as workmanship of no consequence. On the contrary, they are of first importance for any player who wishes to develop skill in improvising. No music by Mozart is more characteristic than the Variations on Gluck's *Unser dummer Pöbel* (Our Dumb Public) or his final set, *Ein Weib ist das herrlichste Ding* (which I freely translate, A Woman's the Darlingest Thing), showing in miniature the same humorous and inventive pathos as its opera companion of the same period, *Così fan Tutte.*

For an account of how much Mozart was able to accomplish in one day, I borrow from his letter written at Augsburg, October 24, 1777: "At the monastery . . . I gave a symphony and played the Violin Concerto in B by Wanhal with universal applause. . . . In the evening at supper I played the Strasbourg Concerto. . . . Afterwards they brought a clavier. I preluded and played a sonata and the Fischer variations. Then someone whispered to the Dean that he should hear me play organ-fashion. I said he might give me a theme; he would not, but one of the monks did. I began andante and in the middle (the fugue was in G minor) I began in the major quite playfully but in the same tempo and then returned to the theme but backwards; at last it occurred to me that I might try the playful style for the theme of the fugue. Without more ado I tried it and it went as accurately as if measured by the tailor. . . .

"Finally someone brought me a sonata, which was fugued, to play. I said: 'Gentlemen, this is too much; I must acknowledge I shall not be able to play the sonata right away.' 'I think so, too,' the Dean said eagerly, '. . . it would be impossible for anyone.' I said, 'I shall try.' And as I played I heard the Dean shouting behind me: 'Oh you rascal!'"

At a concert two days earlier, Mozart wrote to his father, he had played "all of a sudden a magnificent sonata in C major, out of my head, with a rondo at the end—full of din and sound." Alfred Einstein describes this C major Sonata (K. 309) as being like the transcription of a Salzburg symphony for a Stein piano. The sonata was written down afterwards from memory, and Mozart later gave it a different slow movement. Arnold Schoen-

berg once devoted a course of seven summer lectures to analyz-
ing this sonata.

Beethoven improvised at the piano; he seems to have shown
slight interest in any other keyboard instrument. Several of his
early sets of variations seem to be, like Mozart's, records of an
improvisation set down after the event. The simple but affecting
slow variations and boisterous finales answer closely the description of his youthful playing: that he would first move his listeners
to tears and then, laughing uproariously, beat out a rough and
witty dance. Go to the early piano variations by Beethoven, to be
found in Volume 2 of any collected edition, and try them; observe how many are worked up to this pattern.

The summary model of eighteenth-century free improvisation
is a Fantasy by Carl Philipp Emanuel Bach, the last of his eighteen examples—the others combine to make six sonatas—written
to accompany his book *The True Art of Playing Keyboard Instruments*. The Fantasy speaks a rhetoric of arpeggiation and
declamatory modulation, a glorified instrumental recitative or
musical prose without melody or tune, meant for the clavichord.
Mozart's four keyboard fantasies are in the same convention.

Beethoven has left one complete example of an improvisation,
his Fantasy opus 77. It records the search for a subject, the trial
and rejection of several ideas which are found unworthy, and the
eventual settling on a theme for spinning a series of variations.
The opening nonthematic scale is reintroduced several times, as
if to tie the improvisation together. Thus two of the chief forms
of improvisation, fantasy and variation, combine to anticipate a
stylistic habit which recurs in the *Hammerklavier Sonata* and the
Ninth Symphony, the introduction of several successive themes
that are played with and discarded in favor of another.

Having fondled the thought that there may once have been a
period of consistently ingenious and refined improvising, one may
guess with assurance that the period of improvisation was not
more inspired or dignified than the period of memorization. The
groping after passages which do not exist can be more bumbling
and empty than the loss of a few measures in public recital. The
rigid following of a fixed improvising pattern, French conserva-
tory style, can bring forth music as deadly dull as any uninteresting composition. Recall by contrast the extraordinary improvisa-

tory skills that appeared during the first decades of American jazz.

In improvising, esthetic consistency and the proprieties of harmonic grammar are soon at war with the effort to say anything at all. Yet the loss of true improvisation as a technique cannot be replaced from among all the amenities of a musical education.

Jazzmen today have lost the convenience of a common idiomatic vernacular and become polite, imitative, and eclectically musicological. Organists follow a system of modulatory doodling, intended like Muzak to be heard without attention.

▶ *Muzak:* a commercial system of canned and piped music installed in public places to promote the relaxation of employees and patrons by discouraging sustained thought. In Muzak elementary sentences are constantly starting, only to fade into vacuity. The proportion of sensitive to desensitized listeners can be estimated by the commercial success and prevalence of Muzak.

The reversal of the importance placed on the three types of performance occurred during the lifetime of Franz Liszt, who may be thought of as the creator of our musical era, including the standards of performance which we take for granted.

Until the new era inaugurated by Liszt's virtuoso career, all keyboard players made an art of reading at sight. When Beethoven or Mozart played formally in the presence of an audience, though he might continue to improvise, he had always a sheet of music paper before him on the instrument, to indicate that he was playing a prepared composition.

On his first concert tour the eleven-year-old Liszt, in Vienna, asked Beethoven to supply "a theme on which to improvise at his concert tomorrow." As Liszt's virtuoso career widened, he became the first pianist to depend entirely on his memory in playing public recitals. Towards the end of his long life Liszt was able to read at sight the piano concertos by Edvard Grieg and Edward MacDowell, to the admiration of the composers. In Liszt's career, as in that of no other musician, the performing skills of the past and future were combined.

All of these manners of improvising or reading and elaborating on written notation required of the player an easy skill in the

harmonic principles and conventions of *thoroughbass*, as fundamental to interpretation of music at that time as the ability to
read a score is, or is thought to be, at present. Both skills have
been honored as much in the bluff as in the accomplishment.

Along with his knowledge of thoroughbass, the keyboard
player was supposed to have at his command a technical versatility of conventional figurations, embellishing passages, and ornaments, with which to fill out any composition as his taste directed
and give his playing dynamic expressiveness.

The prevalence of improvised figuration and embellishment in
the reading of notated compositions is demonstrated by the urgency of François Couperin's plea that any who perform his keyboard *Orders* shall not tamper with the notes but play them as
written. Yet comparison of the first three *Orders* with those which
follow will show to what extent Couperin relied on the competence of a performer to dispose of his embellished notation according to the conventions of the period. Only in these first
Orders does Couperin write, for example, the variant manner of
double, to be used when a movement is repeated, or indicate the
direction in which chords shall be arpeggiated, upward or downward.

Couperin recommended that beginning pupils should learn to
play simple pieces from memory, so that they might give more
thought to their fingers. This same recommendation, transposed
to the highest levels of execution, is still used to justify memorization, on the assumption that no keyboard player, with the notes
before him, can thread the intricacies of a concert performance
unless he watches his hands. The common belief of pianists that
they are able to play more freely without the notes is confirmed
neither by the occasional catastrophes of forgetting which they
suffer nor by the experience of those who do play with the music.

The prestige of improvising has been transferred in some degree to its look-alike, the virtuoso performance in public without
notes. No matter how strictly the player may have his score by
rote, he feels that in some mysterious fashion he is not tied to it.
This false improvisation can become one of the glories of performance. It is the airy medium also of every sort of interpretive
bad habit.

Exceptional performers do develop exceptional memories. The
pianist must be able to reproduce more notes from memory than

any other soloist. Ferruccio Busoni once wrote in a letter to his wife that keeping the notes in his head was the greatest burden of recital playing. Today's habit presumes that any pianist who has trouble remembering the notes must be an inadequate artist.

A student who has been trained to memorize is likely to give up the instrument sooner than one who has been trained to read at it for his own pleasure. That is one reason why few pianists mature beyond the point where music ceases to be a possible career.

A good listener will keep in mind that music is what he hears, not the score he reads. Exact reproduction of the score does not of itself produce good music, nor is a free and independent reading necessarily bad. A good player tries to reveal in performance what he has discovered in the score. A superficial performer can bring to the same score no more than his superficiality.

Note-playing can be made easy just in proportion to how much the performer concentrates on accuracy to the exclusion of those distinctive chances of performance which are the glory of great playing.

The art of public virtuosity has made playing from memory a convenience, since the traveling virtuoso limits himself to a prepared repertoire, and a means of showing off.

The wise Amateur will know better than to emulate the virtuosity of performing from memory, except as it may come to him naturally or be convenient to do so. Béla Bartók read from the score even when performing his own compositions. The beloved pianist Myra Hess performed interchangeably with or without notes. To know the literature of the keyboard, we should start by learning to read it. We should return as amateurs to making music for ourselves, recapturing the feel of the music-maker, the personality of the instrument.

THE INDISPENSABLE
MUSIC

The literature of music for the keyboard can be divided in two parts: music to perform and music to read.

Music to perform is the smaller part and its success the more recent. The great early organists, Paumann, Schlick, Frescobaldi, performed before crowds; music for the organ, sacred or secular, is in a sense performance music. The invention of performance music in the modern style may be attributed to the gentle master Muzio Clementi, who believed, as he wrote in later years, that he was doing no more than adapting to the keyboard the *bel canto* style of Italian singing.

Clementi wrote to display the instrument, as *bel canto* displays the voice. Mozart wrote in the older tradition music to be played at the instrument in its own speech. Clementi, arriving in Vienna, was invited by the Emperor to play a contest with Mozart. Afterwards Clementi praised Mozart, who did not return the admiration.

Some time later Mozart wrote to his father: "Now I must say a few words to my sister about the Clementi sonatas. That they are valueless as compositions anyone who plays or hears them will recognize. There are no noteworthy or striking passages apart from sixths and octaves and I beg my sister not to be too much taken with these lest she spoil thereby her quick, firm hand and ruin its natural lightness, suppleness, and rapidity. For what is the object of these passages? They must be executed with the greatest speed (which nobody, not even Clementi, can achieve) and the result is a horrible hash, nothing else in the world!"

Mozart was merciless, and uncompromisingly ill-tempered; and Clementi's music—we know which sonata he played before the Emperor—not nearly so bad as in Mozart's description. The sixths and octaves may have been doublings thrown in at the moment, for they are not in the sonata. Whatever actually happened, Mozart had foreheard in Clementi's playing the display music of the next generation, Czerny's *School of Velocity* which trained the incipient performer to bravura flights of the fingers in every interval and every position, the priority of the performing mechanism.

Music to read constitutes by far the greater part of the keyboard literature, including nearly everything written before Clementi and much written afterwards. An Amateur at the keyboard will, for practical reasons, be wise to direct his attention mainly to this large literature, though he should have a thorough acquaintance with display music and should not hesitate to dig into it at the piano as well as he is able.

The split between the two types of composition becomes most evident in dealing with the compositions by Chopin. Though he was himself a composer and performer of the older type, who improvised at the keyboard and expected his written music to be read, his compositions were taken up by performers of the newer attitude, who exploited them for display. For this reason, an amateur, reading Chopin's music, will have at first in his ears a style of playing which obtrudes itself between the composition and the listener. He will do well to put this aside and explore the music of Chopin for himself, according to his own judgement of it, as independently of what he hears in public recital as if Chopin had been indeed two composers, the one a contemporary of Mozart and Clementi, the other a contemporary of Liszt. He will reach in this way a juster appreciation of Chopin's real attainment and learn to evaluate Chopin's compositions for what they are, while setting them apart from the shallow flood of imitative display music which succeeded them.

The sophisticated student can widen and confirm his understanding of eighteenth-century conventions of altered rhythm and embellishment by studying Chopin's carefully notated adaptations of them in his music. He will be the more aware of these conventions if he has studied them in C. P. E. Bach's *The True Art of Playing Keyboard Instruments,* a book which both Chopin and Beethoven kept beside them for a reference and teaching manual. He will observe Chopin's careful attention to the sound of folk music, in his mazurkas and polonaises; within his narrower scope he is as careful as Bartók.

For the true Amateur a complete knowledge of Chopin's keyboard music is indispensable, though he will probably never learn to master to his own satisfaction more than a small portion of it.

Ferruccio Busoni, if one may match his isolated comments with his practice, believed that after a pianist has mastered Beethoven he may go on to Liszt and the piano concertos by Mozart, but that the ultimate refinement is in playing a *Song Without Words* by Mendelssohn or a *Nocturne* by John Field. Whether the opinion be true or apocryphal, it should be held in thought by the true Amateur, who otherwise may be inclined to overestimate the worth of piano performance according to its noise, or its size, or the difficulty of the composition. Having this estimate firmly in mind, the Amateur will apply a like scale of values to the reading of music more substantial than that of Mendelssohn or Field.

He will therefore rank very highly the *Impromptus* and *Moments Musicaux* by Schubert; he will reject the evident coarseness of much Brahms, holding in higher esteem that part which is not coarse. He will discriminate in favor of the rare master who performs the work of Liszt fully and without obvious display against the hordes of opportunists who have imposed a false image upon a too often parodied composer. Having completed this cycle of appreciation, he will never again agree with the snobbish vulgar who overestimate Chopin's music or run it down for the wrong reasons. And he will have a just estimate of what is most admirable in nineteenth-century keyboard music. It is that use of the piano which imparts a new refinement of tone-production, learned from the clavichord, to the eighteenth-century formal inheritance. (Brahms, for example, constantly amplifies his harmony with octaves, whereas Chopin uses octaves in the older manner, for their open resonance.)

Apart from the refinement of playing, the nineteenth-century keyboard literature—in which I do not include the work of Bee-

thoven, who completes the long evolution of keyboard music
through the seventeenth and eighteenth centuries—would be less
interesting than that of the two preceding centuries if Franz
Schubert had not managed to create, during his few years, a succession of piano sonatas the best of which deserve to rank with
the highest achievements of the keyboard art.

These sonatas differ from Beethoven's in requiring a much
higher degree of that refinement of piano-playing peculiar to the
nineteenth century. A full appreciation of the Schubert sonatas
does not usually precede but follows a thorough appreciation of
Beethoven; because one can be excited by Beethoven without
song, but to be profoundly stirred by Schubert one must appreciate to the full the nineteenth-century refinement of pianistic
song.

For an amateur, the best approach to Beethoven is to hear and
read and having read to follow in score, as it is being performed,
each of the thirty-two Beethoven piano sonatas. When I say
"read" I do not in any way imply "perform." A useful skill in
reading no more involves a high competence in execution than
ability to follow a piano score involves the ability to "hear" the
score as sound. While any collection of the sonatas will do well
enough to begin with, none, however portentously edited, will
serve the reader so well as what is called an *urtext*.

▶ *Urtext:* the *ur* is derived from *ursprünglich* (original). An
urtext may mean the composer's original, unrevised manuscript (requiring therefore the guess of an editor to clarify
each dubious notation); or it may mean any one of the composer's several copies or revisions of the manuscript, over a
period possibly years long (with, again, the guess of the editor in dubious places); or it may signify a collated edition of
some extant manuscripts (and the editor's guesses); or it may
refer to the first published edition, edited by the composer
himself, or published after his death, or surviving in a published edition he may not have approved or known of; or it
may signify a copied score believed to be a fair copy of a
lost original; or it may mean something that is not consistently any of these but the best text which can be put together
out of available sources in the opinion of one or more rea-
sonably expert editors. In every case, by the time the work

has reached print in a definitive and accepted urtext edition, it embodies an editor's opinions, his interpretations, and sometimes his markings. Nevertheless, with all reservations, if one has an urtext of Beethoven, Mozart, or any other composer, one will not go wrong in preferring it to any other edition. For Chopin there are now several accredited urtexts.

Besides knowing Beethoven's sonatas, one should look well into his piano variations. The later and better known of the variations have all been recorded, but the earlier and less known have not, a strange omission considering the general popularity of Beethoven's music and the amount of it that is on records.

Among these earlier piano variations even the true Amateur is likely to feel a sense of letdown. If Beethoven from the first composed with grandeur, why did he confine his public playing, apart from outright improvising, to such compositions as these? He did not himself publicly perform his sonatas.

The answer is that these early sets of improvisations represent the spontaneous flights of spirit in which Beethoven customarily improvised, that they are a good measure of his public improvisation and may, as I believe, be in many instances the writing down afterwards of improvisations which had pleased him. The Twenty-four Variations on *Vieni amore* by Righini, composed in 1790, at age twenty, is known to have been Beethoven's favorite performance piece during his first years at Vienna. The music is idiosyncratic Beethoven, prophetic of his last period, his major creative accomplishment before the Piano Trios opus 1 and the Piano Sonatas opus 2. It is interesting to see in how many ways these early variations resemble Beethoven's last and largest work for piano, the *Diabelli Variations*. Beethoven did not develop as a composer so rapidly as J. S. Bach, Mozart, or Schubert, but in a musical culture where the outstanding composers all pointed in one direction he very boldly and in complete independence went a different direction. More than any other composer he understood the full implications of those aspects of Clementi's art to which Mozart objected; he saw them not as means of display but as structural elements of different shapes, weights, and degrees of tensile strength, capable of supporting a denser composition. His borrowings from Clementi are of less significance than what he was able to accomplish at first grasp by crossing the inheritance of the Bachs and Mozart with the Italian operatic keyboard style of Clementi.

Apart from the *Vieni amore* set, the early variations preserve for us the composer's natural idiomatic vernacular at the piano, his habits of spontaneous musical speech, out of which grew his more formal compositions. This idiomatic twang can be heard through even the loftiest passages of his most inspired compositions, so that one is always aware of Beethoven's living presence.

To enjoy fully these early piano variations one will need to develop a fair amount of that genuine musical sophistication which includes a sense of musical humor and an awareness, technical and aural, of what is really going on. They show the young country cousin's thorough contempt for the obvious responses of musical dilettantism. Beethoven delighted in provoking false tears and false excitement; he rollicked in deceiving his listeners' feelings and upsetting their decorum.

When we have reached the sophistication necessary to enjoy these demonstrations of the skill of this extraordinary young man, we shall take an entirely fresh attitude towards all the false emotionality and nonsense that have been piled on him. We shall know him better than his idolators, appreciating the toughness of his sensibility, his awareness of tradition and sure hand in shifting around traditional forms and ideas. We shall recognize above all the complete unlikeness of his musical intelligence to that of Mozart, or the Bachs, or Haydn, each of whom maintained reserves of politeness which Beethoven disdained. We shall understand that the overwrought emotionality of his daily living and of occasional letters was above all what he labored to keep out of his music, though he could not do so entirely. He did not, above all, confuse his personal emotions or his feelings about a composition with the work of art. He did not by a marginal comment or a program note summon furies or angels to inhabit his notation; his esthetic otherworld is as definitely placed as Bach's theology. Claude Debussy, at the height of literary music-making, wrote succinctly: "There was not an ounce of literature in Beethoven . . ."

The keyboard art of Beethoven begins in the early variations as it ends in the consummately reverent and comedic *Diabelli Variations,* a masterpiece so appalling to subsequent generations of pianists that, apart from exceptional readings by Hans von

Bülow, Brahms, and Donald Tovey, it did not enter the keyboard repertoire until after it had been recorded by Artur Schnabel and made familiar enough to be accepted.

► It is hard to understand why that most inclusive and precarious form of composition, equally balanced at its best between structure and texture, the *theme and variations,* has never been granted the critical pre-eminence which it deserves. Variation form in its several aspects has been the most long-lived of the keyboard forms, the only one to have an equal place in each period throughout the entire history of the keyboard art.

I believe that neglect of the variation form may be ascribed to a mistaken idea that, as distinguished from sonata form and fugue, it is not strict. The freedoms within sonata form and fugue practised by the classic masters, but not by textbooks, are at least as wide as those of variation form. Mozart's variations are stricter than his sonatas or concertos.

If the Bach *Goldberg* and Beethoven *Diabelli Variations* (the latter a close-studied adaptation, though in no sense an imitation, of the former) had entered the critical field of reference earlier than they did, some of this lack of critical estimation might have been corrected. Critics might then have valued the strict variation form of Mozart as a measure of all others.

There is good reason to presume that the variation works for the keyboard by the masters of each period are the best sources for knowledge of idiomatic style in the music of their time, weakness as well as strength, and deserve as thorough study as the fugues and the sonatas.

One may enjoy, too, botanizing among the three sets of the Beethoven *Bagatelles,* keeping in mind that the first set (opus 33) consists of early and very early writing, the second set (opus 119) of early and late middle writing, and the third set (opus 126) of later writing. The first and second sets may be regarded as assembled notes for possible compositions; the third is a masterpiece not less than the best shorter sonatas and as difficult to perform.

The true Amateur may now be left to discover for himself that

the opening movement of Beethoven's *Sonata Appassionata,* said
to have been precipitated as a two-hour improvisation after a
walk in the country, may be as calculatedly dispassionate as it is
commonly felt to be emotional. Heard so, it is the more interesting. Beethoven did not invent the title or dream the romantic
narrative of his so-called *Moonlight Sonata;* like its companion
piece of opus 27 and several others of the sonatas, early and late,
it is a study in sonata design after eighteenth-century models.
From it came the later Fantasy Sonatas, opus 109 and opus 110.

Beethoven expertly simulates farewell, loneliness, and home-
coming in one of his most objectively designed sonatas (opus
81a). To understand this in no way detracts from it as music. His
Funeral March Sonata, opus 26, is a complex parody, originating
in a funeral march heard at a theater, but having in mind the
unusual shape of Mozart's Piano Sonata in A major and at the
same time the new strumming style of composition, out of which
came the Schubert sonatas; its shapely child is Chopin's *Funeral
March Sonata,* but Chopin wrote seriously whereas Beethoven
amused himself. The complex relationships among these three
sonatas, and the choice and order of their movements, should
furrow the brow of anyone who believes in the academic sim-
plicities of sonata form.

Another Beethoven sonata (opus 31:1) makes great play with
Italian operatic devices (Clementi's *bel canto*), but Schubert took
it quite seriously for a model. The seeming frenzy of the fugue
of the *Diabelli Variations* is borrowed directly from a subsection
of the *11th Contrapunctus* of Bach's *Art of Fugue.* (Such cross-
references illuminate the creative landscape; they prove nothing.)

Musical appreciation reaches often beyond entertainment to a
sense of the tragic and the devotional but less often to an awareness of the sublimely comic. (Bach never fails to find some
sprightly little tune to accompany the Holy Ghost.) At a point
where the fugue of the *Hammerklavier Sonata,* opus 106, seems
about to burst apart in dissonance and chaos, the principal theme
calmly makes an entrance back end forwards, a commentary as
drastic and studied as the speeches of Lear's Fool.

The true Amateur will eventually satisfy himself concerning
all these and many other matters by reading the whole of Beethoven's keyboard music, however difficult and however badly.
He may do the same for Schubert, but he will learn less from

the lesser music by Schubert than from the incidental music of
J. S. Bach, Mozart, and Beethoven. Of these composers he will
be careful to read with attention every note.

When listening to the separate works of a major composer or
reading his music, you should make an effort to locate each composition in historical relationship and sequence. It's a good idea,
too, to copy in a manuscript book works you cannot afford but
wish to own. So doing, you watch the changing lights of the seasons pass over the fundamental landscape of the composer's
mind. By following the growth of a composer through the evidence of his music, one can accept the authority of his more demanding later idiom as a projection of the same content more
slightly ventured in his earlier work; at the same time, one's
pleasure in the more spontaneous earlier idiom increases. The
little finale of Haydn's A major Sonata (Peters no. 11), put together of a scale and a smile, is reflected by the laughing scales
of the finale of Beethoven's boyhood *Dressler Variations;* is it not
the same scale that returns to become the finale of the *Hammerklavier Sonata?* An awareness of the unique content of the
work of each composer, of his esthetic consistency underlying all
deviations of style, and of the common idiomatic vernacular
shared by composers of any period, or in relation to a common
instrument or speech or ethnic background, will often be as revealing as technical analysis of a composer's compositional
method or a psychological exposure of his presumed emotions.

It is curious how many scholars, as well as pianists who perform a little Mozart, give lip praise to the great series of Mozart's
piano concertos, while failing to set them in context with the
piano sonatas and the piano variations. The first six of the mature piano sonatas (Köchel nos. 279 through 284) were composed
when Mozart was preparing to set out alone to make his fortune; they were the best he could write, carefully graded in
difficulty and adjusted to different types of interest, the sixth, in
D major, being the most learned. Of the first of these sonatas
(K. 279) Alfred Einstein wrote: "This is how he must have played
when he was in the vein and improvised a sonata." Beginning
with the D major (K. 284) the sonatas are companion pieces to
the concertos, several being in the style of a concerto without
orchestra, including tutti, solo, and cadenza.

The reader should guard himself against the extreme fluency

of Mozart's keyboard writing. It conceals difficulties as real as those of the larger works by Beethoven and Schubert. Mozart's incidental keyboard pieces are of no less substance and significance than his variations and sonatas.

The true Amateur will recognize in the enormous achievement of the Mozart piano concertos, the central fifteen composed between 1782 and 1786, the formal apex of all keyboard writing, an accomplishment equal in scope to the four volumes of Bach's *Keyboard Exercises* (*Clavierübung*) or the thirty-two Beethoven piano sonatas. Since concert pianists do not regularly perform these concertos and try too often to import into those they do play a subliminal Beethovenian emotionality, it is all the more important that a true Amateur should read them for himself, in piano reduction, as thoroughly as he reads any music. To familiarize oneself with the orchestration, one should try to hear each of the concertos in a live performance; with some effort and careful selection one can assemble a better than adequate library of recorded performances.

To claim that Mozart unemotionally wrote pure music may flatter one's taste as foolishly as to claim that Beethoven wrote purely in emotion. The ebulliently witty, perceptive, and already embittered young Mozart of the letters did not often display openly the emotion of his A minor Sonata, written at the time of his mother's death in Paris. He did not deny his feelings but subdued them, so that they appear in ways less evident to the inattentive. He was still putting on a bright front, hoping for a breakthrough to success and financial independence, when he died. I do not know any witty music sadder or more consummate than the last set of Mozart's piano variations (K. 613). At the apex of his art, when the previously successful annual series of his subscription concerts was collapsing, the Piano Concerto in C major (K. 503) speaks in a voice more imperial than that of Beethoven's *Emperor*, stricken besides with the further perspective of defeat. Beethoven moves to an outward release of emotion, cathartic and purgative; Mozart, to an inward reckoning, from which there is to be no release.

After so much talk of great style and great emotion, the reader of music may be content to turn aside from tragic and comic extremes to indulge his delight in the contemplative discoveries of Haydn, a composer whose musical economy explored extraordinary methods while avoiding all extremes. We are accustomed to speak, after Wagner, of "Papa Haydn," as in his later life his admiring young friends addressed him, as if his art and will, after long attendance upon duty to three Princes Esterhazy, had grown servile or at best conciliatory.

His letters prove a worthier estimate: the best minds of Europe esteemed him to be as noble as his prince. Not Beethoven but Haydn was the composer who freed music from its long subservience to church and rank—by creative authority, not by rebellion. (A new and persisting subservience to the public audience had just begun, but Haydn did not share it.) Kings, academies, the rising bourgeois and their new musical institutions in Europe and Britain glorified him with awards, titles, commissions, and devoted admiration. He was the most honored and, until Stravinsky, the most widely esteemed composer during his lifetime in musical history.

In the midst of acclaim this reserved and humble but decisive composer went his musical way, developing early a close attention to the careful working out of thematic figures which sets even his largest workmanship apart from the subjectively dramatic outpouring of Beethoven and the aristocratic finality of Mozart. Haydn's introspective method, outwardly revealed in the adagios of the *Seven Last Words* and the slow openings of some of the later symphonies, does not lend itself well to extended forms, but the close analysis of its working upon a subject imparts to each detail of his design an expressive personality, so that the effect of his art should be contemplative rather than exciting. While other composers pile up form and ideas towards climax, Haydn may draw out an entire movement from a single figure, as if pondering the outcome of a unique event. Instead of following his music in the common fashion from climax to climax, one must listen with him closely, phrase by phrase and note by note. For this reason he was a constant innovator. The experience of disciplining ourselves to follow the exigent growth of the less traditional music of our own century has sharpened our attention so that we are able to listen more closely to the art of Haydn.

One should play his music deliberately, rather slowly than otherwise, and not at all with the fast indifference long thought to be good enough for his sonatas—they have so few notes!—devoting careful attention to each carefully notated rhythmic device, so that the movement speaks at length lyrically and with ease. His sonatas provide a compendium from the later period of embellished and altered or expressive rhythm. He writes out much that the preceding composers expected a player to do of his own experience and imagination, notating for example many cadences which another composer would have expected the player to improvise.

Read for oneself, his sonatas take on a conversational intimacy that reminds us of his genius for friendship. One cherishes his wise humor, as one cherishes the keyboard art of François Couperin, for its good company. There are fifty-two piano sonatas, and sonatinas, and divertimentos for piano by Haydn, a few doubling as sonatas with violin obbligato. Not one is uninteresting. A true Amateur will know well all of them.

(The Peters urtext edition includes also one editorial peculiarity that, I doubt not, would have irritated Haydn: the use of a circumflex accent to indicate an appoggiatura, a confusing emendation which merely interferes with the accustomed responses.)

To appreciate how much skill enters into a Haydn piano sonata, read that small critical masterpiece, Donald Tovey's essay on Haydn's Pianoforte Sonata in E flat, in his *Essays in Musical Analysis.*

▶ Donald Tovey played in London in 1900, at the age of twenty-five, recitals that included the Bach *Goldberg Variations* and the Beethoven *Diabelli Variations,* both still as unknown to the public audience as they had been at the time of Beethoven's death seventy-three years earlier. Besides performing this exemplary repertoire, young Donald wrote to accompany it the first of the many long program notes that will outlive his musical compositions. His discussion of the *Goldberg Variations* has never been bettered. English critical prose contains nothing more economical and inclusive. The precocious young pianist later became conductor of the Edinburgh Symphony; for its concerts he continued writing his unequaled program notes, collected as *Essays in Musical Analysis.* The comprehensive maturity he had achieved at twenty-five aged without widening in vision. He underestimated the composers of the seventeenth century and the

Mozart piano sonatas, and found no entry into the new creative means of the twentieth century.

Donald Tovey lived so completely in dead music that he wrote of it always as if it were living, while living music passed swiftly beyond his ken. His amateur critical contemporary George Bernard Shaw was better equipped than he to deal with Schoenberg. Though Tovey knew every trick of the masters, he could never learn as a composer to play their game. He survives as one of the most readable of musical commentators and a figure of warning. Knowledge, ample knowledge of how the past made music will never enlighten a man to be a composer, unless he is willing to throw off the burden of his knowledge and gamble on his own fresh venture into the unknown, as Schoenberg and Webern did, both experts in analysis no less competent than the man who ended his admirable career Sir Donald Tovey.

Through the years, Haydn and François Couperin have become my two most intimate companions at the keyboard. And in consequence I find myself listening for the interior art in the music of Chopin that is obscured by too much activity on the surface.

François Couperin, the most famous member of a French family of organists, wrote four books of keyboard pieces, made up of twenty-eight collections, each called an *Order*. The first *Orders* are assemblages of pieces, with no apparent intention that they should be played through in the unified style of a suite. They were musical Conversation Books, resembling earlier collections of lute pieces in which compositions for a single instrument were simply gathered together.

Couperin's first *Orders* are large assemblages; after that there begins to be an appearance of some collective arrangement, as of a book of lyric poems, unitary pieces so strung together that they may be read in sequence, with a grouping system by key. This was done so that a single meantone tuning of the harpsichord would suffice for the entire *Order*. (A single tuning in meantone will suffice for the majority of the *Orders;* to play them all to best advantage one would have to retune in more than one sharp or flat variant of the basic tuning. See Appendix 1: "Temperament and Tuning.")

By the *Sixth Order,* in the Second Book, a common mood has

been created; the entire *Order* hangs together as well as any suite. The procedure is not consistent; some of the later *Orders* revert to a collection of independent lyrics. The very large *Eighth Order,* culminating in the well-known *Passecaille,* followed by a short allegro like the finale of the Chopin *Funeral March Sonata,* belongs among the chief masterpieces of the keyboard.

At the end of the Second Book comes the dramatic *Celebration of the Grand and Ancient Order of Minstrels,* a suite within an *Order,* including a Parade, a couple of Airs for the dronelike *vièle,* a dance of Jugglers and Mountebanks with bears and donkeys, a limping procession of service-worn Invalids, and a final Disorder, caused by the animals. This is the one series of movements by Couperin that is usually played in sequence. I would suggest that the *Sixth Order,* the *Eighth Order,* and all the *Orders* of the Fourth Book are of a sufficient homogeneity to be better played as suites.

The four books are a treasure house of delight, charm, wit, and that most precious and overlooked ingredient of enduring musical companionship, humor. Like the young Beethoven, but with a more courteous grace, Couperin relished laughter at the keyboard.

Counterbalancing the lighter pieces one finds movements of orchestral fullness and truly French instrumental coloring, satires, classical landscapes, rusticities, ironies. A subtle set of variations in the Third Book, *Thirteenth Order,* presents in each variation a trait of character behind a colored mask: "Virginity" behind a mask the color of invisibility; "The Benevolent Cuckoos" (cuckolds) behind yellow masks, and so on. This is followed in the *Fourteenth Order* by a sequence of bird studies, suddenly abandoned.

Couperin's keyboard music spoke to an inside circle who could appreciate both the niceties of musical treatment and their relation to the sometimes cryptically entitled subject. Since we are not privy to all the secrets of this closely integrated society, where gossip supplied the chief offset to fashionable theology and the comparison of sermons, many of Couperin's titles convey to us only a generalized significance and occasionally no meaning at all. Beneath the usually sparkling surface we feel often the private melancholy of a genius whose two principal sacred compositions are settings of the Lamentations of Jeremiah, and who, like his contemporaries Racine and La Fontaine, could not say all he wished but must convey it by rebellious indirection.

One should give no less attention to Couperin's eight keyboard Preludes, in the principal meantone keys, an epitome of seventeenth-century keyboard art at its most expressive abstraction. Some readers will prefer, in this line, the preludes and other compositions of a slightly older contemporary, Jean-Henri d'Anglebert, pupil of Chambonnières.

For the *Orders* there is only one acceptable edition, that edited by Brahms (the composer) and Chrysander, and published by Augener. I would advise, for a first purchase, buying the Second Book. The Breitkopf and Härtel edition of the Preludes includes the complete text of Couperin's *Art of Keyboard Playing* and his notes and instructions, with many examples, for the correct reading and expressive fingering of indicated passages in the *Orders*. Couperin was a serious and definite taskmaster.

Correct playing of Couperin is one of the special keyboard skills, but it is not beyond the reach of a true Amateur. One should know his work entirely.

Johann Sebastian Bach is the one other composer whose keyboard music should be read unceasingly. (In saying this I set at one side the English composers of the virginal books, who should be read together and as fully as one is able to enter into them.) Historically and temporally, he stands at the center of the keyboard art. The whole of his viable work is larger than that of any other keyboard composer. He was the only composer to create a body of music for the organ equal in importance to the piano concertos by Mozart and the piano sonatas by Beethoven. He was probably the most complete master of performance at any keyboard instrument except piano. (He did try improvising on the several new pianos at the court of Frederick the Great, that great day for music when the famous monarch received him as an honored guest. The three-part Fugue at the beginning of Bach's *Musical Offering* may preserve one of these improvisations.)

In the opinion of his sons and the immediately succeeding generations, Bach was an old-fashioned composer in styles already archaic or going out of date. This was what Mozart meant when he spoke of playing "organ-fashion" (see quotation on page 12). In Vienna, at the home of the Baron von Swieten, Mozart, Haydn, and Beethoven heard and read much music by Bach and

Handel. Each in his own way revived the language and idiom of the older music, with a decisive alteration in contrapuntal and polyphonic practice. From that time until the present day the influence of Bach has been subverting scholastic teaching and inspiring composers to their most daring unorthodoxies in a manner and to a degree that might have astonished but would certainly have shocked him, for he was a pillar of orthodoxy. It is indeed his orthodoxy, carried to his radical extremes, which has made his influence so persistently revolutionary. The new harmonic-structural style of sonata form, which at first rejected him, was infiltrated and in the later work of Beethoven shredded and re-created by the dissonant and enharmonic implications of his counterpoint (because of which Berlioz detested his music).

For us his compositions are the continental divide between the classic and the preclassic, between the relatively known and the relatively unknown halves of the five centuries of keyboard music. The false understanding and performance of his music established and perpetuated by a century of pianists playing in an unlike style has set a barrier between us and this earlier half of keyboard literature. To recover what is still lost we must reacquaint ourselves with the true art of Bach's keyboard practice; to recover this true art we must reacquaint ourselves with the works of his predecessors, in their own styles which culminated in the art of Bach. The two aspects of this recovery need to go together, and I believe that amateurs can contribute to it as much as professional musicians, who profess not to know what is still lacking.

The true Amateur will therefore try to venture every keyboard work by Bach, including all that he can manage of the organ music (which may be read at the piano, with, when necessary, an extra hand for the pedal part), the greater and lesser suites, the partitas, the early pieces, the books of teaching pieces with their little dances, all the preludes and fugues great and small, the chorale preludes, variations, trios, and duets.

There is no best edition of Bach's keyboard music. One should assemble many editions for comparison and inclusiveness, including certain of the recent English editions. A good library will contain the Bach-Gesellschaft edition of the keyboard works (obtainable cheaply in the Lea Pocket Scores). Busoni's idiosyncratic editions deserve thoughtful study.

I have an enduring, technically incompetent liking for Busoni's own later compositions, the *Elegies* and sonatinas, the second set of *Chopin Variations,* and the Toccata.

Having summarized the composers whose keyboard music should be read completely, let me go ahead to speak more rapidly of other composers whose keyboard music should be known in part. It is a long list, and I shall not try to make it complete. Also I shall give more freedom to my prejudices.

Once started, one will and should read all keyboard music composed before the end of the sixteenth century that one can find in any collection. I would recommend for a first purchase the collection *Early Keyboard Music,* Volume 1, published by Schirmer. Through unevenly edited, it is the most satisfactorily complete collection of essential music from near the end of the sixteenth to near the end of the seventeenth century, except for François Couperin, whose work appears in the less satisfactory Volume 2. A beautiful original, beautifully reprinted, which should be in the library of every keyboard player who can afford it, is *My Ladye Nevells Booke,* from a presentation manuscript of the keyboard music by William Byrd written up until about 1590. It includes Byrd's large suite *The Battell,* one of the first and certainly the best of all examples of musical news-reporting.

One should try each piece with the intent of discovering its individuality and style, using any available information but playing it as if one had heard no subsequent music. Keep firmly in mind that these composers were not anticipating or striving towards styles, forms, habits, harmonies, or techniques that we know well but they had not imagined. Assume instead that these composers were well pleased by whatever they accomplished and that their best music thrilled them no less than the best music of later periods thrills us; then try to find out why.

It is a very different attitude than we find in our music schools, where too many answers are provided and the necessary questions are not asked—or, when asked, are discouraged and put aside.

With few exceptions, this very early keyboard music will seem at first melodically slight and harmonically empty. It does not speak our language; we can be fairly sure it speaks its own. So the fun commences. You can spend years at it, crisscrossing back and forth from piece to piece, picking up a feel of the style, a passage here and there that falls naturally into rhythm. Critical writing of the period provides less information than for the seventeenth and eighteenth centuries. You are on your own. Public performers, when they do play at this music, try to make it seem as like the standard repertoire as possible. It should seem instead very unlike.

But there is subsequent comment through which one can look backwards. "And there is no greater grace than breaking the time in the minutes, and still holding it punctually upon the main, to conserve the grand beat or measure," Roger North, who had grown up playing the older music, wrote at the end of the seventeenth century. Disregarding the editor's qualification that this concerns the new Italian practice of *rubato*, let us try it in every way that it may be found in the earlier music: in English dances using the "Scotch snap" which we still hear in bagpipe-playing; in running passages letting the passing notes fall away from or lean towards the beat notes, using great liberty in slow movements (which are often shown to be slow by an increase of ornaments); in polyphonies freeing the separate voices to move in horizontal independence, as if sung by individual singers held together only by someone tapping to mark the principal beats— but not metronomically or with careful matching of the vertical relationships, as choral singers are unwisely trained to do today.

". . . it is not of great import how the breaking is managed," Roger North instructs us, "provided the generall equallitys are maintained; on which account it is that the capitall masters, in their performing, capreole it in such a manner as any one would think they kept no time at all, and yet they never fail their gross measures."

That is the heart of it. In the modern reading of this music it is all time and no "capreole" (as of the curvetting of horses or the jumping of a little goat), and no one would ever "think they kept no time at all." So mark the beat and put away the metronome. Isn't this very nearly the same measure as New Orleans jazz?

Better to overdo than to be cautious. Our purpose in reading is not to perform but to discover, and we are not required to satisfy an audience. Playing it safe in the wrong style, as harpsichordists generally do nowadays, will tell nothing, except to show, in our terms, the thinness of the vertical harmony; better to be wrong, aiming at the right style.

One should never cease reading in the Elizabethan virginal books, realizing that these contain and speak for a self-sufficient keyboard art. A good share of the pleasure of reading widely in music comes from grasping and evaluating new expressive possibilities and stylistic differences. Play the idiom of the music and not its appearance, which has been regularized in the modern printing as it was not in the original.

To cover the entire field of keyboard music, one must accept many unsatisfactory editions. Some I find that I can use by translation; others I cannot. Formerly, if you wished to own the complete keyboard works by Orlando Gibbons, you could buy a set of volumes in which care for the exact notes was matched by an equal care to remove all the original indications of embellishment—as if these might mislead the player or as if he could not, if he wished, do without them. In such a case, my solution is to use a better edition of any separate piece that is to be found, for instance in *Parthenia,* or the *Fitzwilliam Virginal Book,* or, especially for Gibbons, *Benjamin Cosyn's Virginal Book,* and try to work out my own embellishments for the remainder. Some editions of the older music, for example the only edition I have found of the keyboard suites by John Blow, have been damaged by the editor beyond my retranslating.

▶ I have seen two once-reputable editions of the Bach *Goldberg Variations* from which all indications of the ornaments have been removed. This great work fortunately came to popularity through a recorded performance played on harpsichord by Wanda Landowska. The first recording of the *Goldberg Variations* was an event as decisive for the future, and the recovery of the past of music, as the first performance of Stravinsky's *Rite of Spring* or the conception of the twelve-tone method. Landowska's example has set this work apart from the greater body of sixteenth-, seventeenth-, and eighteenth-century keyboard music, as the one major composition in which the player is expected, because of his listeners' expectations, to account for all notated embellishments.

The seventeenth century was formerly dismissed as a period of transitional experimentation between the end of the polyphonic era and the rise of the German classical tradition. It was in truth a period of experimentation and seminal intercourse among new ideas. During the seventeenth century the new forms of the harmonic era were created.

We should expect to find the composers of such a period, though local in tradition, receptive to fresh ideas from surrounding traditions. The disturbed political and diplomatic atmosphere increased, as if by heating the mixture, the rapidity of molecular interchange.

The seventeenth-century German music for the organ is a literature in its own right, more prolific or better preserved than the organ works of the English, French, or Italian composers— except Frescobaldi. The German keyboard music of the seventeenth century is easier to read, regardless of style, than the more individual works of the Italian and French composers. It requires less elaboration and embellishment by the player than the compositions of Frescobaldi or Alessandro Scarlatti, and its rhythms and ornaments are more easily comprehended than those of the French composers. The keyboard works of Purcell and Blow, which seem at first acquaintance too simple, if not charmingly trivial, are in fact not at all so. Properly performed, with a decisive rhythmic swing and correct ornamentation, they will be found much more worth reading than they appear on the page.

I recommend in the same way a recently discovered collection of small suites and keyboard pieces by Buxtehude, and the collected fantasies by Telemann, which invite the reader to experiment with textural detail in the altering of rhythm and the addition of expressive embellishments. What has been learned from reading Couperin and Bach can be applied more easily to these slighter compositions, which so played can be made lovely in sound and continuously interesting; whereas strictly read as they show on the page they remain unchangeably thin and dull.

The works of Chambonnières, d'Anglebert, and Louis Couperin are not representatively published in general collections (the Schirmer *Early Keyboard Music*, Volume 1, fortunately includes excellent examples); their works can be obtained in complete editions with a little trouble and expense. They require and will reward careful individual study. The style is much stricter and more formally ordained than the English.

A complete playing knowledge of Handel's keyboard music is advisable, but I do not believe it necessary if one knows thoroughly the two volumes of the Suites. But one should know the great theme, with its little set of original variations, of which Brahms made too much. Here, as with Purcell, the texture will take on increased richness and interest as one learns not to dash off the music but to play it more slowly and rhythmically with correct and amplified embellishment. One should have in mind that for some amateurs and musicians the music of Handel is the correct antidote to that of J. S. Bach, the perfect balancing of harmony and texture in a keyboard style.

The complete Domenico Scarlatti of the ten-volume Longo edition should be gradually accumulated in the library of every true Amateur; the smaller but more accurate edition of sixty sonatas, edited by John Kirkpatrick, furnishes a useful offset to Longo's editorial excesses.

I have not made my way completely through the keyboard works by Soler, Domenico Scarlatti's Spanish contemporary—not his pupil—or those by the Portuguese composer Seixas. Here my readers, if they can develop a playing style for what has seemed to me, with a few remarkable exceptions, a rather bare music, may outdo me. My taste is far from infallible. My friend the composer Lou Harrison would prefer Handel, Soler, and Seixas to my choice of J. S. Bach and Domenico Scarlatti. Our difference of taste has had much to do with the historical shaping of this book.

Lou Harrison's own Six Sonatas, as well as several other pieces he has composed for harpsichord or piano, effectively re-create in twentieth-century idiom the technical interest of the early eighteenth century. His Suite for Piano, like Schoenberg's *Dance Suite*, opus 25, brings together the eighteenth-century suite with the serial language of the tone-row.

Other examples of such stylistic transformations successfully brought off (they are rather rare, and most such efforts are no more than imitations) are Ravel's *Tombeau de Couperin* and Stravinsky's Piano Sonata. At a further remove, John Cage's *Sonatas and Interludes for Prepared Piano* may remind the innocent listener of Scarlatti or Soler. (The necessary equipment and diagrams and measurements for "preparing" the piano are supplied with purchase of the Cage music. For a person who likes to play around with the technical innards of things, the Cage pieces offer a fascinating opportunity.)

The eighteenth century divides into two equal halves, each the equivalent for keyboard music of any other full century: the first half ending with the death of J. S. Bach in 1750, the second half rising from the already mature writing of C. P. E. Bach and the early works by Haydn. One should read all available music by C. P. E. Bach and by his youngest brother and pupil Johann Christian Bach, known respectively during their lifetime as "the German Bach" and "the English Bach." They carry forward the vertical split in eighteenth-century music, between the Germanic tradition epitomized by J. S. Bach and the Italianate tradition epitomized by Handel and Domenico Scarlatti. These traditions, cross-fertilizing, produced, in the Germanic line, Haydn, and in the Italianate line, Clementi and the early Mozart. Lesser composers, Italian, German, and French, among them Padre Martini, Galuppi, and Schobert, should be examined; each was both popular and influential.

► Since I wrote this chapter I have obtained the complete urtext edition of the *Sonatas, Free Fantasies and Rondos* by C. P. E. Bach, reissued by Breitkopf and Härtel, and my enthusiasm for these compositions has immeasurably increased. Besides a number of very individual and powerful sonatas, there are many rondos in style unlike those of any other composer. Whether or not these will "go" in public performance I cannot be sure; much will depend on the authority of the playing. There is nothing tepid or small about the best of these compositions. For private or intimate reading they are among the most fascinating and idiomatic music of the literature. They are indeed all style, a formal music of the Age of Reason that is never vapid. I would now include "the German Bach" among those composers whose keyboard music should be known entire.

Another composer of equal validity in the same style is Johann Gottfried Müthel, one of the last pupils of J. S. Bach and later a pupil of C. P. E. Bach. Only a small amount of his extant music has been published. His *Duetto* for two pianos and three solo sonatas (see Bibliography, p. 281) are among the best examples of embellished music in the French clavecin tradition carried over through the German clavichord to the early piano. These are large compositions well worth knowing and playing.

A major French composer, Jean-Philippe Rameau, summarized in his keyboard works the disappearing clavecin tradition, while his theoretical studies looked beyond the eighteenth-century classics to the nineteenth-century emancipation of harmony from thoroughbass. The articulation of his compositions seems to present fewer problems to present-day readers than that of Couperin, probably because of his richer vertical harmony. As with modern playing of J. S. Bach and Handel, the effect is deceptive.

Here begins the history of piano music, in which I should not need to guide the choices of any true Amateur, merely reminding him that the best music for reading is not always the same he hears most often in performance. Include in your repertoire a few sonatas by Clementi. Dussek and Hummel are of less interest. Weber's graceful sonatas have charm for the light-fingered. A more important but limited keyboard lyricist is John Field; you should know his *Nocturnes* thoroughly but not his sonatas and concertos. Do not pass over Czerny's delicately colored *Etudes*, though there is small fun in playing them. Now that we are in the period of the finger-exercise, let the Amateur keep in mind that for him music should be a recreation, a discipline perhaps, but not labor.

Look well into the not always attractive library of compositions by Franz Liszt, containing a variety of peculiarities and experiments by no means all unsuccessful. If you have patience, spend some of it on the bare steppes of Alkan; better players than ourselves have found profit in him. Among other such composers are Saint-Saëns, Reger, and Medtner.

I must confess that I do not enjoy reading Brahms or Debussy so much as I value expert playing of them. Debussy is well known by performance and recording, but the early works of Brahms and his less-known sets of variations deserve exploring. Schumann is as friendly as Haydn, though I find him less companionable; he communicates a mood but seldom thinks in it. His lyrical charm is best heard in suites of short movements such

as *Carnaval* and *Scenes from Childhood*, though it is capable of
the larger eloquence of his Fantasy.

Nor am I among those who revel in such oddities as the piano
works by Gottschalk. To enjoy such music at the keyboard one
needs a more than ordinary manual dexterity, which cannot be
made up by awareness of the style to the extent that is possible
with music of more content. There was a time when Grieg
seemed to George Bernard Shaw, in comparison with his contemporaries, a giant. That time is long past. His Piano Concerto is an example of a type of nineteenth-century display music
made to sustain itself in spite of any deficiencies or omissions in
the orchestra. As with many familiar nineteenth-century masterpieces, its power is not in its content but in its durability. In this
style, the Piano Concerto by Tchaikovsky is as well-weathered as
the county courthouse. His piano pieces, widely used for teaching, emphasize thump at the expense of rhythm.

Putting aside the difficulties of nearly all twentieth-century
keyboard music, which are not to be mitigated, you should give
attention to Satie and to Ravel, examine if you cannot read successfully the several piano works by Schoenberg, and do whatever you are able to with Scriabin, an important keyboard
composer who may be said to have followed the right insight in
the wrong direction.

For an amateur the principal keyboard composer of the twentieth century is Béla Bartók. You should do the best you can to
read his works completely, starting with the wealth of smaller
works which should be within any amateur's skill.

The more conservative composers of our century have written
a large literature of attractive and technically helpful smaller
pieces for piano, in every style, though none that I know so
stimulating as the works by Bartók.

For the other larger composers of twentieth-century keyboard
music, they are at the end of the trail, technically erudite, genuine composers but idiomatically styleless. It is the idiom of a
style, the tone of voice of something still being said, that mediates between past and present in Ravel and Stravinsky, and
faintly in Fauré. An exception must be made for the keyboard
works by Prokofieff and Hindemith, both of whom have their en-
thusiasts among virtuosos, students, and composers. I would
recommend a knowledge of their writings, though I cannot com-

municate any personal enthusiasm for them. Prokofieff, himself a brilliant pianist, wrote to his own taste and to that of such contemporary masters of the piano as Vladimir Horowitz and Sviatoslav Richter; the music displays technical virtuosity with a minimum of substance. If it be self-condemnation, let me admit that I find the piano music by Hindemith unbearable, except for his Chamber Concerto. Read his piano sonatas, *Ludus Tonalis,* and keyboard pieces and make your own decision. Do not let my taste dissuade you.

As for the two piano sonatas by Charles Ives, the most capacious keyboard compositions of the twentieth century, only the most exceptional playing can manage them.

Among the more significant, if not all equally important, American compositions for piano are the Sonata by Charles Griffes, the *Sonata Seria* and *Sonata Pastorale* by Ingolf Dahl, and the Piano Variations and Sonata by Aaron Copland. Another, writing in my place, might recommend the Sonatas for piano by Samuel Barber and Elliott Carter, and Copland's *Fantasy for Piano.* The early pieces by Henry Cowell, with tone-clusters to be played by depressing the keys with the forearm and pluckings and swishings of the strings, should be known, both for themselves and for their drastic influence on present-day uses of the piano.

Among Latin-American compositions, I would recommend the Preludes and other keyboard works by Carlos Chávez of Mexico and many pieces of varied sorts by Heitor Villa-Lobos of Brazil.

A pantonal survey of contemporary keyboard music may be found in the many issues of *New Music Quarterly,* a magazine of musical compositions, edited by Henry Cowell and Gerald Strang, which continued for some twenty years, subsidized by Charles Ives.

In this long survey I have tried to provoke you to re-evaluate musical opinions commonly held, to tempt you beyond the common repertoire, and to place emphasis where I believe it should be placed. I was fortunate in coming to maturity at a time when the musical horizon was continuously expanding at an unprecedented speed, when nearly the entire historic legacy of Western music was being discovered to us as a performed, recorded literature in sound. Later, after the Second World War, there was an equally unprecedented publication and republication of the entire musical literature in score. No one coming now to music as an amateur can repeat the exhilaration of those years of unfolding discovery and exploration.

The literature is still there, the greater part known but still uncharted and unvisited. Even as I write, my discoveries are continuing, and I have not hesitated to include mention of them. Now go beyond me and make your own discoveries.

Technicalities

: 4 :

SCALES, MELODY,
RHYTHM, HARMONY,
KEY, TUNING

If you find this chapter more complicated than you like when you read at it the first time, don't bother with it, and by all means don't read the two Appendixes, but just go on with the succeeding chapters. You don't have to read this book through from front to back. I've tried to design and build the chapters so that each carries its own weight; when necessary, what you need to know is repeated. Sooner or later you may decide to come back and read this chapter clear through or more closely. After the second or third try, when you realize that everything in this chapter is extracurricular, if not illegal, you will commence feeling as much at home in it as Brer Rabbit in his briar patch, and you may even wish to read both the Appendixes.

All of the world's music has been composed of scales. A *scale* is a succession of notes moving upwards or downwards by steps. Some scales move upwards and downwards on the same notes; in others one or more of the notes may be different in downward as compared with upward movement. It will make the technical aspects of music much easier to grasp if you realize that a scale is only a particular form of melody, either traditional or selected for one occasion, out of which a musical system or a composition grows.

A scale need not be composed of notes which can be written. Tap three or four surfaces around you, the chair arm, the side of the chair, a table top, a book lying on the table; each will produce a sound slightly higher or lower than the others. Percussion composers of the present day rank scalewise as many as a dozen seemingly identical Ford Model A brake drums or a row of flowerpots or coffee cans. By arranging these sounds in rising or descending order you have composed a scale—it's as simple as that. By arranging melodically the four sounds lying within reach of your hand you are able, using a little imagination, to become a composer.

If you wish to write out your composition, you may choose any symbols that please you, for instance the letters Q, R, S, T, to signify the upward progression of the four sounds; T, S, R, Q is then the downward progression. Q–R, R–S, S–T are each an interval or step of the scale proceeding upwards, and the same is true in reverse downwards. Q–S, R–T, Q–T are also intervals and can be sounded in either direction, upwards or downwards, according to the melodic pattern you wish to compose.

Now select four other surfaces, determine the scale of progression upwards and downwards, and apply to these the same melodic pattern. Although the melodic pattern is the same, the affect or character of the melody will be different, because the sounds composing the intervals are not the same. The sounds themselves will differ in quality, since they are produced by striking new objects, and the distances between the sounds, the intervallic steps, will be larger or smaller in each instance.

We are now deep into musical theory and composition without having struck a note. So go at once to the piano and try the same system, with four notes at the keyboard instead of four surfaces. Using the four notes, play your composition at the piano. Then put down the lid over the keys; rap the wood under the keyboard, the rail in front of the keyboard, the lid over the keys, and the piano top: play your composition again. (John Cage has composed a song accompaniment by this means.)

In each case the *melodic pattern* is the same; the sounds and the intervallic relations which compose the *melody* differ. You have learned, like most of the world's peoples, to make music without harmony, using melodic scales of your own invention. You can whistle your little piece to four pitches of your choice or sing it to four vowels or syllables or words. You have set up as a composer and are in business.

You may find that it will be easier to follow visually the rise and fall of intervals if you write the sound-symbols in a stepwise pattern.

Now transfer what you have learned to the keys of the piano, each of which has a letter-name, and learn the system of notation which indicates these letters (or notes of the scale) by symbols on the stepwise system of horizontal lines and spaces called a *staff*. Go right ahead composing and practise writing the notation, so that you can repeat and preserve your compositions. It is one-finger composition (played one note at a time), but so is much of the world's music and always has been. The music with notes printed perpendicularly one above another in vertical relationship on the staff, that we are accustomed to think of as MUSIC, is in fact a special and exceptional type of music peculiar to the European culture and no other.

Now buy the first book of *Mikrokosmos* by Béla Bartók and start reading the first pieces. These are five-note compositions, using only five notes side by side on the keyboard in stepwise position; the notes lie directly under your fingers. You can't miss.

Many of the great traditional systems of music use for notation no more than a set of letters written in succession, without visual arrangement upward or downward. The *inflection* of these notes, by adding conventional groups of notes that are not written or by ornaments or graces (what older English musicians called "gracing"), was learned in these systems by years of exact practice, so that the pupil was trained to do exactly what his master had done before him. Such systems of aural transmission, some of them centuries old, are slowly disappearing under the impact of Western culture, because learning in that way consumes too much time.

The earlier jazz musicians improvised around familiar tunes, the younger ones learning from the older. Many of them could not read music; they spoke or sang music through the voices of their instruments. They sang words with an artificial voice and style, as if playing them on an instrument. They played and sang slides and microtones which cannot be written down in our notation.

Systems of diacritical marking are also used to help the student

remember the correct conventional method of playing and inflect-
ing each letter-note in its place. Some systems allow the player
considerable freedom in inflection; others require an exact reproduction of each tone and microtone.

Earlier keyboard composers permitted great freedom in in-
flecting the music by gracing and embellishment, following generally accepted models. Since players were not of equal competence in using their opportunities, the composers wrote out
more and more of the musical text as they wished it to be played,
expecting that in those places where inflection was still permitted,
the players would limit themselves, by learning the conventional
models, to using only acceptable and expected embellishments
and graces.

These conventional passages of inflection were gradually absorbed into the written texture and structure of the composition,
so that we play classic music today almost without being aware
to what extent it is made up of conventional idiomatic figures and
patterns of inflection used by the composer as if he or the player
had improvised them. So Chopin wrote: "When your completed
work gives the effect of an improvisation, you will make the
greatest impression." The composer thought his composition in
simple melodic and harmonic relationships, like our notated
melodic pattern in letters, and then inflected or performed it by
substituting for or adding to each note in the pattern a conventional group of notes resembling the syllables or words we put
together to convey an idea in writing or conversation. Or, with
experience, he substituted his own original idiomatic groupings
for the more conventional groupings.

We compose writing; we improvise conversation. A good writer
composes and improvises at the same time, by a practised feeling
for combining words and phrases without clumsiness or confusion, forcefully and gracefully. Some persons write in correspondence even better than they speak, by a natural feeling for such
combinations in literary form—and because they allow themselves
more time for "composing" correspondence. Some illiterate persons speak in verbal melodies of memorable expressiveness and
charm. In sixteenth- and seventeenth-century European speech
and writing, and among peoples today who take more time than
we do to express themselves, ideas are inflected away from the
direct statements we prefer into substantive patterns of elegant

indirection and elaborate reference that are felt to be more graceful and meaningful. (So poetry and myth grow out of language.) The ideas they wish to express occur to them in the natural melodic context of their habitual language. To pass beyond this context and write or speak of ideas not habitual to one's language, one must overcome difficulties, sometimes going so far as almost to invent a new language, tied to the speech one knows by no more than the customary rules of syntax—even these may be stretched. Such are the languages of systematic philosophy, theory, mathematics.

The reversal of the balance between idiomatically conventional and composed language in keyboard music occurred at no one time, but in the maturing experience of composers striving to substitute for the conventional elaboration of relatively simple ideas a completely ordered, original expression that would enlarge the idea as nearly as possible to the whole scope of the composition. That is why some of the great works of art in music convey, like a Mozart concerto, no other idea than their own self-sufficient existence, while in a few works the idea, whether or not we can convey it in words, seems, as with Bach, to energize every note of the composition or, as in late Beethoven, threatens to explode the structure into fragments.

Among the generality of more recent composers these demanding requirements, which they respected and wished to emulate, set up a division between sweet, simple, tuneful, and often mentally lazy music, which is called popular, and would-be serious music, bulging with an imitation of mental muscularity and strung out all over the place, like painting and sculpture after Michelangelo. Mention no names.

You see how rapidly our knowledge can grow from tapping on a table: how a scale can become the body of a thought or be transfigured into idea. We have observed how a single note may be inflected by a conventional figure or phrase of several notes, and that this is what the bulk of music is made of.

For expressiveness there must be rhythm. When you were tapping that melodic pattern on the table, chair, and so on, I'll bet that you didn't make every note equal in volume or intensity of sound, or in shortness or duration, and that the space or time of the successive intervals between the notes was not always the same. Some of the notes you emphasized and some you didn't.

5

If you weren't thinking too hard about what you were doing, but just doing it as you liked, then probably the rhythms were very free. If you were being self-conscious because it was the first time you had ever composed, then the rhythm may not have been so free.

Rhythm is one of the factors that make up dynamic expression. The word "rhythm" itself would be good enough, but too many people think of rhythm as beats and counting, pulling the music together into strict time while you listen to a metronome. So when I use the term *dynamic expression* to include all the other elements besides time that contribute to making music expressive, I mean *rhythm* in its broader sense.

Concerning good rhythm in performance, Percy Scholes writes in *The Oxford Companion to Music:* "The rise and fall of the intervals of the melody, and the greater or lesser pungency of the chords of the harmony, create in the mind of the genuinely musical performer and listener a desire for tiny hurryings and lingerings such as could never be expressed in any notation. . . . These operate to modify the demands of regularity without destroying the feeling of regularity; such slight but purposeful departures from regularity suggest life as opposed to mechanism.

"As such modifications, though following general principles that would perhaps be susceptible of modification, are yet infinite in their variety of possible detail, rhythmic treatment of a composition offers one of the most notable means of the unconscious expression of personality and of mood. It is certain that no two master-performers have ever yet performed the same composition in the same rhythmic manner, and it is even doubtful whether any master-performer has ever performed the same composition twice in quite the same way."

In determining correct rhythm the metronome has its place, and exact counting of the measure will also be necessary. As soon as you have determined what the rhythm is, you should put the metronome away. The ear takes over, translating the exact temporal and metrical relationships you have worked out into dynamic expression and the pattern of notes into a melody.

Beethoven warmly endorsed the clockwork metronome invented by Maelzel, much the same that we use today, and wrote out metronome indications for the tempi of many of his movements. Coming back to these indications at a later time and in a different mood, he found them uncomfortable and gave up using the metronome. In our own time the great pianist Josef Hofmann advised that the best place for a metronome is in a closet.

To train your ear to rhythm, listen to good conversation, to expert dramatic speech, and to every performer of music in every kind or style or tradition. Listen with your ears and with your whole body; listen as it were inside the music, not on the surface, until your whole body lets go and responds by contrary feelings of movement to the counterpoints of rhythm. Rhythmic counterpoint is a descriptive rather than an exact term, signifying the different rhythms going on in the music at the same time, as well as the horizontal variants in each melodic voice.

The multifarious, subtly differentiated voices, intensified by accent, by volume, by displacement of tones, by phrasing notes in groups which lie forward or lean backward from the beat; the placing of silences, the little breathing-pauses of Couperin and the larger breath-taking pauses of a folk singer; always working together to clarify, to articulate, to hold backward or press forward the seemingly exact fall of the beat—which is not always beaten but sometimes silent or implicit—transform the larger body of the movement, and often by relationship a sequence of movements, into a dynamically expressive and rhythmically integrated melody, though it be in many parts.

The beat, or fall, of the unified melodic complex must seem to be exact, like waves breaking on a beach, subject to changes of rhythm the composer has indicated by his dynamic markings. I like the word *fall* better, because *beat* implies a drum or a strong accent, whereas the *fall* may be no more than holding one note rather longer than the others, a silence, or a barely noticeable accent.

"The correctness of my time astonishes them all," Mozart wrote in a letter to his family. "The tempo rubato in an adagio with the left hand keeping strict time was quite beyond their comprehension. They always follow with the left hand." The accompanying hand, that is to say, keeps strict time, while the singing hand sings free. But the strictness of the accompanying hand at once governs and sustains the free flight of the song; and this strictness is itself a constant slight flexibility, a giving forward and pulling back, within the seemingly strict metric accent.

And Mozart again: "In what does the art of playing consist? In playing the piece in the correct time with all the notes, appoggiaturas, etc., with the appropriate expression and taste so that one believes the player has himself composed it. . . . Moreover it is also much easier to play a piece fast than slow; notes can be dropped out of passages without being noticed; but is that right?"

Couperin and Ives both divided their compositions into *verse* and *prose,* verse being metrical with a regular accent and prose unmetrical with an irregular accent (see Couperin's Preludes and the first movement of Ives's *Concord Sonata*). The division applies throughout music, though in some periods and styles more than others. As distinguished from the earlier European choral music, the music of the keyboard centuries tends to be more metrical than otherwise. One should read metrical music, as one should read verse, especially when it is rapid, with a constant definite varying of the phrase and the phrase accent across the beat. Played so, a slower reading will convey the inner moving of the parts and will seem more rapid; when this practice has been made habitual, the absolute speed of the performance can be increased, with exhilarating effect. Only so can a true adagio or largo be played as slowly as it should be and gain in interior movement.

The reader may now add to his little compositions such metrical and rhythmic devices as may please him, keeping them in simple mathematical relationship by count so that he can easily notate them. But now let him work backwards: first reading the simple rhythmic notation of the first five-finger pieces of Bartók's *Mikrokosmos,* and then tapping or beating or whistling or singing his own compositions and notating them in the same way.

(I am assuming that my reader knows or will go to the trouble of learning musical notation. This book is not a teaching manual but a pointing procedure: Look at this, and this! And by pointing it raises questions. Wherever I point, you should continue the process by looking up and arguing with the answers in standard reference works.)

Rhythm should flow, leap, and whorl as naturally as running water, which at first seems very free and then, under close observation, strict and recurrent, yet never exactly to the same point. Rhythm should never be permitted to become mechanical. Even the bass drummer in a band should think a melody. There has been a strong tendency to become mechanical in key-

board playing of the last thirty years, as a partly deliberate pro-
test against the extreme and capricious distortions of time made
by virtuoso performers of the immediately preceding generations. Ostentatious irregularity or distortion can be bad, but an
ostentatious regularity is bad also. One must grant, however, that
for some excellent musicians and some excellent poets the only
comprehension of rhythm seems to be strict and accentual.
(Tennyson, for example, was remarked for his absolutely exact
accentual reading, to which he sometimes beat time with his
hand.)

The notating of rhythm can never be more than a compromise
between the reality the ear seeks and the mathematical mendacity
of a notational system. That is why composers of other centuries
and of other cultures have left so many of the intricate details of
rhythm to be learned by study of tradition and convention. We
today cannot recover dynamic expressiveness by a short cut. Experience will show the reader that any attempt to "explain" the
rhythmic convention by writing out the notation as the editor
believes it should be played will be no more helpful and indeed
more confusing than learning to read from the composer's indications. I have a collection of the minuets by Haydn, edited in
notation by Hugo Riemann; it is almost unplayable, because the
eye is continually being distracted by the editorial emphasis.

When you have mastered melody and rhythm, you have
learned the art of music, except for the special circumstances of
music during the keyboard period.

Listen to the records made by Huddie Ledbetter (Leadbelly)
for their rhythm. Listen to them also for their accompaniments,
played on the twelve-string guitar, basses as elegant as Chopin's.
This is music made entirely of harmony, without counterpoint, so
self-sufficient that, unlike most harmonic accompaniment, it is
not ruffled or influenced from its purity by extreme deviations in
the melody—the deliberately off-pitch, microtonally sliding, deep-
Southern Negro tradition of speaking-singing that falls across it.
Here is C. P. E. Bach's or Mozart's rhythmic practice, with true
European harmony in full chords on the guitar (as it were, in the
left hand) and a still African, or at least non-European, inflection
of melody going comfortably against it. In idiomatic ability to
digest and transform unlike materials, Leadbelly resembled
Bartók.

So we return to Bartók's *Mikrokosmos*. In the first pieces we have been reading unison melodies, played under the five fingers, moving in parallel octave unison in both hands. This doubling of a simple stepwise melody at the octave is the earliest type of European harmony, *plainsong*.

(If you are thinking that music in five-finger position is too simple, let me remind you that the theme-tones of the final movement of Beethoven's Ninth Symphony can be picked out at the piano in five-finger position, except that the melody goes down to one tone instead of going up.)

In pieces 12 and 17 of *Mikrokosmos* the melody moves at the same time upwards in one hand and downwards in the other; this is contrary movement, and we see that in number 17 it requires the introduction of two sharpened notes in the left hand to make the harmony come out satisfactorily.

In piece 22 we begin reading counterpoint in varying interval relationships and parallel and contrary movement. Counterpoint is the setting together of linear parts or voices in vertical relationships directed by the harmony. (In polyphony, by contrast, the vertical—simultaneously heard—relationships are incidental to the simultaneous horizontal unfolding of melodies.) Wherever two or more notes fall vertically together and are heard at the same time, there is a degree of harmony, desired or undesired, correct or incorrect. The correctness or incorrectness will be in relation to the harmonic context; a number of interesting musical conventions and rhythmic devices have been thought up just to get around undesired harmonies.

Vertical harmony is the grammar and its horizontal unfolding the syntax which result from combining in simultaneous vertical relationship two or more independent musical voices. In pure vertical harmony the independent movement of voices disappears, and there is a succession of chords, which need change shape only slightly to be impressive. *Harmony* is commonly a fluctuating control among the vertical and horizontal relationships of the same notes. In fact, to play harmony you need but learn a few chords and strum them with a rhythmic feeling, occasionally breaking out or spreading the separate notes like a peacock displaying its tail feathers. For many, this is resource enough to fill out a lifetime of musical satisfaction.

We shall do well to understand that there is an integral consistency in the succession of sounds that composes each separately moving part of a composition. This self-harmonized consistency refers to the scale that is being used. Music has no discrete term for it; the horizontal consistency may be composed around a pentatonic (five-note), hexatonic (six-note)—more often called hexachordal, or diatonic (seven-note), or chromatic or dodecaphonic (twelve-note) system, or a modal scale, or a chord used like a scale (as was done by Scriabin), or a scale borrowed from a non-European tradition or microtonally altered, and so on. In spite of this, the vertical relationship may be harmonized according to strict European rule, as Leadbelly does it, with the result that the melodic (horizontal) consistency and the vertical harmony are distinct. That is what happens, for instance, in harmonizing folk song, except that most folk-song arrangers, lacking the skill of Bartók or Leadbelly, confine the free melodies by the formal limitations of their harmonic knowledge, so that the free melodies are made slavish tunes.

Tunes, generally speaking, are built around simple chords melodically disposed. A melody need have no harmony but itself, as we discovered at the start of this chapter. Harmony and counterpoint result from setting the same melody in vertical relationship with itself in varying positions (e.g. fugue), or in vertical relationship with other melodies, or in relation to accompanying groups or progressions of chords, or in relation to a recurring figure in the bass (e.g. variations or divisions on a ground). In a *figured bass* accompaniment or *continuo* part, the player is invited to fill out the single written note of the bass with the correct inflection of additional notes in melodic or chordal elaborations.

At different periods different vertical combinations, formerly outlawed, have become permissible. One reason for this, nearly forgotten nowadays, lay in the temperament (the pitch-relationships of the successive notes of the scale). The earliest formal harmonies were concordances at the octave and the fifth (or its alternative, the fourth: from C to G upwards is an interval of the fifth, from C to G downwards is an interval of the fourth), because these intervals were the only perfect concordances in the Pythagorean temperament, which governed music at this period. Music reference books commonly define *concord* or *concordance* in terms of the more consonant or less dissonant intervallic and chordal relationships of tones in equal temperament. A concord or concordant interval (or chord) is, strictly, perfect or beatless (e.g. the octave in equal temperament, the octave and fifth in Pythagorean, the octave and major third in meantone, the triad in just intonation) or includes, by extension, combinations of intervals with small number ratios in just intonation.

All intervals in equal temperament are discordant, except the octave. *Consonance* comprises those intervals and combinations of tones thought to be consonant according to the convention of the time (e.g., in equal temperament the very discordant major third is called consonant). *Dissonance* is whatever exceeds the conventional, or tolerated, field of intervallic relationships described as consonant. The "emancipation of the dissonance" merely dispensed with the rules which distinguish consonance from dissonance, so that all twelve tones of the chromatic scale may be used as a common musical *field,* subject to whatever rules the composer chooses to establish.

As composers desired more vertical concordances—there being at the time no permissible formal harmony except by concordance—a new temperament was worked out, called *just intonation,* with concordances at the octave, the fifth, and the third (which read downwards is a sixth). To tune just intonation on a keyboard instrument, that is to say, one must *temper* the theoretically perfect scale of mathematically exact just intonation, by tuning one or more of the intervals more narrowly. Any keyboard tuning of just intonation is therefore a temperament.

Theorists and composers have tried by many methods to build a keyboard instrument which would permit a perfectly concordant scale of mathematically exact just intonation to be tuned. Such an instrument was built in the sixteenth century at the court of Ferrara, and there are reports of others in each of the succeeding centuries. The best that I have heard is a celesta, tuned to a very pure just intonation, built for the composer Lou Harrison. The overtone resonances are as rich as those of bells and more accurate.

The scales used for the earlier music were called *modes.* In European music, a scale is the division of a single octave into a stepwise pattern of intervals. Earlier European scales had fewer notes, lacking some or all of our sharps or flats. The full twelve-note scale came into use during the sixteenth century—we could argue that point for a week, but the full use of the twelve tones in relation to one another becomes evident in such a composer as the sixteenth-century madrigalist Gesualdo. The singers of these madrigals adjusted their vocal pitches so that discordances (which we scarcely notice in a modern performance) became concordant; they sang by ear and intention in a true just intonation which was not a temperament. But fixed-pitch instruments could not be so altered, and the conflict of pitches between voices and instruments could be strident.

This at once very exact and very free practice was soon curtailed by new rules of vertical harmony and a new temperament, or system of tuning, called *meantone*, developed primarily for keyboard use, which kept the concordant or perfect third but narrowed the fifths so that these were no longer concordant but were instead noticeably dissonant. Meantone tuning, which has many practical advantages, soon overran all of Europe, coming afterwards to England.

With meantone, mildly dissonant relationships, being no longer avoidable, began to be acceptable and were soon being heard *as if* they were concords. Habits of inflection were devised to avoid or prevent more extreme discords, and singers lost the skill of adjusting their pitches to pure concords.

English keyboard composers seem to have retained the Pythagorean tuning in perfect fifths and imperfect thirds until Purcell, tempering the fifths slightly at the extremes of the cycle to permit such a degree of modulation as is required for playing the controversial *Hexachord* by John Bull (*Fitzwilliam Virginal Book*, no. 51; *Ut, Re, Mi, Fa, Sol, La*).

All standard modern treatises of harmony and harmonic analysis take for granted tuning in equal temperament (the tuning used from the start of the nineteenth century until the present), even where it is known or should be obvious that the music being analyzed was written for a different tuning, having concordances or consonant relations where we have discordances or dissonant relations. The meantone major third, for example, is a concordance; the equal temperament major third is an equal and invariable sharp discordance. Yet we continue in theory and practice to treat the major third as a concordance and to call it consonant. Because the fifth in just intonation was a concordance, we have rules for avoiding parallel fifths, as if these passages would stand apart from the texture because of their concordance, even though fifths have not been concordant since the adoption of meantone. It is probable, too, that composers had tired of parallel fifths and welcomed the new art of controlled dissonance—as we may soon tire of extreme dissonance, which is really discordance, and welcome back the richer sonorities of more perfect concords.

These are some of the confusions of our harmonic theory, which could be quickly cleared up by some study of tuning, instead of being left as they are, surprising and confusing.

Apart from theoretical confusion, what are our real losses? We do not hear the pure concordant sonorities of medieval and Renaissance choral singing interpenetrating like the lights of stained-glass windows the darker texture of the moving voices, held distinct from one another by nonconcordance. Instead, we hear all vertical relationships the same in a tepid pseudoharmonic whine of false relationships which we think of as the medieval sound. The true relationship sounds less archaic and harmonically less peculiar than our misuse.

In keyboard playing we have lost the sweet sonorities of the perfect fifths in Pythagorean and tempered Pythagorean, which with the sweet tone of the true virginal, plucked well out from the bridge, must have made the Elizabethan and Jacobean keyboard music like a garden in flower, while for us it is only uniform green leafage. And we have lost the remarkable voice-leading of concords mixed with varying degrees of dissonance provided by meantone, the varieties of key-coloring in any one tuning which could be altered with a change of tuning. We have scarcely explored meantone, the most long-lived of the keyboard tunings.

Anyone can quickly train himself to tune meantone on one register (set of strings) of a harpsichord. Pythagorean and tempered Pythagorean are no more difficult. A harpsichord register has one string for each note. Tuning a piano, which has three strings for each note, or a double-strung clavichord will be more troublesome. Although J. S. Bach could tune a harpsichord keyboard in fifteen minutes, he had at the time of his death, presumably distributed in every corner of the house, two clavecins, which were likely large two-manual instruments in French style; three ditto (as the *Specificatio* of the Estate has it), which may have been smaller or single-keyboard instruments; two lute-harpsichords (presumably with gut strings, the others having metal strings); and one *Spinettgen,* or little spinet, probably to be set on a table. It seems reasonable that the purpose of having so many instruments in this musically busy household would have been the need to keep several instruments in different or variant tunings and at distinct pitch levels, since no instrument will keep in good tune if you change the tuning very often.

If, like myself, you have only a single-manual spinet, you will have to plan to spend a few months with the English music, tuning tempered Pythagorean, and other months with the meantone literature. Once you have done so, however, your ear will readily discriminate the necessity of the correct tuning.

Besides their complacent assumption that a *well-tempered* tuning is the same as *equal-tempered,* which is a mistake, historians of music have been content to presume that J. S. Bach, once he had worked out his well-tempered tuning, never went back again to compose or play in meantone. The evidence would show that well-tempered is only one of perhaps several solutions Bach considered and tried experimentally.

J. S. Bach's solution of the problem of a well-tempered tuning made possible harmony and modulation in full chords in all twenty-four keys, while preserving some color differentiation among keys—which would have seemed as necessary to Bach as it does not occur to us. Played in well-tempered tuning, Beethoven's two Preludes through all the keys, opus 39, change color in each modulation, whereas in the undifferentiated equal temperament the modulations are paper-exercises, meaningless for the ear. Well-tempered tuning is not equal temperament but a distinct tuning in unequal intervals.

Equal temperament, the mathematical division of the octave into equal intervals without regard to acoustical concordance, was known to ancient mathematical theorists but seems not to have seriously interested musicians until the rise of the modern orchestra towards the end of the eighteenth century. Equal temperament came into vogue with the increase of instruments in the orchestra and the growth of technical interest in the possible developments of modulation and counterpoint by means of larger bodies of instruments and orchestral mixtures. Well-tempered would have been an acoustically preferable and more musical choice, but the interval relations require a very subtle ear in

tuning, since the fifths are progressively narrowed to mid-point
and then progressively widened to return to the starting perfect
fifth. Use of this tuning by orchestral musicians would have
caused even more imperfect agreement among players than we
shrug our shoulders at. But the substitution of orchestral color
for key color set in motion another train of events which would
inevitably destroy the harmonic key-system.

To describe economically the principle of *key* in the European
harmonic system, I shall quote again from *The Oxford Companion to Music:* "Key is a quality that gradually crept into European music during the sixteenth century and began gradually to
creep out of it from the beginning of the twentieth. . . . The
principle of key is that of the construction of melody and harmony, at any given moment, out of a scale of which all the notes
bear a strong and easily recognized allegiance to a chief note
('key-note' or 'tonic'). The same scale can be taken at different
pitches, and consequently any melody or harmony in one key
can be taken also in another key, the effect being precisely the
same but for pitch. The melody or series of harmonies may move
from key to key ('modulate'), but the piece will return to its
original key to end. In fact, the feeling of 'home' is the essence of
key. The key-note is the home note of the scale and the opening
key of a composition is the home key. . . . There are ways of
using incidental notes extraneous to the key without destroying
the 'home' feeling; such notes are often called 'Chromatic', the
notes of the key itself being 'Diatonic'."

This is not strictly true. Some composers like to start in the
wrong key for the fun of concealing the right key; but "wrong"
and "right" are in relation to the home key. Experts in form are
connoisseurs after the event.

The definition is true only for equal temperament. In meantone, and to a less degree in well-tempered, each key sounds a
different pattern of unequal intervals, producing a distinct key-
coloration. The loss of such individually distinctive key-coloration, which transforms the fixed-pitch music of this period with
subtle coloristic distinctions impossible to imagine until one has
heard them, is the great loss we have suffered in changing from
meantone to the equal intervals and indistinguishable keys of
equal temperament. (Gustav Mahler said the same to Arnold
Schoenberg, who told it to me.) Meantone and well-tempered

compositions exploit these changes of coloring in ways that cannot be made up by the heavier harmonization and chromatic
dissonance used in equal temperament.

We see that harmony is a much broader and less definite
matter than the subject we read about in harmony textbooks,
which have to do only with the manipulations possible in equal
temperament.

For each of the twelve notes within the octave there is one
major scale or key and one *minor* scale or key. (If you think that
musical theorists know exactly what this simple statement means,
you'd be surprised.) These are the two principal types of key-
scale into which composers after the sixteenth century gradually
reduced their harmonic opportunities.

The term *minor* serves also to indicate a lesser interval: the
interval of two white keys lying side by side on the piano keyboard with no black key between them, or the interval between a
black key and the white key at either side of it, is a minor second.
The term *major* serves in the same way to indicate a larger interval: the interval between two white keys side by side on the
keyboard divided by a black key, or two black keys divided by a
white key, is a major second.

We must now pause to observe that a *key* on the keyboard is
the lever you strike to produce a tone; key, thus used, has nothing to do with a key in harmony. You can call a key-lever a "note,"
as some do, if you keep in mind that it is not a written note (e.g.,
"strike a note on the keyboard").

A half-step interval is commonly called a *half-tone*, although it
is not a tone but an interval; a whole-step interval is in the same
way called a *whole-tone*.

We may now risk saying that a *major scale* pattern runs upwards by two whole-step (major second) intervals and a half-step
(minor second) interval and three more whole-steps and a half-
step. A *minor scale* pattern runs upwards by one whole-step and
a half-step and two whole-steps and a half-step and two whole-
steps. This is called the *natural minor* and is the one you mean
when you talk about "major and minor."

There are also the *melodic minor*, the *harmonic minor*, and the
relative minor, which I suggest that you forget about.

The *whole-tone scale* has six instead of seven notes because it
includes no half-steps. It has only two practical positions, depend-

ing on whether you start with a white or a black note (key-lever) on the keyboard.

Observe, however, that a *white note* means in notation one in which the enclosed oval of the note symbol is white (usually a half-note or a whole-note) and a black note means in notation one in which the enclosed oval of the note is black (a quarter-note or less).

While we are battling out this confusion in terms, which is one of the principal flaws of our musical methodology, let me add that Americans commonly speak of a note as a tone, whereas the English prefer, with scorn, to call a tone a note.

The English, with their genius for beautiful language, however imprecise, unnecessary, or confusing, like to speak of a *breve* (a double whole-note, which was once, as its name indicates, the short note of musical notation), a *semi-breve* (meaning a whole-note, not a half-note as the name suggests), a *minim* (meaning a half-note), and so on.

As the great musical comedienne Anna Russell remarks hysterically, after describing for fifteen minutes the plot of Wagner's *Ring of the Nibelungs*—"You know, I'm not making this up!"

Music is a beautiful and reasonable art, founded on simple physical facts of relationship among sound-vibrations, which can be described exactly in plain mathematical terms, as Pythagoras first described them 2,600 years ago.

Anyone interested in this subject will do well to obtain a copy of a book by the American composer Harry Partch, *Genesis of a Music*, and read as much of it as he is able. The book is published by the University of Wisconsin Press. It is one of the most reasonable books ever written about the bases of musical tonality and is therefore almost entirely overlooked, avoided, or deliberately disregarded by experts.

When you have mastered this chapter, you will be considerably better informed and freer of misinformation about music than I have been during most of my long musical career.

STRUCTURE
AND TEXTURE

A theme is the tune or melody that sets the music in motion. If it is the only theme, it is the subject. A subject may consist of several themes, and a movement or composition may have several subjects.

A textural theme consists of a melody or figure capable of furnishing its own accompaniment. There are two distinct types of structural theme. The first, or classic, type consists of a tune or motif or a combination of motives and can evolve around as little as a single interval. One may call this type of theme analytical, because the material of the theme is able to be taken apart and used separately, or the entire theme may be reorganized, for example by composing a different melody on the recognizable rhythmic shape of the theme or by keeping the familiar harmonic units of the melody while altering the rhythm. The second, romantic or nonanalytical, type of structural theme consists of an unalterable melody or melody and accompaniment.

Schoenberg wrote: "From Bach I learned . . . contrapuntal thinking; that is, the art of inventing musical figures which can accompany themselves." Textural themes are often in two sections, the whole theme or each section being capable of combining in various positions of vertical relationship (harmonically or polyphonically) or of being mirrored in some instances by a contrary statement (upside down or backwards) of the same notes. Although these possibilities are never fully realized by the textural themes of Orlando Gibbons and no more than occasionally by those of J. S. Bach, they underlie all textural composition, as well as all applications of textural method by structural composers, and continue lively as ever in works by Schoenberg, Webern, Stravinsky, and Charles Ives.

Beethoven has left one such textural theme unexploited, that of the first *Bagatelle*, opus 126, a subject with which one might attempt another *Art of Fugue*.

In textural composition, harmonic relationship is subordinated to the positioning of the voices; its working out is conditioned by the harmonic possibilities set up by the intervallic relations of the melodic theme, taken in melodic order. When the intervallic relations deny any key, the resulting composition must be without key, not polytonal (i.e. in many keys), as Schoenberg and Webern recognized with misgiving. Since much folk melody is without key, a similar result occurs in the music by Bartók which is derived from folk-melodic materials.

As the textural theme is not simply the original statement but its potential, so the classic theme by structure is not the tune, the motif, or the interval, but the unit, which is exposed, analyzed, and recombined, and which may often bring forth new themes. The logic of a structural theme is displayed against the background of its reconstruction in unfamiliar positions and in relation to the progress of the harmony. The moving voice or voices are conditioned harmonically by the successive positions of the bass, in short figures or long passages or plateaus. The progress from one position to another by modulation, transition, or variation sets up a journey of events, dramatized by their successive relations with one another and with the original key.

In structural music any rise or fall by a chromatic interval in the bass can severely influence the harmony. Whether such a change is to be a storm or a breeze over the waters depends on the harmonic complication. In textural music, by contrast, the chromatic rise or fall of the bass obeys instead of determining the context.

Any structural composer, as he enlarges the scope of his method, finds more use for texture, to expand the incidental developments of chromaticism, as counterpoint or modified fugue, the structure supplying a framework for the texture. Textural composition can continue only so long as the theme permits; the addition of themes allows added sections and in some instances a final combining of themes. Thus a fugal movement, in structural composition, is likely to contain the opposing theme group of a sonata movement, so that the fugal theme, however predominant, is seldom the sole determinant. This happens often with Beethoven.

The utmost effect of structural music is brought about when the harmonic control, after having been most thoroughly threatened by an eruption of textural independence in the moving parts, is firmly and finally reasserted by the composer by means which make clear that, however far afield he may have wandered, he has never lost direction. This drama and reassurance, combined, explain the emotional authority of Beethoven; no matter how tragic the events his music figuratively suffers, he is never defeated in the end. When the harmonic control slackens or falls away without emphatic reassertion, the denouement occurs brokenly, as pathos.

The second, romantic or nonanalytical, type of structural theme, consisting of an unalterable melody or melody with accompaniment, cannot be manipulated texturally or with analytic economy by structural concentration, having to assert its full length by sequences of juxtaposition, no matter how inworked by devices or methods from other systems.

Critical theorists, having in mind the economy of classical structure, find the resulting composition unwieldy, as it may be when it reaches the extremes of Schubert. Problems of length displace the priority of modulation and transition. Schubert's lyrically inlaid subjects seem to have solved the problem merely by their presentation, but their unalterability becomes the more evident as the composition grows, though the unequaled inventiveness of Schubert in his later compositions turns even this condition to emotional and esthetic advantage. Liszt, Mendelssohn, the Chopin of the sonatas and concertos, still more their lesser contemporaries, show the defect of the dilemma without Schubert's compensations; at their best they cannot make so much virtue of the defect as Schubert does.

The temptation to apply inherited analytical and textural devices to unalterable themes causes the unwieldiness of composers who try, as Liszt did, to apply to such an unalterable theme the textural transpositions of Bach. The technical rationalizations of

6

this problem by Brahms, which he resolved conservatively, when carried to their conclusions eventuate in the unresolved dissonances of Hindemith and Schoenberg.

The application of textural methods is one subject of nearly all Bach's exemplary music, so that ideally the student will learn how to read and spread out a figured bass by mastering the elaboration of thematic possibilities in independent composition. The theme of Bach's *Goldberg Variations* is the bass, around which, from the first presentation, melodies are elaborately woven. We have reason to believe that Bach and Handel were able to expand upon a figured bass to an extent unequaled by their contemporaries.

Schubert and Liszt often raised their accompaniments to greater prominence than the sustaining melody, but without altering the subject or the method of structure by juxtaposition. Chopin wrote that "with me the accompaniment has always equal rights with the melody and often must be placed in the foreground." The elevating of the accompaniment plus the resulting interest in harmonic coloration eventually destroyed the governance of the bass, so that the composition wandered freely on its harmony but not within it.

Bach uses structural devices in all extended compositions, which could not otherwise have been successfully extended: by key relationship; by plateaus of modulation; by introducing additional themes, each extended separately; by combining themes after such initial presentation; by contrasts of rhythm and style; and by return or *ritornello* of a section.

Handel mediates between textural and structural composition, the movements of his larger compositions as well as the whole body of any set of variations being organized each around a single distinct idea, whereas Bach thinks almost invariably in the meaningful related textures of an entire work or group of works. The tendency to think by separate movements breaks up the continuity of Handel's keyboard suites, making them the more congenial to an age when the movements of a concerto, in performance, would be divided by groups of songs and other performance events. Whereas the whole of any Bach suite or partita, and indeed the whole of each book of keyboard music as Bach planned it, flows together as a completely interrelated organization, no matter how many diverse ideas may enter into it.

In the piano concertos by Mozart, themes, ideas, fragments of a subject are thrown out by the orchestra, by the piano, picked up separately, gathered, interwoven: here is an art that can be followed but never really analyzed. One can describe what seems to happen, what appears to have occurred, but not how or why it happened. Here is neither Bach's formal unrolling of the design fully foreseen to best advantage in its theme nor Beethoven's subjectively dramatic exposition and clash of opposing tensions, holding together like the stresses of a building. Mozart is the supreme *improvisatore:* throwing out the threads of idea and gathering in the complete idea, the form—not an idea of the form.

The shape of a textural composition is its span, though the tendency to increased embellishment and to the quickening re-entries of the theme that are called *stretto* may produce a more complex elaboration in the second half than in the first. Very large textural compositions tend to be organized sectionally, each part being separately worked, the accumulative elaboration being sometimes directed to the center rather than to the end: thus, therefore, and thereafter, like a Shakespeare play.

A structural composition is put together by contrast of independently organized movements, the structural development working normally towards climax. Mozart preferred sometimes to let the material run thin at the end and almost vanish. The shape of a large structured movement is obtained by contrast of forms, each section or movement being itself separately blocked out, usually in relation to the controlling harmony, on successive plateaus of recession and return in relation to the principal key. A structural master expresses himself by the climactic progression of events, where a lyrical formalist such as Boccherini merely progresses.

In Beethoven's music the extremes of recession between the moving voices and the bass introduce sensations and ideas of conceptual space, opportunities which the nineteenth-century composer lost by filling them in harmonically, while the twentieth-century composer of antitraditional intention separates the attributes of tone in space (pitch, loudness, timbre, and duration) from the harmonic determinant, to make these expressive for their own sake. Silence, a rhythmic breathing in Couperin, becomes in Beethoven a dramatic moment, and in more advanced twentieth-century composition a determining factor of the design.

The design of a classically structured movement is determined by its bass, upon which the harmonic blocks move from position to position. The texture of a structural music, however elaborately counterpointed in all parts, will require an increasing assertion of the leading voices, as these move into harmonic independence of the harmonies asserted by the bass. Structural music is therefore less stable than textural music, because the increase of harmonic independence in the voices threatens at all times to disrupt the harmonic control, unless this control exerts itself by imposing limits on the independence óf the voices. The former is more characteristic of the late works by Beethoven, the latter of Brahms.

The keyboard art of Beethoven will be more easily enjoyed in public performance than that of Bach by so much as it deviates from a whole integrity of texture into a moment-by-moment immediacy of structure; and the keyboard art of Bach is more satisfying for the reader than that of Beethoven precisely because of its integrity of texture.

EMBELLISHMENT

The problem of returning to a lost idiom of art and trying to think again in a natural manner a rich and varied body of interpretive conventions arises in every branch of art history. In reading the "March of Horsemen," one of the movements from William Byrd's episodic suite of news-music, *The Battell*, we should play quite slowly in the rhythm of the horse's gracefully heavy amble, under the weight of a part-armored horseman—putting out of mind entirely the romantic steed.

The Dutch historian Johan Huizinga wrote of the Flemish master painters Jan and Hubert Van Eyck: "The Van Eycks were utter realists as far as form is concerned, but we know as good as nothing about their spirit. Everything that modern, estheticizing art criticism concludes from their works regarding their spirit is fantasy and paraphrase." The same can be said of modern surrealistic interpretations of the paintings by Hieronymus Bosch. Careful study of each portion of the surface gradually discloses that the naturalistic or surrealistic detail is made up of meaningful embellishment: moral homily, theological exposition, figures of damnation and salvation, woven around with folk tale and myth, a book of symbols intelligible in one way to the illiterate, in another way to the learned, and quite possibly in yet another set of meanings to the initiate.

In reading music, we do not merely explain an interpretation to ourselves or others; we create it. The composition is the sound-realization that we make of it; it is our understanding of the composer, his intentions, his symbols, the atmosphere of meanings that he lived in. For the listener, the third party, the music

can be only what he hears. The measure which we play contains
a measure of ourselves; we must not let this engulf the composer's
greater measure. Like anthropologists living among the folk they
study, we must subdue our habits and prejudices; we must be all
ears, eyes, and awareness. And amid all this sensitiveness to
everything that is going on around us, we should strive to be in
spirit as we need to appear in our actions, quite unself-conscious.

"In the history of music," Huizinga tells us, "the concepts of
art and craftsmanship are even more closely related than elsewhere." Among the imitations of natural sound that permeate the
music of the fourteenth through the sixteenth centuries there was
another spirit, and for this Huizinga quotes Sir Thomas More
praising the church music of his *Utopia:* "For all their music, both
that they play upon instruments and that they sing with man's
voice, doth so resemble and express natural affections, the sound
and tune is so applied and made agreeable to the thing, that
whether it be a prayer, or else a ditty of gladness, of patience, of
trouble, of mourning, or of anger, the fashion of the melody doth
so represent the meaning of the thing, that it doth wonderfully
move, stir, pierce, and enflame the hearers' minds."

During the sixteenth through the eighteenth centuries this attitude took the name Sir Thomas gives it here: a doctrine of the
affections, the *affect* originating in types of symbolism but having
much of the meaning we give that word in psychological interpretation. With meantone tuning, the key was chosen and recognized
to be an enhancement of the affect.

Modern musical education has spread over this art a fog of
visual misunderstanding, known as *faithfulness to the score,* the
score being the notes as seen arranged on the printed page. The
conception of music as structure has so overshadowed the feeling
of music as embellished texture, that we think of the art as if it
were an exercise in precision, fabricated strictly to the blueprint,
out of which, because the composer put emotion in, emotion
flows.

Belated romantics complain of today's "intellectual music."
What was ever more emptily intellectual than repeating endlessly
the same works in the same manner, frothing them up by a pre-
tense of applied emotion, as we expect of public performers
nowadays!

Was not a truer intellectuality the ability to amplify, at sight, in performance, the figured bass line of an extended composition —say, a cantata for chorus and soloists in several movements? Present-day players are seldom aware how little art and what unenlightened scholarship have gone into grubbing together the written-out arrangements of those basses provided by standard performing editions.

In European music the melodic tradition and the conventions of embellishment emerge together from the distant historic past. The melody is the mnemonic and popular aspect; the conventions of embellishment are the esthetic or interpretive aspect, by which the common melody is given individuality and significance. In ancient Jewish and the earliest Christian music, notes were set to words, the rhythms being articulated and made expressive by the speech rhythms of the words. (The same tunes, adapted to the flowing Semitic melodies of Hebrew, grew into cantorial singing; adapted to the more square-cut quantities of Latin they became Gregorian chant.) The release of emotion occurred in the wordless, embellished *alleluias*. With increasing freedom the musical patterns signifying emotion were applied to the setting of the words, so that the musical meaning or decorative embellishment and elaboration took on a distinct and individual significance. This reversal of the balance between liturgical enrichment of the words and a musically illuminative gloss on every initial reached its climax not within the Roman Catholic Church, which has consistently opposed subordinating text to music, but in the B minor Mass by the Lutheran J. S. Bach and the *Solemn Mass* by the Deist Beethoven. Yet I believe there would be few who would say that the elaborate musical glosses by Bach and Beethoven do not double and redouble, for anyone who comprehends the Latin text, the theological (God-knowing) content of the liturgy.

We speak of *interpretation,* meaning the adjustment of a composition in performance according to some inner enlightenment of the performer or conductor. Except in our time, interpretation has signified the embellishment, varying, and elaboration of an accepted melody or composition by a performer according to his taste and ability. With increasing accuracy of notation and the printing of scores, the composer began to assert himself as the predominant interpreter and to insist that only those embellishments indicated by signs or definitely permitted within the tradition should be played. The contrary tradition, for example in Arabian music, throws an ever greater stress on the accumulating of embellishments by the performer.

The habit of present-day performers and musicologists is to presume that composed music which has all its notes written out is in some way better than music requiring embellishment by the performer; and that implied embellishments, to be added by the player, although definitely in the intention of all music composed during the sixteenth, seventeenth, and eighteenth centuries, in Palestrina as in Handel, in Mozart and Clementi, in Beethoven and Chopin, are somehow irrelevant, esoteric, and seldom to be attempted in practical usage.

Because player, critic, editor, or musicologist has trouble reading or performing knowledgeably all notated embellishments, for example in Couperin or Gibbons, he is not justified in writing them all out in his own single-minded interpretation or in pretending that they should not be played.

Passages of conventional figuration can be stiff and poorly integrated or they can be used with a great creative imagination. For a player reading from a figured bass, such additions were at the least an idiomatic convenience. Such figures are the stuff of idiomatic improvisation, and the distinction of the best music of our classical-romantic tradition stems from a proper understanding of them. Fully written-out classical music includes a large measure of conventional figuration. The figures are common even in twentieth-century music, for example Gustav Mahler's highly emotional use of the turn.

The omitting of such improvised elaborative figuration in present-day performance of works by Corelli, Vivaldi, and Handel is as inexcusable as if the performers were leaving out passages of written notes. Good intonation and a luscious vibrato are no substitute. The effect is illiteracy with a high-toned accent. When J. S. Bach transcribed for keyboard the middle movement of the Violin Concerto, vol. 7:2, by Antonio Vivaldi, he added at the start of the movement indicative embellishment.

During the later eighteenth century such composers as J. C. Bach and Haydn were attempting to preserve by notation the conventionally altered expressive rhythms, which had been previously taken for granted as the normal mode of playing. In the same way later generations of jazz musicians have tried to preserve in their arrangements rhythmic habits that originated in the anonymous musical folk speech of the Negro and were codified by convention in practice long before they were roughly written out.

When J. C. Bach borrowed for a violin sonata the melody of the *Praeludium* of his father's B flat Partita, he dotted it in the style of his later generation to emphasize the delayed stroke of the upbeats. It is probable that father Bach played the melody in similar fashion but without dotting it—and with more free melodic variation.

The effort to preserve by notation the dying conventions of altered rhythm went hand in hand with the attempt to preserve the usages of embellishment by writing it all in, as Haydn tries to do throughout his piano sonatas and their notated cadences. Comparison of the notation of embellishments in a sonata by Haydn with the writing out of embellishments in a modern edition of an eighteenth-century score will show how little the more recent scholar appreciates either the purposes of embellishment or the significance of eighteenth-century "good taste."

For organs and harpsichords of varying registration, tuning, or mechanical efficiency, or among organ, harpsichord, clavichord, and piano, the manner of embellishment will differ. In compositions expecting meantone tuning, an embellishment might be interpolated to conceal the presence of a discordant "wolf" note. Or consider the stylistic distinctions between Mozart's keyboard works written in Germany, for piano, and some of those written in Paris, probably for *grand clavecin,* or between the German and Italian versions of passages in the piano sonatas.

Anyone who has learned to recognize by ear the proper uses of embellishment will know that an embellishment is good only when it is expressive of its rhythm and a rhythm proper only as it conforms to the notated implication of its embellishments. Having grasped this fact, he will try to make embellished music come alive. His comprehension of the older writings about what seem dreary technicalities will read suddenly like current information. When he plays, his style will be his own but now authentic in intention, derived to his taste from the newly integrated feeling for the composer's indications and rhythmic devices. He will be able to read more simply or more elaborately as he pleases, to vary the repetition and enjoy his skill in doing so, while he improves his taste with pruning. He will understand why in former days mere note-players were thought to be poor uninformed creatures without skill or taste.

Our common manner of performing the older music would be, for a player of that time, as inept in its lack of style and misreading of expressive passages as it might be astonishing for its digital precision and speed. Style means individuality of expressiveness, and musicians of that period had more style, having more means of variety to work with, than the best of our merely reproductive virtuosos.

Composers today do not eschew embellishment and altered rhythm but write out each note precisely to the minutest disposition. Metrical changes in successive measures are a commonplace. The written appearance of such precisely notated music sets up patterns of difficulty which seem inherent in the make-up of the composition. Such is the end of metronomic time-counting and exact reproduction of the notes as written. The results of the older convention were as complex but the notational methods relatively simple.

The musical notation of the sixteenth, seventeenth, and eighteenth centuries is as exact, as accurate, and as explicit as any notation since that period. (This does not imply that we know all the answers.) The notation gives the intended rhythm, tempo, emphasis, phrasing, and embellishment, wherever these restrict the conventional interpretation of the idiom. It differs from nineteenth-century notation in leaving the emotional affect to the performer, while giving exact visual rather than verbal signs of the composer's intent. In performance, the taste (or recreative imagination) of the player was reckoned as of nearly equal value with the creative data, the composition. Haydn reported in a letter his delight at hearing a young friend play one of his major piano sonatas as individually as if she had composed it.

Good readers contributed more ornaments, embellishments, and elaborations than were indicated. One indication may suggest a series of like ornaments; or the indication may be repeated by the composer where he wished to ensure that the ornament be not omitted. In playing the slower movements of such artists in rhetorical declamation as Bull, Froberger, or Handel (for which Mozart's *Suite in the Style of Handel* [K. 399] offers an excellent commentary), one should take care not to anticipate or conceal the climactic rise of a sentence by slipping in an ornament where silence will be more eloquent; to remember that a slight rhythmic shift in the progression, like a shrug, may be more expressive than a trill or shake.

In many cadential figures the ornament is taken for granted. (Unless he finds it written out, the present-day player seldom exploits the chance to improvise a cadence. Wanda Landowska has given several examples of improvised cadences in her recorded Mozart and Haydn albums.) Where an unusual interpretation or an exact melodic design is required, the entire figure may be written out. The opening of a piano sonata in G by C. P. E. Bach (*Sonaten und Stücke*, Peters, no. 9) duplicates the opening of the second movement of Beethoven's F minor Sonata, opus 2:1. Bach writes out the embellishments to clarify the rhythmic merging of this figure with the succeeding passage, which is syncopated. Beethoven's embellished figure leads melodically, with no danger of rhythmic misunderstanding, into the succeeding measures, the embellishment being indicated by the conventional signs for a turn followed by an *appoggiatura*.

Rhythmic deviation (altered or expressive rhythm) may be exactly notated but is customarily left to the performer's judgement. This is the first, the simplest, the most expressive, ultimately the most subtle, and the chief embellishment not only in music of the centuries when it was recognized as an embellishment but in any music, the "breaking and yet keeping time," as Roger North described it. Phrasing, emphasis, and tempo were derived by taste, and by the composer's indications, from accepted idiomatic habits.

A common body of method existed and was accepted, with wide deviations in practice, by the majority of seventeenth- and eighteenth-century musicians both in improvising and in reading at sight. In considering the deviations, one should consider also what tuning was likely to have been used in either case, since what may be excellent in one tuning may not be so in another. Many of the basic principles were so widely accepted in their period, though afterwards altered beyond recognition or discarded, that they were seldom discussed or explained by contemporary players, who thought of them as natural (in the nature of music) and unalterable.

The same was true of the earlier generations of American jazz and of its origins. Like the earlier jazz players, Roger North at the end of the seventeenth century liked the sound "dirty" rather than cleanly related: as when two violins play together, "it is better musick when one goes a litle before or behind the other, than when they play . . . to a touch together. For in that, nothing is gott by the doubling, but a litle loudness; but in the other way, by the frequent dissonances there is a pleasant seasoning obtained."

To arrive at some idea of these principles, one should seek the root-forms common to the larger body of recorded variants. It is needful to assume also that habits often inveighed against are proved, by that fact, to have been in general usage.

"What comprises good performance?" C. P. E. Bach asks in Chapter 3 of his *The True Art of Playing Keyboard Instruments.* "The ability through singing or playing to make the ear conscious of the true content and affect of a composition. Any passage can be so radically changed by modifying its performance that it will be scarcely recognizable.

"The subject matter of performance is the loudness and softness of tones, the snap, legato, and staccato execution, the vibrato, the arpeggiation, the holding of tones, the retard and accelerando. Lack of these elements or inept use of them makes a poor performance."

"Vibrato" refers to the playing of C. P. E. Bach's preferred instrument, the clavichord. The "affect" of a composition is its expressive content.

Note the mention of arpeggiation; the breaking and melodic distribution of chords both upwards and downwards, though essential and derived from good continuo playing, are nowadays more avoided than attempted. "For the sprinkling or *arpeggio,* the proper genius of it," Roger North explains, "must have pauses, for liberty of that kind, which hath an egregious effect, as either in leading the air, to possess a voice with its key, to enter *petit* fuges or intersperse *ritornello's.* But in a great consort, tho' struck full at every note, it is lean and soundless. If one can but say there is such an instrument heard among them, it is all. One may fancy it clink like a touch upon a ketle; but a gross base at every stroke kills it, unless there be used a litle of the *arpegio* . . . in the intervals of the other bases."

The treatises and examples provided by seventeenth- and

eighteenth-century musicians and theorists are factual, accurate, occasionally voluminous, but incomplete, because each offers in detail a single contemporary point of view. Where little or no information exists, it is better to avoid carrying backward a convention from today; instead, using the available data, try to work it out for yourself.

Try always to imagine contemporaneously, so that your mistakes, when you make them, will be in the right direction, sometimes the very errors a less sophisticated contemporary would have fallen into for the same reasons. We know the value of learning to think and speak a foreign language, even with dubious grammar and a thick accent.

I have compiled in Appendix 2, "Rhythm and Embellishment," a set of basic principles which can serve as root-types, and their relationships; from these, and the notated examples supplied by many composers, a present-day player can learn to think a wide repertoire of rhythmic and ornamental variants. The best compilation of source materials is, as I have written before, *The Interpretation of the Music of the 17th and 18th Centuries* by Arnold Dolmetsch.

The Instruments

THE ORGAN

The organ is the largest, the most complicated, the most nobly panoplied, and many will contend the most inexpressive of instruments. The organ makes up in atmosphere and in grandeur what it lacks of intimacy. In the words of Roger North: "All that that's good and great in Musick is founded upon that, whose *copia* is infinite; and magnificence, as well as variety and mixture of sounds unbounded. It is a conglomerate body of Harmony, and by wonderfull, I had almost say'd miraculous art, brought intirely subject to the twice five digits of a single person, sitting at his ease afore the mighty machine."

The organ is the eldest of the keyboard instruments that has remained continuously in service. The original organ, built by a Greek engineer in Alexandria and afterwards improved to vulgarity by the Romans, had the wind pressure controlled by means of a three-chambered water tank and so was called a *hydraulis* or water organ. By sliders and valves the player could choose the pitch and registration of each tone, to the extent of adding or omitting an octave pipe or in some larger organs a double-octave pipe.

This powerful, strident organ became in its later Roman development not less coarse and unpleasant than an American motion-picture organ of the 1920s (a dinosaur that died quickly) and was used for much the same mob-spectacular purposes.

The early medieval organ dispensed with the water chamber and the valves, probably for lack of engineers and facilities. The sliders let the wind directly into a rank of pipes, which with uncontrolled wind pressure must have blasted, faded, and

wavered constantly; the sound would have been rackety at all
times and in a big organ with plenty of bellows could be ear-
splitting (demonstrating that at this time music was made to the
glory of God and not for the pleasing of the congregation). Yet
because lovers of an art will accept as the ultimate esthetic
achievement whatever is accepted by the fashion of their time,
the music of this period—when fashion changed more slowly than
it does now—was praised in language more absolute and beautiful, because written by poets, than any that is written now by
critics.

The timbre (though of course not the quality) of such an
organ was estimated rather shrewdly by my friend Gerald Strang,
composer and acoustician. Wishing to perform a fourteenth-
century motet by Guillaume de Machaut, accompanied by organ
on one tone for forty measures and then on another tone for
twenty measures, a decisive if simple modulation, he tried sustaining the two tones on several seemingly well-qualified instruments, among them a modern organ, without being satisfied by
the result. At length he asked that one of the singers sound the
two tones on a piano accordion, and the effect was right.

In medieval organs all pipes were the same width, whatever
their length, so that the lower pipes sounded too coarse and the
higher pipes, by comparison, too ethereally soft. Such built-in
registration matched the registration of the male choirs, as well
as the general balance of the contemporary instruments, with
the result that vertical harmony, as we understand it, was
effectively nonexistent, the voices moving in linear and metrical
freedom between the successive positions of vertical concordance.

In the thirteenth century levers, so stiff they had to be struck
with the fist, replaced the heavy sliders. The levers were controlled by buttons on a narrow keyboard, or the levers themselves
projected like modern keys. As action improved, the levers
were able to be played with the fingers.

At this time portative organs came into use, being slung from
the shoulders by a strap, the bellows pumped by the left hand,
the keyboard projecting outward from the body and played by
two or three fingers of the right hand. The habit of fingering a
keyboard instrument with the two or three middle fingers, omitting the thumb, began with the playing of the portative organ
and continued into the sixteenth century.

By the end of the fourteenth century solo stops came into use, matching the growing independence of other instruments in doubling or replacing voice parts in ensembles. By the sixteenth century the addition of overtone pipes (mixtures) enabled organists to join qualitatively in polyphonies of several parts, instead of merely supporting them.

By the seventeenth century, the earlier, strongly speaking stops were being replaced by lighter, transparent mixtures, which grew more refined in texture, though not lacking edge and penetration, during the lifetime of J. S. Bach. Such is the instrument now spoken of, in building modern imitations, as the "Praetorius," "Silbermann," or "baroque" organ. Praetorius was a seventeenth-century organist, composer, and musical theorist; Silbermann, a friend of J. S. Bach who designed and built keyboard instruments.

When several pipes blend above a common fundamental tone to produce a distinctive registration, the effect is called a *mixture;* a selection of assorted tones or mixtures or both is called a *combination.* On a modern organ, preset combinations are controlled by pushbuttons.

During the nineteenth and early twentieth centuries, combinations replaced mixtures, as the orchestra of many disparate instruments replaced the blended groups of the string orchestra and *concerto grosso.* The ultimate instrument, proving that the last stage of an evolution is not necessarily the best, was an organ put together of several hundred combinations, each thrown into play by a tabular lever on the rank surrounding the keyboard.

One cannot really orchestrate an organ, as one learns by listening to organ symphonies of the later nineteenth and early twentieth centuries; nor can one make organlike combinations of mingled orchestral instruments, as one learns by listening to major organ works in orchestral transcriptions. The latter has been the more successful, though the effect at best does not and should not resemble that of an organ.

Igor Stravinsky, speaking of the composition of *Symphony of Psalms* in one of his conversations with Robert Craft, says: "I thought, for a moment, of the organ, but I dislike the *legato sostenuto* and the mess of octaves in the organ, as well as the fact that the monster never breathes. It is exactly the breathing of wind instruments that is one of their greatest attractions for me."

Yet I must say, in fairness and gratitude, that many like myself heard our first orchestral music simulated on an organ before we had ever heard a symphony orchestra even on a phonograph record.

Much has been done in organ-building to reproduce the authentic disposition of the organs on which Bach and his great contemporaries and immediate predecessors played their music. A *disposition* is the total collection of registers built into any organ by the choice of its sets of organ pipes; the written disposition is the *specification*. For every stop or separate registration of an organ a different set of pipes must be installed. An organ of Bach's time was already a large instrument, though small in comparison with the multi-keyboarded monsters which came into favor during the later nineteenth century.

For such great mechanisms, still surviving and still being built, a literature was indeed created, almost entirely by organists of enthusiastic but doubtful gifts. This literature continues to be played, though few can be found who seek it. It is a cruel joke of history on the modern organist that the most enduring literature of his instrument was created for an organ which the modern organ could, figuratively, put in its pocket. Only a small part of the monster organ can be properly used to perform the organ works by Bach, his predecessors, and his contemporaries. The significant organ works written since their time can be listed on a single page of print. Chief among them are the organ works by Mendelssohn and César Franck. So reluctant is the nineteenth-century organ to change its habit of speech that the Organ Variations by Arnold Schoenberg, written sixty years after Franck's death, can be mistaken, even by a skilled ear, for "something by Franck." The confusion is not in the writing but in the sounding of the instrument. The published registration is not by the composer but was made by an organist at the publisher's request; the composer expressed his thorough dissatisfaction with it.

The effort to revive correct playing of the organ music of the seventeenth and eighteenth centuries has resulted in as many inconsistencies as are built into the modern organ the organists would like to get away from.

Nobody knows, for instance, how a good organ of that period, in prime condition, would have sounded. Such organs survive, some of them in excellent playing condition. To keep their voices fresh, however, these venerable instruments have been many times reconditioned, and in reconditioning the preference of subsequent ages in the voicing of organs has had its way with the original voicing. A few smaller, self-contained cabinet organs may retain their original voicing, as they have kept their original tuning.

Not long ago, an American organist who has devoted profitable years to recording old music on contemporary organs discovered in England an instrument on which Handel is said to have played. That this instrument was in prime condition was attested by the fact that it still kept the meantone tuning that Handel would have expected. The virtuoso organist rushed to London, communicated with his recording company, engaged a large orchestra and conductor, and made ready to record on this organ once blessed by Handel the whole of Handel's concertos for orchestra and organ. Then, at far more expense than would have been risked to bring the work of a living composer to performance, the organ was rebuilt completely with new pipes tuned to equal temperament, but with care to provide a mechanical device by which the local organist, if he prefers his Handel in the correct tuning, can shift back to play the original meantone pipes. All having been taken care of and provided, the virtuoso, famous for his pursuit of the authentic instrument, recorded the Handel organ concertos at the keyboard at which Handel had once sat.

A similar devotion has been expended in constructing instruments of contradictory dispositions and haphazard sound which are called "baroque" organs. The quality of these musicological rebirths is often far better than that of the no longer fashionable monsters. What is in fact being constructed is a new and esthetically more useful modern organ. Such organs are tuned incorrectly for the "baroque" music that is to be played on them; they are usually provided with electrical actions that respond quite unlike the original; and the pipes are voiced according to modern standards, since nobody knows how else they should be voiced. And the wind comes without interruption from a motor.

The organ of the seventeenth and eighteenth centuries was built with what is called a tracker action, communicating, pianowise, the impulse of the keys to the controlling mechanism through a set of levers. By this means the player's hand directly controls the sounding of the pipes. This may seem a small matter, but any pianist who plays for the first time an electrical organ will be rendered uncomfortable by the arbitrary timing of the musical response. He depresses the key, and the electrical machinery in its own time blows the whistle. Arguments concerning the extent to which natural organ-playing is hampered or improved by the direct mechanical operation of a tracker action have been going on ever since the great and saintly organist Albert Schweitzer wrote a book damning all electrical organs as bad company for good music. The argument continues, but some devoted connoisseurs are now building new organs with old-style tracker actions.

In modern organs the standards of nineteenth-century gentility have so modified the sounding of the pipes that the tone emerges from them without any whisper of escaping wind—without, that is, what an orchestral conductor calls "attack." "The fault of the _____ Symphony," Igor Stravinsky said to me one time, "is that it has no attack." What had been thought until recently an ultimate refinement in the playing of this famous orchestra was now a cause of criticism.

Organists in search of the authentic "baroque" sound have therefore begun refitting the genteel monsters to which their personal careers have tied them with new Dutch and Scandinavian pipes, designed to release the tone supported by a sufficient push of wind to provide an attack. This is unquestionably an improvement, since an instrument without attack can keep time but not rhythm.

As to the wind source, to ask for the return of former conditions would be as disreputable as agitating for the return of slavery. Until an electric motor was provided, all organs had to be pumped by hand-bellows, and a human being was needed to do the pumping, not only in performance but during any practice. When we read of Mozart or Liszt visiting a local organ and improvising at it two or three hours to the gratification of the local organist, nobody mentions the feelings of the local organ-pumper. Yet I am convinced that the quality of an organ pumped, however faithfully, by hand must have been different from that of an organ which gets its wind without fail from an electric motor. I doubt that anything should be done about it.

The authentic "baroque" organ was built, as often as not, without a pedal keyboard to be played by the feet. Cabezón in

sixteenth-century Spain had a pedal keyboard of a sort. Frescobaldi in Italy is said to have had one, and Sweelinck in Holland
also. German organs had them; English organs did not. Bach had
a pedal keyboard and wrote for it lovingly and lavishly; Handel
had not and did without. In the critical literature of the period
are disparaging commentaries against the organ-playing of
Handel, because he did not play with his feet, and in favor of
Bach, who was able to. But the pedal keyboard that Bach did
possess and use with famous virtuosity was not like the modern
pedal keyboard, which permits "fingering" with the heel as well
as the toe; it was so small it could be played only with the toe.
Organists in search of the authentic instrument should not neglect
this disadvantage.

To be an adequate instrument, an organ should be designed
uniquely for the building in which it is to be heard and it should
be properly placed in the building. The organ is a church instrument; it does not usually sound so well in a concert hall. The
acoustical arrangements of a concert hall are and should be unlike those in a church. The true purpose of stained glass in church
windows is not to ornament the wall with glowing pictures but
to fill the interior space with an atmosphere of colored light. The
true purpose of an organ in a church is not to enable the organ
works by Bach to be enjoyed as studies in counterpoint but to
fill the interior space with a radiance of tone.

If the swell box enclosing the smaller pipes is set at right
angles to the nave, so that the notes produced from within trail
by a substantial fraction of a second the intended-to-be-simul-
taneous notes from the exposed pipes, the organist may hear his
performance correctly, but listeners in the body of the church
will hear acoustical chaos. To deliver the notes accurately to his
listeners, the organist must play them inaccurately for himself.

The earlier makers of stained-glass windows intended the
colors of the glass to combine in pleasing mixtures of atmospheric light—instead of the indifferent pictures on glass one looks
at today. The designers of the finest organ music intended that
the linear mingling of the voices, themselves mixtures, should
combine not so much in clarity as in radiance of sound. Radiance
should not be confused with acoustical vagueness. The earlier
composers for the organ passed their careers in churches. C. P. E.
Bach reports that his father had a very sharp eye, as well as ear,

for the acoustics of a building. What an organ will do musically is of far more importance than an Organ Committee's decision whereabouts the organ can be fitted so that it will look its money's worth.

A well-played organ should respond musically as an organ and like nothing else. Any other effect is more or less a trick. Would piano-playing today be in any way improved if pianists had continued using the paper stop, which buzzed like a snare drum, or the lute or harp stop suitable to a plucked instrument like a harpsichord but not to an instrument with hammers, or the attachment which beat the underside of the soundboard like a bass drum?

Organists also spoil the clear registers of organ music by excessive use of the swell pedal, drawing attention to individual notes by means more suitable to orchestra or piano. The present-day organist's trick of achieving clarity by a continuous semi-staccato is another pianistic imitation unsuited to the instrument.

An amateur who does not possess any type of organ need not deny himself the pleasure of reading organ music. For that part of the literature which was written for the manuals only, the piano will suffice, though one should keep in mind that, in the crossing of parts, voices which are written lower on the staff may, when correctly registered, sound higher on the organ than parts written above them on the staff. Playing organ on the piano requires a good musical imagination, as well as charity towards the quickly failing voice of the piano.

For the pedal parts, since much of the best organ music cannot be played within reach of the ten fingers, the player will have to borrow a third hand. Few of the chorale preludes of Bach's *Little Organ Book,* however simple in appearance, can be brought within the compass of two hands. Three-handed playing of organ music at the piano opens a new literature, and the usually rather easy pedal part is a good starting-place for an adult beginner.

Most of us would enjoy having more access to an organ than is likely to be permitted us. We may try to satisfy the desire in one of three ways.

One is to obtain use of or purchase what is called an electronic organ, which produces pitches by the same general means that cause any improperly manipulated electronic sound-generating apparatus to whistle or shriek. The pitches these instruments produce, accompanied by such overtones as the electrical machinery proudly adds to its pure fundamentals, do give distinguishable melody, usually accompanied by the sort of undulating murmur we are accustomed to hearing as the indefinite offertory of organs when played to fill the vacancies of a church service. Some manufacturers have been improving their electronic organs, and the convenience of size, compared with a pipe-organ installation, ensures increasing use of them.

There is also an instrument, related to the electronic organ, at which an unskilled player can pick out a tune with the fingers of his right hand, while pushing buttons with the left hand to produce predetermined harmonies. For any true Amateur such a device is beneath contempt. I am not informed whether such tone-machines come with reversed keyboard for the left-handed.

I recall Arnold Schoenberg speaking in conversation about a small musical instrument for amateurs that he was sure would be invented. A description exists in a published letter of this period, 1949:

"If one did not remember the splendid organ literature and the wonderful effect of this music in churches, one would have to say that the organ is an obsolete instrument today. No one—no musician and no layman—needs so many colors (in other words, so many registers) as the organ has. On the other hand, it would be very important to have the instrument capable of dynamically altering each single tone by itself (not just an entire octave-coupling)—from the softest *pianissimo* to the greatest *forte*.

"Therefore, I believe that the instrument of the future will be constructed as follows: there will not be 60 or 70 different colors, but only a very small number (perhaps 2 to 6 would certainly be enough for me) which would have to include the entire range (7–8 octaves) and a range of expression from the softest *pianissimo* to the greatest *fortissimo*, each for itself alone.

"The instrument of the future must not be more than, say, 1½ times as large as a portable typewriter. For one should not strike too many wrong keys on a typewriter either. Why should it not be possible for a musician, say, to type so accurately that no mistakes occur?

"I can imagine that, with such a portable instrument, musicians and music-lovers will get together in an evening in someone's home and play duos, trios and quartets; they will really be in a position to reproduce the idea-content of all symphonies. This is, naturally, a fantasy of the future, but who knows if we are so far away from it now?"

The third and, in my present opinion, the most satisfactory type of commonplace organ is the harmonium or reed organ, the wind pumped by foot pedals. Unlike an electronic organ, a harmonium has both timbre and attack, and it is seldom quite in tune. Every separate interval on such an instrument can be a separately recognizable experience. Thus the music, while seldom exact, has character in abundance.

Since a considerable literature of organ music exists for manuals alone, the harmonium player need not regret the lack of a pedal keyboard. The harmonium is one of the best instruments on which to practise free improvisation, if only because the tones can be sustained until others have been chosen to replace them. So long as the wind continues and the note is held, the tone continues sounding, while piano tone quickly fades. A harmonium is provided with several stops, permitting change of registration to make up for the almost invariable impulse of the sound.

Another way to make up for the lack of an organ is to own a clavichord, the regular home-practice instrument of organists until the close of the eighteenth century. Some organists would set two clavichords one above the other and add a foot-operated clavichord with pedals for practising the larger organ compositions. Bach's Trio Sonatas, customarily played on the organ, may have been written for the pedal clavichord.

8

THE CLAVICHORD

The clavichord is the loveliest in tone and the quietest, the most private, and the most difficult to play well of the keyboard instruments. In these days few public performers play it at all; not many amateurs play it well. Arnold Dolmetsch, who revived it by building new clavichords and performing on them, played it, out of great knowledge, exactly as he pleased. I recall reading that there was an old clavichord in his home when he was a child, and that the tradition of clavichord-playing had never ceased in his family.

Like the other keyboard instruments with strings, the clavichord consists of an oblong box strung lengthwise. It differs in that the strings, bridged at one end, are damped by being wrapped with felt at the other end and do not sound until touched by a tangent, a strip of metal inserted vertically into the back end (or shank) of the key-lever. The tangent both strikes the string, producing vibration, and serves, so long as it is held touching the string, as a second bridge, so that the string may sound. This extremely primitive mechanism produces little volume but has the virtue of causing the string to vibrate undamped at its full length, giving off the entire range of overtones, the richest and softest sonority produced by any of the keyboard instruments.

The clavichord key communicates the actual "touch" of the finger on the key, by means of shank and tangent, directly to the string, enabling the player to manage several important effects not possible on any other keyboard instrument. (No corresponding "touch" is possible with the piano mechanism.)

The first of these effects is vibrato (in German, *Bebung*), a wavering of tone across the pitch like that on a bowed instrument. If the damper pedal is the "soul of the piano," the *Bebung* is no less important for the clavichord. The vibrato is caused by slightly increasing and decreasing the pressure of the finger on the key, by sideways motion, thus directly altering the pressure of the tangent on the string. The clavichord player must not only strike the key with proper force to bring out the exact volume he wishes, but he must hold the key down so that the tone will continue sounding, while he very lightly agitates the key-lever to produce the breadth and speed of vibrato he wishes. Playing one tone on a clavichord requires little pressure; a full chord compounds the requirement—almost geometrically; one may have much trouble controlling the sudden varieties of pressure needed to retain a correct, even intonation.

By pressing the tangent more firmly against the string the player can increase the tension, raising the pitch of the tone. The least deviation in pressure on the key-lever while holding a sustained tone will at once change the pitch. This enables the player to emphasize one voice of the music by raising it in pitch very slightly above the others. Raising the pitch imparts a slight dissonance to the melodic line, altering the relationships throughout its entire overtone series.

It is possible that players may have tried raising the pitch very slightly across all the tones, so that one passage might be lowered while another was being raised. Because the "correct" pitch of a note on the clavichord depends on the degree to which all the keys are depressed while being tuned, an exact tuning across the keyboard demands a very considerable precision and judgement. Large clavichords are normally double-strung, so that two strings must be attuned for each note. A minute difference between the pitches of the two strings may have been preferred, to intensify the tone. Clavichord-playing very likely increased the aural acceptance of continuous slight dissonant relationships, which made possible an easy transition to the consistently dissonant relationships of equal temperament.

▶ In music of many cultures alteration of pitch by microtonal waverings or melodic inflection is often more significant than exact sounding of the tone. These microtonal waverings, without vibrato, may be more exact than our usual instrumental intonation. Modification of pitch was an important practice in polyphonic singing. Until the advent of keyed wind instruments in the early nineteenth century, pitches on these instruments were more variable and less exact than they are now.

In modern times the influence of the piano has stiffened the habit of inflexible pitch at the expense of a more desirable modification and blending. In orchestral playing, exact intonation, though seldom if ever heard, is theoretically necessary for the proper combining of instruments. In string-quartet playing the musicians alter the intonation to produce desired combinations; therefore string players are seldom quite in tune with the piano when they play together. Rudolf Kolisch, violinist, chamber musician, and masterly performer of the classical and contemporary Viennese literature, insists that string music composed for equal temperament should be performed every note to the exact pitch, as on piano.

The harpsichord is, like the piano, an instrument of exact pitch. That is probably still another reason why chords on the harpsichord were intended to be broken, arpeggiated, or spread out in melodic pattern, especially in playing continuo, so that they would mingle with the greater variability of the voice and obbligato instruments.

Ears that demand an exact pitch will prefer the piano with its emphatic fundamental and low range of overtones. An expertly tuned harpsichord pleases many listeners because it does not strongly emphasize the bottom of the tone and doubles the range of higher overtones. With an instrument feather-quilled in the preferred older style, the upper overtones are intensified. This is desirable for and helps to explain the thinner writing of the earlier harpsichord literature.

No other keyboard instrument equals the variability of pitches and combinations of altered pitches possible on the clavichord, when it is played, as it should be, slowly. (The best examples of what "slowly" means for multifaceted listening are to be found in the earlier examples of Southern boogie playing on piano and guitar—never anything hurried.) Seat a pianist at a clavichord, and he will likely show

off his finger dexterity to the criticism of his ears by whiz-
zing away on the light action as rapidly as he can.

Because the clavichord was much used as a practice instrument,
being in its smaller form a portable instrument, like a portable
typewriter, it was often built small and *gebunden:* meaning that
several keys struck on a single string. Each of the tangents that
shared the use of a single string struck it at a separate point, producing a separate note, according to the length of the string from
the bridge to the point where it was struck. Only one of these
notes could be sounded at a time, limiting the usefulness of the
instrument but increasing the ingenuity of the player in learning
how to disperse the sounding of simultaneous tones.

In his *Life of Johann Sebastian Bach* the biographer Johann
Forkel tells us: "He liked best to play upon the clavichord; the
harpsichord, though certainly susceptible of a very great variety
of expression, had not soul enough for him; and the piano was in
his lifetime too much in its infancy and still too coarse to satisfy
him. He therefore considered the clavichord as the best instrument for study, and, in general, for private musical entertainment. He found it the most convenient for the expression of his
most refined thoughts, and did not believe it possible to produce
from any harpsichord or pianoforte such a variety in the gradations of tone as on this instrument, which is, indeed, poor in tone,
but on a small scale extremely flexible." ("Poor in tone" means, of
course, poor in volume of tone.)

The clavichord is a private instrument. In some Italian homes
a small room or alcove called the *Paradiso* was reserved for it,
with space for no more than one or two listeners. Yet though the
tone is amazingly quiet, and difficult to record adequately without overamplification and consequent distortion towards a
guitarlike twanging, the resonance on a good instrument well
played can fill a small area with an extraordinary richness of
sound.

Cecil Clutton observes, however, in *Musical Instruments
Through the Ages:* "The remarkable qualities of the large German clavichords of the second half of the eighteenth century, as
exemplified at their best by Hass and, doubtless, Silbermann, are
very little known in England today, and this is a great pity, because they have a musical range—both in compass and general

capability—far beyond the miniaturist approach to clavichord making and playing which is now fashionable in England. Even Beethoven sonatas by no means come amiss to a Hass clavichord. . . . The similarity in tone between a Hass clavichord and a Stein pianoforte is most striking, and the Stein is perhaps only twice as loud as the Hass. Almost its only corresponding loss is that no vibrato (*Bebung*) is possible upon it."

The later keyboard writings by C. P. E. Bach give evidence that he felt able to perform on the large clavichord with a wider dynamic range and greater confidence that the instrument would speak strongly throughout the upper keyboard (to high F) than either Haydn or Mozart.

An amateur who wishes to play the clavichord today, however charmed by its tone, will be disappointed by its lack of responsiveness to his unskilled management. If his ear for style is acute, he will soon be aware that by far the greater part of the harpsichord literature can be played satisfactorily on clavichord only by careful stylistic adjustment. The earlier Spanish, the Italian, and the German keyboard literatures adapt well to it; the French and British do not.

In popular parlance the clavichord is thought of in connection with the title of J. S. Bach's *Wohl Temperierte Clavier,* commonly mistranslated "The Well-Tempered Clavichord." The German word *clavier* means either "keyboard" or "keyboard instrument." The title refers to the well-tempered tuning which the pieces demonstrate, not to the instrument.

The period of the clavichord as an independent solo instrument, which may have begun with J. J. Froberger, ended with C. P. E. Bach's generation. Among the later works composed for it are the earlier keyboard sonatas by Haydn.

Playing the Haydn sonatas on a modern piano loses the higher overtones obtainable both on the clavichord and on the earlier piano with its leather-covered hammers and lighter stringing. But play an early Haydn sonata on the clavichord, and you will hear at once the higher overtones, corresponding to the winds and brass, which render it like a little symphony.

9

THE PIANO

An amateur who has few musical opinions may as well start exercising them at the piano.

Pianos come in a variety of styles and in two principal shapes; the grand and the upright. There is also the square piano, the handsomest of domestic instruments; any extant specimen survives in peril of being converted into a desk. Earlier in this century, piano dealers burned them in heaps to make way for new sales.

The grand, the oldest type of piano, has its strings running horizontally away from the keyboard; the upright has its strings vertically behind the keyboard. That is all the real difference in pianos, whatever else anyone may do to make them different, like putting the strings up vertically into the air (zebra piano) or sinking them vertically to the floor (studio upright) or making the bass strings too short to produce a true fundamental tone (baby grand) or building the frame so large that the bass strings become too thick and rigid to give off more than a few of the lowest overtones and one must balance the art between percussive violence and illusion (concert grand).

There is also a difference in actions, much written about but unlikely to influence our practice, unless we are so fortunate as to own a well-rebuilt piano as much as 150 years old or a reproduced eighteenth-century piano. The chief difference today is between normal and slightly faster actions; each has its partisans.

To make the piano sound, one strikes the keys with fist, finger, forearm, or the feet of a kitten. However one does so, striking depresses the key, which activates a set of levers (the *action*) inside under or in front of the strings, throwing the hammer against the strings; when hammer strikes strings, the strings vibrate, producing tone.

A widespread illusion persists that the manner in which the player touches the keys ("touch") influences the tone. In fact, from the moment the hammer flies free of the levers touch can do no more about controlling the tone. What counts is the speed imparted by the key to the levers and thus to the striking speed of the hammer. That is the only way that any pianist, using any means of striking, can control the individual tones. The art of piano-playing is to control the relative striking speed and placement of the impact by such minutely contrasting gradations of volume and temporal disposition that the listener believes the player controls the tone absolutely.

Whether the pianist agitates his arms in swoops or merely strikes the keys with well-disciplined fingers, or like the American composer Henry Cowell depresses them in clumps with fist or elbow (tone-clusters), the musical consequence and affect depend on the player's skill in depressing the keys at varying speeds so that the relationships among tones will be slightly louder or slightly softer, as well as slightly sooner or slightly later. Only the clavichord permits control of the tone by exact finger-touch, by way of key-lever and tangent, on the string.

In addition, the pianist has the use of two or three pedals. The right side pedal (*damper, sustaining,* or *"loud" pedal*) controls the dampers. These are felted blocks which lie on the strings to prevent them from sounding. When the levers throw the hammer at the strings, they raise the felted damper block for the corresponding note and hold it raised above the strings, so that the strings continue vibrating and the tone sounding, though with rapidly diminishing volume, until the finger is removed from the key. By depressing the right pedal the pianist lifts all the dampers from all the strings, so that they resonate with the struck strings, giving off corresponding sympathetic vibrations. Unless this general release is carefully controlled, tonal chaos results. Beethoven greatly increased and improved the use of the damper pedal. Pedaling in the modern manner, after the note, may have begun with John Field and was continued and improved by Chopin.

The skill of pedaling is to raise and lower the dampers in such a way that only those tones and sympathetic vibrations continue

8

sounding which one wishes to hear together at the same time. When the dampers are down, only the strings struck by the hammers vibrate; when the dampers are raised, all the strings vibrate in sympathy with those that are struck. This susurrus of free vibration enriches the tones by adding impartially consonant and dissonant overtones.

▶ Between *consonance* and *dissonance* there is no actual point of difference. A piano accurately tuned to equal temperament has no consonant interval except the octave. Thus all the piano music we hear is dissonant, in varying degrees, according to the harmony. The only real distinction has to do with the degree of dissonance that the listener has been conditioned to receive pleasurably, as if it were consonance. A more experienced listener appreciates a greater range of dissonances. All classical formal structures involving modulation are built on appreciable distinctions involving degrees of dissonance.

Good keyboard tone depends on the variety, relationships, and linkings of tone managed by use of the fingers. A good pianist uses the damper pedal always a little but most of the time sparingly. When you listen to a pianist, you should watch his feet as well as his hands, but the meaningful experience is not seeing but being able to hear what he is doing. Most of the hand-raising, arm-swinging, head-tossing a pianist shows you is bluff. A truly concentrated pianist attends strictly to his business with a minimum of display, and you can see him listening.

The left pedal, commonly called "soft," shifts the entire action to one side so that the hammers hit only two strings instead of three. The ordinary modern piano has three strings to each note. Older pianos often had two strings to a note; the Italian for "use the soft pedal" is *una corda* (one string).

The distinction between the "loud" and "soft" pedals should not be thought of in relation to volume of sound. The right pedal sustains the tone and enriches it by harmonics from the other strings, whether the volume is loud or soft; the left pedal alters the tone while reducing it, by eliminating one string. Subduing the resonance alters the quality.

Thus a pianist has at his disposal two complete sets of tone-color or registration, one using three strings, the other using two. He can play the entire range of volume using either set, to produce quite distinct effects.

The middle pedal keeps a single tone sounding after the finger has left the key, by holding up the damper for that one note. Some pianos do not have this.

Not all pianists are instrumentally insensitive, but the ordinary pianist who has been taught to produce notes at the piano and afterwards "interpret" them as music seldom learns to control all the varieties of tone of which a piano is capable. Such a pianist muddles along within a broad tonal plane of what is called *mezzoforte* (middling loud), getting louder or softer without any real distinction in quality.

Classical music, the best of it, indicates clearly what is wrong with the *mezzoforte* approach. A clear distinction is made at nearly all times between *p*, meaning *piano* (soft), and *f*, meaning *forte* (loud). These two planes of volume are again subdivided between *pp* and *ppp* (softer and very soft) and between *ff* and *fff* (louder and very loud). Thus a pianist should have at command six levels of distinguishable volume. (But *ppp* and *fff* are more usually nineteenth-century editorial emendations, seldom found in a seventeenth-, eighteenth-, or early nineteenth-century score, although C. P. E. Bach used them in his later writings.)

If the prevailing indication is *piano*, the pianist will chose a wider plane of softer sound and set his *forte* higher. If the prevailing indication is *forte*, he will allow more room for gradations of strength or loudness. Or, put another way, if the piece demands gradations of softness, the range between *ppp* and *p* should be increased by taking the *p* with more volume than if the prevailing gradations are between *p* and *f* or between *f* and *fff*. One often hears a player who has boxed himself into too narrow a range to be able to play, without forcing it, more loudly or more softly. The most ethereal *pianissimo* by a skilled pianist will be usually measurably louder, as well as richer, than the strained, thin *piano* an inexperienced player tries to squeeze the tone down to. The planes of volume overlap, so that what may seem an adequate *piano* in one place will seem an adequate *forte* in another; and the ear, having no chance to compare them directly, will believe them different qualities.

There are several types of piano-playing. The classical Ger-

man style puts the composition first and controls tone and registration more by phrase and dynamic groupings than note by
note. It is the style of the sonata-player.

The international virtuoso style thinks of the composition in
relation to the instrument and its voice. A true virtuoso has to
be by necessity the most sensitive of instrumentalists. He is not
to be considered therefore the most sensitive of musicians. The
range and variety of his tone threaten the continuity of design in
a classical sonata. For him the virtuoso composers of the nineteenth century, following Clementi, invented a new keyboard
style, combining the *bel canto* of Italian operatic singing with
imitation of the orchestra and individual instruments. But since
the piano lacks the distinctions of timbre peculiar to voice and
orchestral instruments, the vocal and instrumental effects of
virtuoso playing are achieved by an extraordinary suggestiveness.
A piano so played becomes a very complex percussion instrument, producing an almost infinite differentiation among qualities
and volumes of tone within the relatively narrow range of which
the instrument is capable.

Some twentieth-century composers and pianists have taken to
abusing the piano as if it were *nothing but* a percussion instrument. Only one composer, Béla Bartók, raised the percussive use
of the piano to an art high enough to rank him in the great line
of composer-pianists.

Another type of piano style is ascribed to John Field, the Irish
composer-pianist, whose European travels brought his elegantly
relaxed adaptation of the *bel canto* playing of Clementi to the
inspiration of Liszt and Chopin and then to Moscow. The inheritance of this style, sometimes called the "string of pearls," persists
in Russian music to the present day. It cares less for the phrase-
by-phrase tonal linking of the German style and the note-by-note
differentiation of the international virtuoso style, but puts in place
of these a long line of rather indiscriminately beautiful tone. It
is perhaps the most satisfying type of piano-playing for listeners
who have not learned to discriminate the inner workings of keyboard expressiveness and who find sonata-style or virtuoso-style
playing difficult and cold because of the demands these make on
the attention.

An amateur alert to distinctions will listen to all types of
pianists in search of performance skills and types of expressive-

ness which add to musical experience. He will observe the manners of *crescendo* and *diminuendo* (growing louder or softer note by note, a skill that comes to full use only with the piano); he will learn how tones may be run together and how they may be kept sharply separate. He will remark the dry and the melodious *staccato*, having to do with the length of time each note is let sound, and the many kinds of *legato*, which link or bind the tones together. A pianist with a well-managed legato fingering can dispense with much unnecessary pedaling. And he will learn that refinement of tone, the *sotto voce*, that my friend the pianist Richard Buhlig, in playing Beethoven, described as "the tone that has no tone."

Piano music is an art of tonal planes, of linear surfaces and projections, bound together in such a way that each is set apart in relationship to the others. This tonal relationship within fixed time is another aspect of rhythm.

It is in the multitudes of possible inflections by minute differentiations of volume between the successive tones, in several voices at the same time, that the piano surpasses other musical instruments.

Every keyboard instrument has its unique sound. A piano in perfect condition is likely to sound as impersonal as a butler. One reason for putting a piano in good condition, or training a butler, is to reduce unwanted interference. A stage butler is not a real butler, because he talks out of turn. A piano which obtrudes its personality in a way that it is not supposed to disturbs a good pianist.

For an amateur a piano can be as interesting as its personality, and an eager amateur's piano soon has one. We amateurs are sometimes fascinated by the individuality of a piano, even by its out-of-tuneness, the sad, or cheerful, or neglected, or responsive way it has of sounding as it does. We will sit diddling at a piano with an unexpected quality, just to get acquainted, enjoying its reminiscences of high living or abuse, the hints that its unusual qualities will bring out in familiar music.

An amateur is usually better off with a piano that has an easy action. He has work enough to do just to get the right keys down. He plays with his finger muscles, helped by the weight of his hands, whereas a professional, playing with far greater strength and weight from arms, shoulders, and back, needs the resistance of the keys to help him control the fine discriminations in striking which govern the throw of the hammers against the strings.

Softer striking produces more high overtones from the strings, hard striking produces more of the lower overtones. The piano is, of all the keyboard instruments, the most deficient in overtones. The timbre of a tone is given by the resonating of its overtones. Therefore the secret of what pianists like to call "touch" lies in the correct mingling of louder and softer timbres, in a chord or a succession of chords or a running passage, to give the utmost play to the harmonics, while guiding the ear by a slight emphasis of the leading tones. Many hard-fingered pianists, who believe that a note is a tone, just as it is notated in black ink on the printed page, never find this out.

In recent years some builders have been producing copies of pianos of the period of Mozart. These instruments are more lightly strung at less tension than nineteenth-century and later pianos, so that they produce higher overtones and have a timbre somewhat between the clavichord and the modern piano. The action, simpler than that of later pianos, is as rapid; the hammer should not be heavily felted (the original hammers were bare wood or wood covered by leather). Played on such an instrument the middle registers of thinly harmonized early piano music sound more eloquently than on a modern piano; the tone merges with string-tone instead of warring with it. In sonatas and trios the instruments combine, instead of standing apart as they do now. Piano and harpsichord mingle at the same level of volume, gracefully singing together through the concertos for harpsichord and piano by C. P. E. Bach, instead of requiring the unnatural adjustments for balance needed in performing such twentieth-century concertos for the same instruments as those by Frank Martin and Elliott Carter. A more widespread use of the early piano would implement a more correct style of playing the keyboard music of the later part of the eighteenth century and would very much alter our conception of the sonatas and trios by C. P. E. Bach, Haydn, and Mozart.

10

THE HARPSICHORD

Nearly anyone nowadays who plays the harpsichord has played the piano first. That is the cause of the present-day misunderstanding of the instrument. It explains also why modern harpsichord players and builders have preferred, with few exceptions, an instrument that is not authentic.

The keys of the piano activate a series of levers which throw the hammer at the strings. The keys of the harpsichord directly raise a perpendicular shaft, called a *jack*, bearing on one side like a thorn a horizontal plectrum that plucks the string as the jack rises. A simple spring at the back lets the plectrum slip past the string when the key is released and the jack falls.

Plectra can be made of several materials. Some modern instruments have nylon plectra. The two ancient types are still the best: quills cut from feathers (crow, eagle, turkey, each in my experience equally good) and plectra of shaped leather, sometimes known as "buff." In earlier instruments the feather quills were preferred; in modern instruments the leather plectra are often supplanted by nylon. For a virginal or spinet, or one register (upper manual) of a larger harpsichord, I recommend feather quills; they are surprisingly durable—as durable as nylon by test —and no more difficult to cut, replace, and adjust.

The ancestor of the piano was an oblong box across which were stretched strings that were hit by small-headed hammers held in the two hands: the *dulcimer*. The ancestor of the harpsichord was a similar box with stretched strings which were plucked: the *psaltery*. Both are widely played today.

The Italian word for dulcimer is *cembalo*. When the harpsichord took over the literature of the dulcimer, it also took over its name and was called incorrectly *clavicembalo,* meaning keyboard dulcimer. Thus began the confusion between plucked and hammered string instruments which has never ceased. If the Italians had preferred the name *arpicordo,* from which comes harpsichord, things might have gone better.

To make matters worse, the French called the harpsichord *clavecin;* the Germans called it *Flügel* and later used the same title for a grand piano; the British called it in one form *virginal,* in another form *spinet,* also borrowing from the Italian *harpsichord* and *cembalo,* as well as *clavicymbal* or *cymbel.* And the medieval and later Spanish use of the word *clavicordo* seems to have referred not to a clavichord but to a spinet harpsichord.

In comparison with a piano, a harpsichord is a rather simple apparatus, having only a few hundred instead of a few thousand parts. Harpsichords come in three types.

The simplest consists of stretched strings lying at an angle lengthwise within an oblong box. A straight line of jacks is adjusted between the two bridges, one at each end of the strings, in such a way that some of the strings are plucked about a third of the way from one bridge and others at varying distances, as well as can be managed. This is the instrument called originally, in England, *virginal* or *virginals—a pair of virginals* being somewhat like a pair of pants. They were made also in real pairs, one instrument fitting inside or beneath the other.

The problem in designing any harpsichord is to adjust the *plucking-point,* where the jacks rise to pluck the strings, in such a way as to produce an even scale: one in which the quality or register of the tones from end to end of the scale will be fairly alike. Trying to improve the disposition of the strings and plucking-points, builders bent out the back wall of the virginal box, giving the instrument a pentagonal shape, and increased the length, to provide longer strings and a better choice of plucking-points. A well-designed virginal, having the strings plucked some distance from the bridge, gives a very sweet tone.

The alternative is to pluck the strings very near the end, close to the bridge. This gives the tone that the French call *nasal.* The *nasal* tone is more intense, drier, and capable of a greater variety of suggestiveness. Such tone is especially characteristic of French clavecin music, as the sweeter tone is more characteristic of the earlier British music for the virginal.

When the instrument was given a triangular shape, with the farther point at the player's right and the strings still running crosswise as in the earlier oblong box, it was called a *spinet* (French, *épinette*). The extension of the point to the right gave space for longer bass strings, while reducing the over-all size of the original box, so that the longest side of the triangle fits snugly to the wall and the player sits at the keyboard diagonally to the back. A spinet has only one set of strings and no registers, though it may have a lute stop, partially dampening the strings so that the tone resembles the plucking of a lute. The spinet is the easiest of the keyboard instruments to play and to maintain; in my opinion the best of all house instruments, and the best suited to the keyboard education of children, for whom a piano action is too heavy.

A virginal or spinet came at first without legs and was set on a table or trestle; the player stood up to play, as one sees in a famous painting by Vermeer. After a while players ceased making any distinction between virginal or spinet, using the names interchangeably; nothing was gained by this, and it is just as well to use the right names.

The harpsichord proper is distinguished from virginal and spinet by having more than one set of strings. The shape of the box was changed to conform with the layout of the strings, very long in the bass, very short in the treble, like a slender harp lying on its side in a wooden case. The strings now ran from front to back, as in a grand piano, crossed by the rows of jacks approximately paralleling the keyboard at the front end.

By attaching a pull-stop at one end of each row of jacks, it was possible to move the entire row of jacks to right or left, and to adjust additional rows to pluck the strings at different distances from the end. Thus two rows of jacks could be set to pluck one row of strings, one producing a *nasal* tone by plucking close to the end and the other producing a more mellow tone by plucking a little farther in. In this way a single keyboard could have the use of two contrasting registers (registrations) with one set of strings.

The common early harpsichord with a single keyboard had

usually two sets of strings, one giving an 8' (eight-foot) tone, the other a 4' (four-foot) tone. The 4' sounds an octave higher than the 8'. The 4' strings are shorter and have a separate bridge. By moving the jack-rows, either set of strings may be played separately, or the two can be combined, so that each note played at the keyboard sounds an octave, emphasizing the higher overtones.

The usual registration for a two-manual harpsichord would provide an 8' stop for each keyboard (manual), each having a different plucking-point and a distinct quality of tone, the more mellow probably on the lower manual, and the *nasal* on the upper, plus a separate 4' usually coupled to the main (or lower) manual. The choice of registrations and coupling combinations determined the qualities and possibilities of the instrument.

With meantone tuning, the change of key-coloration and the intervallic variety in each key provided most of the "registration," eliminating the need for the constant changing of stops with which a modern player tries to accomplish a similar result in equal temperament. For this reason, and to accommodate variant tunings or different pitch levels—differences as common then as they are unusual now—the two manuals may have been played separately, without coupling. With correct tuning, the greater part of seventeenth- and eighteenth-century music registers itself for one manual; even when played in equal temperament it is better performed on one manual, with a minimum of registration changes. Everything depends on choosing the right register to play in or, in the case of a single register, adapting the style of playing to the composition. Unlike the piano, which depends on an art of tonal illusion, the harpsichord will speak adequately for itself if the player will let it. That is why, of the four keyboard instruments, a harpsichord is the most satisfactory for an amateur player—especially if he will learn to tune and maintain it himself.

A good player, when reading harpsichord music, will determine changes of registration, not by caprice of taste and the convenience of foot pedals, but according to the evident intent of the composer. An authentic harpsichord has only hand stops and no pedals. For this reason, one can expect the composer to have ordered the successive planes of the music to permit one hand to leave the keyboard at any place where he wished a change of registration. By locating these places, the modern player will know where and when the stops are to be changed.

A peculiarity of modern harpsichords has been the addition of a 16′ stop, an octave below the 8′. Curt Sachs wrote of this in *The History of Musical Instruments:* "Harpsichord players of today may wonder why the fourth stop was not used for a 16′. This was not done for two reasons. First, the instrument was not long enough. Second, there was no need, indeed there was a dislike, for a 16′. No English, Flemish, French, Italian, or Spanish harpsichord ever had one; it occurs exclusively in a few German harpsichords of the eighteenth century. This should be learned by modern harpsichordists who are continually pressing the 16′ pedal in Couperin's *Pièces de Clavecin* as well as in rounds of the *Fitzwilliam Virginal Book.* . . .

"Moreover, it cannot be too often repeated that the harpsichord, generally speaking, had no pedal to facilitate the change of timbre and power. . . ."

The 16′ pedal, as we use it now, was for all esthetic purposes invented and popularized by Wanda Landowska during the first half of the twentieth century. It is an intermediary between the piano and the harpsichord, an attempt to preserve in harpsichord registration the more heavily weighted timbre of the concert grand piano.

For a short run the 16′ can be impressive, but used constantly to supplement the normal registration of the instrument it weights the tone, dulls the bright coloring of the higher harmonics, and gives a false report of the composer's intention. Remember that the harpsichord speaks most naturally in its 8′ register; many traditional instruments possessed no other. There is, however, a little spinet, called *spinettino,* which has only 4′ tone.

Besides stops and couplers, harpsichords come equipped with a muting device which presses loose felts against the strings to damp them lightly, giving a tone like that of a harp or lute. The quality is interesting and has abundant historical authenticity, though now overused, as are all changes of registration on the harpsichord.

Many small harpsichords have a so-called "Bach keyboard" of four octaves plus two notes, from C two octaves below middle C to D two octaves and two notes above middle C. In the bass, this will suffice for nearly all keyboard music until towards the end of the eighteenth century, provided that one uses a *short octave*, as was common practice. To do so, one tunes the lowest C sharp to B below, or B flat, or A, as the notation and harmony require. You will find that the composer has taken this practice into account and will seldom embarrass you by requiring you to play the C sharp. At the upper end of the keyboard, unfortunately, a similar economy operates contrariwise. The keyboard used by Haydn and Mozart goes up to E, instead of D. And you will find very few keyboard works by either composer which do not rise to that high E somewhere in the composition. So that if you would like to play Haydn and Mozart on your harpsichord, as I should, you should ask the builder, if he is planning a Bach keyboard, to work into his plans the two necessary additional notes, E flat and E, at the top. (C. P. E. Bach's keyboard rises to F.) This cannot usually be done, alas! on a completed instrument.

All good pianos sound approximately alike; harpsichords should not, varying decidedly in quality and usefulness according to the evenness of the scale, the types of plectra, the weight and length of strings, the choices of register and the combinations these produce. Volume of tone diminishes in the upper registers. A good harpsichord tone will be distinctive and penetrating but not loud. Listeners to recorded harpsichord music often blow the volume up to orchestral dimensions, causing a clangor which falsifies the quality of the instrument and distorts the music.

Modern musicians and their audiences expect that a good instrument should produce a large volume of tone. Musicians and audiences of other periods have thought differently. The volume of a tone pleased them less than its timbre, its individuality, its edge, its fineness. One may doubt whether the clangor of a modern pianist hammering through the finale of Rachmaninoff's Second Piano Concerto would have pleased them at all, though it would have astonished them as much as a steam whistle. They did not expect an instrument to be heard at its full power by an immense audience in a large hall, because they did not usually play in large halls or before immense audiences. The tone of their keyboard instruments was relatively quiet.

The tight stringing of modern instruments reduces the richness of their overtones, but we are so accustomed to hearing a modern solo instrument punching out its fundamental that we do not appreciate what is being lost. A few months of playing at a quiet clavichord or pleasant-speaking harpsichord, tuned perhaps a half-step below present-day concert pitch, may help us to understand the rich amplitude, with quietness, of truly musical sound.

A Brief History
of Keyboard Music

THE SIXTEENTH
CENTURY

In approaching music of an earlier century or of another culture, we should take pains to convince ourselves that the musicians were not less skilled than ours, however seemingly limited or primitive their instruments; that the composers were no less assured in their methods of composing than our classic or contemporary composers. (The ancient Chinese-Japanese bamboo flute without mouthpiece, the *shakuhachi*, is still one of the most versatile of instruments, whether in playing unaccompanied the millennia-old outdoor music of the wandering monks, or in taking its part as a solo instrument in the chamber music of the last three centuries, or in the Westernizing habits thrust upon it by recent Japanese composing.) Earlier composers did not feel themselves lacking the means we know and the solutions we have learned to what were not their problems. They too argued the balance between technique and spontaneity, between intellect and emotion. Their standards of judgement and prizes of admiration were not less meaningful than ours.

Let us go back and approach the art of keyboard playing as if the piano had never existed.

We return to the sixteenth century, to a civilization where everybody sings, freely and with remarkable skill but not in concert style and probably not in what we should think of as a natural voice.

Apart from religious music, of which this period is called the

9

Golden Age—a music more glorious than the decadent religious attitudes it springs from—the prevailing musical content is amorous-melancholy to lugubrious.

Musical skill and erudition have exceeded the limitations of their content. Or one may say that a new content, waiting to be recognized, is inspiring composers to go beyond the traditional limitations of their means. In extremes of taste and varieties of experimentation the sixteenth century resembles the twentieth.

Though public singers, like actors, are by social convention boys and men, the women's voices and musical skills are also highly cultivated. Women join with men in part-singing or on an instrument, as groups today listen to recorded music. Throughout Europe music is cultivated by amateurs with a skill and knowledge unrivaled since that time. Let them be an example to us.

Singers and those who could not sing played at an instrument or carried a lute to pretend with, as a swaggerer wore his sword. Part-writing for voices and instruments (*madrigals* and *consorts*) of a complexity that tests our own most skilled performers was read at sight by these amateurs—a skill that astonishes us, until we think of our own often recklessly casual skill in traffic. So concentrated a public interest could not last long, as we know by the example of amateur sports today. From the start of the seventeenth century this amateur activity dwindles towards audience participation and an imitated professionalism.

The first solo keyboard playing was done at the organ, the organist reading vocal music and embellishing it for his own pleasure. In the fifteenth century, the blind organist Conrad Paumann of Nuremberg became expert enough to travel as a virtuoso performer, playing before large crowds. Paumann is said to have invented the *tablature* notation by letters, also used for lute music; he wrote in tablature his organ compositions in two parts, *Fundamentum organisandi,* as examples for students, as well as organ elaborations of Gregorian chant and popular tunes. Arnolt Schlick, court organist at Heidelberg in the sixteenth century, became both a famous organ virtuoso and an authority on organ-building. His *Tablaturen* for organ are richly embellished melodies elaborating a *cantus firmus,* a melody, usually from Gregorian chant, which appears in long notes of equal value in a lower voice. Neither the modern organ nor the piano can do justice to these compositions, written for an organ of what Schlick called "sharply cutting" sound, full of character and overtones.

The first composer to produce a body of music which still holds a high place in the keyboard literature was a blind Spaniard, Antonio de Cabezón. (In Europe at that time, as in Japan even today, a blind boy who showed promise was often educated to be a musician.) Cabezón's short, formal, powerful preludes and fantasies for organ (composed on the tone or tonal formula to which a psalm was sung) and secular variations and fantasies for keyboard and *vihuela* (the Spanish guitar-lute) epitomize an already rich extravocal musical culture, of which only a small published literature survives. Cabezón's music, fortunately, was published by his son. The composer is said to have gone to England in the train of Philip II of Spain during that ambitious, hyperesthetic monarch's brief conjunction with Mary of England. He may then have met Thomas Tallis, but no influence of Cabezón's distinctive Spanish idiom appears in subsequent English music.

Cabezón's writing for keyboard can be distinguished from his writing for vihuela only by the rather more difficult lie of the lute music under the hands on the keyboard. He wrote in the same tablature for both instruments. The surviving literature would indicate that until the later sixteenth century the lutenists had mastered a greater virtuosity than the keyboard players. It is not a great step from pressing frets melodically and contrapuntally to pressing keys similarly—indeed, for complex music it is a simplification, since the player need not press and pluck at the same time. The lute repertoire merges, almost insensibly, into the keyboard repertoire.

Looking through the collection of sixteenth-century English keyboard pieces called the *Mulliner Book,* one sees that a large part of this music is still closely related to vocal music for the church. But virginal and harpsichord, though lacking the sustained tone, could without hesitation play it all. Outside the sacred edifice they were already inaugurating a new art of secular keyboard pieces, built around popular tunes. The *Hornepype* attributed to Hugh Aston and the anonymous *Lady Carey's Dompe* are harpsichord music solely, the former a marvelous example of the performing virtuosity which had already been attained before the preservation of a written keyboard literature, the latter a skeletal notation requiring to be harmonically filled out and embellished with ornaments in playing.

Filling out of such skeletal notation had begun earlier in the German practice of organ *colorieren,* the inflection of single notes by conventional figuration, a habit that soon extended throughout European music. *Colorieren* and embellishment are derived from similar practices in folk music that go back to aboriginal sources.

In reading the very early European keyboard music, one should not be deceived by archaic-sounding vertical harmonies, as we meet them in modern notation. In our ears these archaic-sounding harmonies seem more "authentic" than the same music properly embellished in its proper tuning. The piquancy of sound results from playing the music in equal temperament instead of the perfect fifths of the Pythagorean tuning or the perfect fifths and thirds of just intonation.

Strange that, with the real thing not so difficult to obtain, experts in performing and writing about this music should continue refusing to try as much as they know, and instead go on determinedly repeating what has been said and done incorrectly in the past.

Having looked through the *Mulliner Book,* try now a wonderful little provincial item, the *Dublin Virginal Book.* The recent modern edition of this book contains in the back the same airs and tunes in earlier Italian settings for the lute. The *Mulliner Book* leaves much to be guessed about the sound of the instrument and the manner of performance. The *Dublin Virginal Book* is made up of folk music, which, when you have mastered its rhythmic intricacies, will swing even on piano. (There are perhaps three pieces which will not, one that is unplayable). The keyboard pieces retain the tricky rhythms of the earlier lute versions but spread into scales and figurations beyond the lute compass.

In the library of keyboard music the *Fitzwilliam Virginal Book* stands for a century; it is a library within a library. On the small evidence we have, we believe that a recusant enemy of the state named Francis Tregian made this collection, during the many years he lived with his family and his instruments in the Fleet prison at London. The collection is named in honor of a subsequent possessor, the builder of the famous library at Oxford, where the manuscript now lies. It was called formerly *Queen*

Elizabeth's Virginal Book in the belief that the Queen once owned it, an incorrect supposition, since a number of the pieces were written after her death. It is also possible that the collection may have been compiled at Antwerp some time after the writing of the last dated composition, the *Ut Re Mi Fa So La* by Sweelinck, dated 1612.

The *Fitzwilliam Virginal Book* is not a printed collection of contemporary music brought together and professionally edited and thereafter made accessible to anyone who would buy it. It was put together by someone who copied in manuscript popular, sacred, and experimental compositions mainly by English composers, a number of them Roman Catholic recusants safe in European exile out of reach of the government of England. (Being a Catholic recusant in England at that time was the equivalent of being a member of the Communist party in America during the 1950s, but more dangerous.) This great collection survived simply by good fortune, its contents indicating how much more music of equal value, in England and other countries, may have been lost. The manuscript was not printed until the last years of the nineteenth century.

The *Fitzwilliam Virginal Book* includes 297 compositions, from the 30 Variations on *Walsingham* by John Bull to witty musical epigrams in two staves by Giles Farnaby. It reaches from Thomas Tallis, several of whose pieces appear also in the *Mulliner Book*, to Richard Farnaby, son of Giles, and includes two works by Sweelinck: from the reign of Queen Mary to that of James I, spanning the entire reign of Queen Elizabeth. It contains tedious pieces in the older, vocal polyphonic style, such as the *Felix namque* composed in 1564 by Tallis, and experimental compositions like the *Hexachord* with modulations and the elaborately contrapuntal *In Nomine* by Bull. It is a treasury of popular tunes and dances, Almans, Corantos, and Gigges, and a jumping dance enjoyed by Queen Elizabeth called La Volta. Besides the many sacred pieces for the organ, there are fantasies and grounds and pavans and galliards of all sizes. One can never learn enough to read or play it all or finish with it. Much of it demands a keyboard technique not easily to be acquired at the piano, but there are little pieces which are fun to read the first time through. It is the first great collection of what can truly be called keyboard music.

Polyphony stood for the old style, tradition, the authority of the Church, weight and solemnity as against liveliness. The madrigal and its country cousin, the part-song, are the true sixteenth-century music, circulating in many editions and often reprinted. Keyboard music was not yet so popular.

In the *Fitzwilliam Virginal Book* are several songs by French and Italian composers, written out and embellished for keyboard solo by the exiled English priest Peter Phillips. The accompanied song and the now liberated accompaniment newly functioning as independent solo keyboard composition (for example, three settings, by Byrd, Giles Farnaby, and Thomas Morley, of the *Pavan Lachrymae*, originally for lute and voice, by John Dowland) are music of the future which comes into predominance with the turning of taste in the seventeenth century.

In the midst of this musical evolution, at the start of the three hundred years of vertical or keyboard harmony (which I shall refer to hereafter as the period of *modern music*) that we accept too casually as if it were the whole of music, the English keyboard art remains isolated among its mutations like Darwin's Galapagos finches, a little influenced from Italy but in every way surpassing that influence, transmitting somewhat more of its authority, by way of Bull and Sweelinck, to the seventeenth-century keyboard art of Europe. It is work of that sophisticated anthropological self-sufficiency that we call *primitive*.

▶ If such *primitive* art is intensely cultivated but static, with a long present but seemingly no future, we think of it as "ethnic," though the ethnomusicologist does not understand his study in that way, nor is that the proper significance of the word.

Ethnic music is music played by "natives" who learn to play only their own music, exactly as it was played by their forefathers, and nothing else. The natives do not expect to be taught music appreciation, because everybody they know, except outsiders, shares the common knowledge of their music. Ethnic musical art depends entirely on tradition, on doing the same thing over and over again, whether or not—as in jazz—the player is expected to improvise. (Current jazz has ceased to be ethnic and has become musicological.) Among primitive musicians the music, if written, is not read exactly

as notated; the notation consists of informational signs or letters, which the player interprets, by adding accidentals, embellishments, unwritten notes, or microtones, according to
the habit of tradition. Few of the world's flute-players except
our own would play a notated tone as we sound it at the
piano, without some microtonal embellishment to make it
interesting. Yet the embellishment may be so exact in the
tradition that two or more flute-players joining together for
the first time will play it alike.

In such a primitive culture the occasional musician who
deliberately deviates or "mutates" from the tradition may
succeed in establishing a parallel tradition of his own.

Western European music (our own) is not thought of as
"ethnic," as Western musicians do not think of themselves as
"natives." Historically, both suppositions may be at the point
of change. The entire European harmonic period of three
centuries, however cosmopolitan it has grown by recent
world-wide imitation, may soon be historically recognized as
isolate, "primitive," and in the larger sense "ethnic." It's fun
to have a share in it while we can still read the music and
play the instruments.

Parthenia, the first collection of keyboard music to be printed
in England, contains the work of three composers: William Byrd,
Dr. John Bull, and Orlando Gibbons. Their reputation as the
three foremost composers of their period in England, in all forms
as well as keyboard music, was downgraded during subsequent
centuries by the prevailing distaste for what was called "gothick"
art. Only during the last century have their formidable gifts as
composers begun to receive an increasing and proper recognition.
Their complete surviving music has been reprinted and somewhat
hesitantly discussed; with all that has been reprinted and all that
has been written about it, one is surprised to discover how little
we really know.

Many of the Elizabethan keyboard pieces now in anthologies
were taken from a bastard nineteenth-century reprinting of
Parthenia, which was for a century the only accessible text.

William Byrd, a composer of the eminence of Vittoria, Lassus,
and Palestrina, was so highly esteemed by Queen Elizabeth, herself reputed to have been a skilled player at the virginal, that he

was allowed to stay in England unpersecuted, though he was a recusant. Byrd was even permitted to engage in litigation, a privilege restricted by law to Protestants, which dull-spiteful activity is his only other recorded interest outside music. It is hard to reconcile the musical character with the biographical account of this seemingly all-melodious genius. (Yet what should we think of Beethoven, if we had besides his music only the tale of his dealings with his publishers and relatives?)

The most beautiful of the English manuscripts of keyboard music, *My Ladye Nevells Booke,* is made up entirely of earlier compositions by Byrd, copied for presentation to the lady to whom the first piece in the collection is dedicated. Dedication during this century and the next was often by making the person's name a part of the title: *My Lady Nevels Grownde.*

There is also a modern collection, *Forty-five Pieces for Keyboard Instruments,* including all the keyboard pieces not elsewhere published. Byrd ranks among the complete masters of the keyboard art, yet we have no more record of his keyboard playing than we have of Haydn's.

Dr. John Bull was a Doctor of Music at both Cambridge and Oxford and the first Professor of Music at Gresham College. Unlike Byrd, who lived in the country and seems to have left the playing of his music to others, Bull was a famous virtuoso who ended his life in exile as organist of the cathedral at Antwerp.

As Byrd is the master, for whom experiment is incidental to achievement, Bull is the experimentalist, whose achievement, like that of Domenico Scarlatti and Franz Liszt, stems from his willingness to experiment. Like them, Bull accomplished as much by the native gift of finger-technique as by mind.

Orlando Gibbons, the last and probably the most deliberate artist of the century which ended with his early death two years after the death of Byrd, passed his career as organist to King James I. Byrd's composition has a prevailing structure, like Beethoven's; Gibbons's composition is textual, like Bach's. Nearly all the keyboard music of Gibbons has an organlike formality, in the traditional polyphonic style, though much of it was intended for the harpsichord. Like Dr. Bull he was a famous performer at both instruments, yet his finger-technique seldom intrudes on the formal deliberation of his mind. A good part of his best work is in *Benjamin Cosyn's Virginal Book*, in company with pieces by Dr. Bull, Byrd, and Benjamin Cosyn.

Among these greater figures who commanded all the resources of music, Giles Farnaby, gifted with rare musical humor, is technically a Schumann, more difficult to get your fingers around than musically demanding, delighting to compose little pieces as ingratiating as they are simple. Farnaby's son, Richard, emulating his father's wit and expertise, a little lacks his grace.

William Blitheman, Peter Phillips, and John Munday are among the other composers of this flowering century of keyboard music, to whose individual styles the true Amateur will wish to bend his enjoyment and skill as he comes among them. Early compositions by Thomas Tomkins, a belated organist and virginalist in the Elizabethan style, appear in the *Fitzwilliam Book*. During the mid-century between Gibbons and Purcell, Tomkins wrote a large number of compositions, including pavans and galliards in a style resembling that of William Byrd, recently published in the *Musica Britannica* series from a Paris manuscript. Though a Jacobean instead of an Elizabethan, Tomkins deserves to be ranked with the major composers of the earlier period.

No one to my knowledge has succeeded in describing, categorizing, or emotionalizing with literary flourishes this keyboard literature of Elizabethan England. Like many intensively developed "primitive" arts it is completely masculine, and was therefore the more delighting to its most puissant amateur, Queen of all true Amateurs, Elizabeth. (Though we must not forget that other queenly Amateur, Maria Barbara of Braganza, Queen of Spain, for whom Domenico Scarlatti composed hundreds of his *esercizi*, that we call sonatas.)

The principal form, as one speaks of sonata-allegro form, was that of the *pavan and galliard*, a solemn dance in duple or common meter in three sections followed by a faster triple-measure dance also in three sections. In full development each section was written out first in simpler and then in more elaborated variation, making a full form of two movements in contrasting rhythm, each movement divided in three rhythmically contrasting sections, each section progressing to the next through its elaborated variation.

All larger pavans and galliards have the repeat, or double,

written out in varied form as an equal part of the composition. In the same way, when playing a Haydn sonata, for example, one should repeat and vary in some measure the six halves of the three movements. In seventeenth- and eighteenth-century composition the repeat is a structural device, in which the player may, if he wishes to, exploit his skill in improvising variation. To eliminate the repeat deforms the structure and admits a lack of musicianly skill. This is what happens in public performance: we hurry to the end of a piece and on to another.

By articulating a strict pattern after the event, we lose the genuine freedom of a form; it is the exceptional Bach fugue or Beethoven sonata movement that agrees with textbook formal pattern. Such schematic description errs by inflexibility: no genuine composer thinks in that way by habit or writes so by idiom.

The internal sections of pavan and galliard were subject to striking alterations of design, so that the effect of a section with its repeat may be as often a quadruplicate as a double. The changing of rhythmic pattern within a compositional unit is likewise not uncommon among the dance and song variations. At full reach, the larger pavans and galliards by Byrd and Gibbons achieve an architectural variety and structure not less than that of the sonata. (I am comparing form, not composer personalities.) Though pavans and galliards, together and as separate movements, were composed in the other countries of Europe, nowhere else did the form attain a design of comparable breadth and magnificence.

While variations and the pavan and galliard were anticipating the rise of structural music during the next two centuries, the *fantasy,* or *fancy,* remained, as in Spanish keyboard music of the same period, polyphonic, disorganized, and diffuse, its style rather dry and its texture little more than a succession of patterns. Yet when played in the tempered Pythagorean tuning, with careful displacement of the rhythms, as for example in sections notated in *tripla,* the texture and coloring of the fantasy can take on a prose eloquence resembling the less metrical twentieth-century music. The test-piece for this skill is John Bull's *Hexachord (Fitzwilliam Virginal Book,* No. 51), a musicological problem which Wesley Kuhnle solved by working out the tempered Pythagorean tuning. During the first half, the *Hexachord* modulates upwards by whole steps at each variation, each modulation altering the interval relationship and therefore the color-registration of the tuning.

There is an interesting smaller *Hexachord* by Byrd, the scalewise ground to be played by a third hand, while the variations exchange popular tunes.

In the fantasies by Orlando Gibbons the style grew more concentrated and purposive and the texture more freely fugal, paralleling the brief flowering of similar fantasies for viols by Byrd, Gibbons, Deering, and William Lawes, a formal development out of the commoner *consort* for mixed instruments. The style reappeared, briefly, in the fantasies for viols by John Jenkins and the young Henry Purcell and was then swept away in a flood of professional violinists and smart new means of musical entertainment imported from the Continent. The gentleman's diversion of music had become the professional's business.

When playing this music, one should avoid setting a single tempo and staying in it through every change of movement in the score. Byrd's *O Mistress Mine* includes a variation with extended shakes for both hands, which can be played only as an adagio or largo, as in a set of variations by Mozart. Varying the rhythm among sections in pavan and galliard will bring out the largeness of the form. Those who play these movements too fast lose them entirely. A marked alteration of rhythm should be practised in all stepwise passages, the passing note pressing sometimes to the note following, sometimes falling quickly away from the preceding note, very freely, to define the movement.

"And there is no greater grace than breaking the time in the minutes, and still holding it punctually upon the main, to conserve the grand beat or measure," Roger North instructs. All other embellishments and graces proceed from this one.

Learn to hear, in imagination, the sinuous, leaping independence of these rhythms, the extraordinary syncopations accented by embellishment, the devil-may-care ragtime of Giles Farnaby's tunes and variations, the idiosyncratic physical vitality of these composers thrusting out of the idiom of their crafting. In the dances it is better to play broadly and risk being vulgar than to stay merely strict and finicky. A good many of these dances were no better than our own coarse ones—except that a better composer makes a better dance—and were intended for the same purpose, to have fun. Hear how the last beat of the leaping measure of a lavolta waits for the jumper to come down. Without these extrametrical devices the texture will be as lifeless, however superficially interesting, as metronomic jazz.

The expressive alteration of rhythm and meter in polyphonic music, or in compositions in slower time, depends on more subtle displacements, having regular or irregular stresses instead of a fixed beat. Play in the same way that Shakespeare's verses should be read, neither speaking flat prose nor counting on the fingers. The bar-line should be no more than a guide for the eye; though it is printed in modern editions according to strict measure, it was not so in the original manuscript or in the printed score of *Parthenia*. The bar-line does not indicate fixed vertical relationship or an accent.

Accompanying chords should be played lute-fashion, either a strum or a broken chord. We need to throw off entirely the chorded vertical harmony and strict metrical counting of our superposed habit. Musicians of other periods kept time by their methods as exactly to their purpose as we do to ours.

There are other composers and other collections of keyboard music from the fifteenth and sixteenth centuries that are of interest: the *Buxheim Organ Book*, the dances and versets published by Attaignant in France, compositions by Neusiedler, Claudio Merulo, the Gabrielis, by North German and Dutch organists. European keyboard music does not come into full view before the start of the seventeenth century. Doubtless there was a larger body of music, as in England, than that which has survived, but none that we have, until Frescobaldi and Sweelinck, bears comparison with the work of the principal composers of Elizabethan England.

12

THE SEVENTEENTH
CENTURY

During the seventeenth century the lute and its literature drop gradually out of sight, while organ and harpsichord continue their interlocking development as solo instruments. If we think of the sixteenth century as continuing until the latest compositions of the *Fitzwilliam Virginal Book*, and of the seventeenth century as beginning with the works of Girolamo Frescobaldi and Jan Sweelinck, there is an overlap. We are entering the century and a half of the international primacy of the organ, to which the harpsichord and, rather more privately, the clavichord play a subordinate role. It is the period that ends in 1750 with the death of Johann Sebastian Bach. Dates are of less importance than ways of thinking music. (So the period 1750–1900 may be called the century and a half of the international primacy of the orchestra.)

Listeners and critics who accept sixteenth-century music as quaint or charming or incomplete, having no larger appreciation of it, make a habit of dismissing the seventeenth-century music as "transitional," meaning that it was on the way towards music which they believe they know how to appreciate. Their tendency has been to regard seventeenth-century music as in one way or another ill-formed or inadequately conceived, a consensus of manners and styles which became valid only after J. S. Bach, during the first half of the eighteenth century, took charge of working them up for critical acceptance. As for the art of embellishment, which is the domain of style in seventeenth-century music, they prefer to know as little of it as possible. Such complacency has been for many the equivalent—indeed the art—of music appreciation.

The period of three centuries, the seventeenth through the nineteenth, is the true period of *modern music*, an art whose retrospect now threatens all other musical cultures of the world. The music of these three centuries became modern by the substitution of vertical key-harmony for polyphony.

In sixteenth-century music there is no real key-harmony; the influence of the mode still prevails. In Pythagorean and tempered Pythagorean tunings and in just intonation there are no real keys; the upward modulating of Bull's *Hexachord* is an experimental and exceptional event.

Gesualdo, Prince of Venosa, writing madrigals in the sixteenth century, could use all twelve notes of the chromatic scale as easily as Arnold Schoenberg in the twentieth century and less self-consciously. Schoenberg, in amused recognition of the affinity, spoke of Gesualdo as "the Schoenberg of the sixteenth century."

Listeners habituated to the relatively common language of the three centuries of modern music, and few who read this are habituated to any other music, take for the musical norm what is in reality the most exceptional period in the history of music, for nowhere else at any time has a similar music of vertically related key-harmony existed. That is why twentieth-century music, at once breaking with key-harmony and reaching out to learn from the other musical cultures of the world, seems to have lost contact with its immediate past. It differs most markedly in having renounced the dramatic conflict, within key-harmony, of consonance and dissonance.

If in key-harmony we modulate from the key of X towards the key of Y by one or more harmonic stations, the harmony of Y will be dissonant in some respects when related back to X but not when related to Y. The farther we remove from X the more we increase dissonance; but so long as we adventure within the realm of Y we are still within the domain of a secondary, and safe, consonance. The terms of harmony are therefore ambivalent in relation to key. Consonance and dissonance are entirely terms of relativity.

But if there are no keys and therefore no sensations of key-relativity, the twelve notes of the chromatic scale can be put together in any way that pleases the ear or mind (what pleases the mind will not always please the ear, at least not immediately); that is what Gesualdo did for his own pleasure, and his madrigals sold in many editions; it is what Schoenberg meant by the "emancipation of the dissonance."

There is another relationship that is more nearly absolute: between concordance and discordance. Until the sixteenth century, music was composed around the concordant instead of the discordant intervals of the scale. From the sixteenth century until the present time, music has been composed around discordant intervals.

Until the sixteenth century, music had been composed for instruments of *variable* intonation, which could, like the voice, adjust pitch slightly to preserve as a concord an interval which would be notationally a dissonance. Gesualdo's musicologically famous dissonances were actually sung as twelve-tone consonances in a scale of concordantly chromatic just intonation. We perform the same music in discordantly chromatic equal temperament, even widening the major thirds to exaggerate the dissonances.

After the sixteenth century, music began to be composed around the *fixed* intonation of the keyboard instruments, on which no interval can be adjusted to preserve a concord. The new vertical harmonic relationship exists by agreement to accept certain moderate degrees of dissonance as equivalent to consonance. Instead of the acoustically correct sonorities of the previous concordant vertical relationship, there is now no music which does not embody and dramatize degrees of dissonance.

The basic structure of harmonic music is dramatic, a conflict between lesser and greater extremes of consonance and dissonance, the farthest remove from the starting key being the height of the drama and the return to that key its logical and emotional conclusion. This discovery was not established in practice until towards the end of the eighteenth century. Composers of the seventeenth century, not having this fact clearly laid before them by example, were constrained to seek other ways of putting their new harmonic idiom to use.

Thus harmonic theory originated, like the violin, before its literature; the literature came into existence by putting the instrument to use. At a certain point in its historical development the expanding implications of the literature compelled drastic alteration, a redesigning of the instrument. Every Stradivarius that is being played today has been taken apart and rebuilt differently from its original shape. Harmonic theory, in the same way, has been several times redesigned and rebuilt. Though we know these facts, music for the older medium is today performed, historically discussed, and analyzed as if it had been written in terms of the newer medium.

The seventeenth-century composers, starting with the means and forms they had, narrowed them from the great freedom of the sixteenth century into the narrower channel of monodic harmony, continuing to wander astray when they felt like doing so. Thus their more consonant passages sound to us thin and undeveloped, while their more vagrant measures please us by their originality.

▶ *Monody* consists of a single moving part with its accompaniment; polyphony is made up of independently moving parts. The distinction, like so many distinctions in musical parlance, is less clear than the general comprehension of what the term signifies. Thus a monodic accompaniment, from Dowland to Handel, may be counterpointed, that is in more than one independent part, but always in relation to the predominating single line of melody; whereas a single voice, as in the compositions for violin alone and cello alone by J. S. Bach, may be either monodic, when the instrument provides its own accompaniment, or polyphonic, as in fugue or gigue.

The music of the seventeenth century was in fact strongly idiomatic. It kept some of the linear interest of the earlier music, with a certain crabbed pleasure in forcing this free line to wear harmonic dress. It developed a highly cultivated feeling for elaborate embellishment, adapted to enlivening the rhythmic and melodic texture to give the instrumental speech a more diverse expressiveness. It exploited in its own way the harmonic possibilities of the new meantone tuning.

The doctrine of the *affections* as a figurative musical speech appeared in Italy but reached its height in Germany, where it combined with the native homely *expressionism* characteristic of all Germanic art. The doctrine presented itself in two aspects. The one aspect was literary, the belief that music is a type of figurative speech, that the expressive figures of music can be more or less directly related to words. This theory fitted well into a period when all language involved circumlocutions and expressive terminology which today seem to us tedious. To put it simply, the texture of composed music reflected very faithfully the style of the dedication to some noble lord or lady which the composer appended, with the engraver's flourishes, at the front of his collection. This method of expression contributed to music a richness of design and elaboration of texture which speak to us in our time far more naturally than their equivalent in verse or prose. Compare for example a formal letter by J. S. Bach with its contrapuntal equivalent in his music.

The second aspect of the affections was less literary but no less widespread in acceptance. This had to do with the fact that in meantone tuning each key has an unlike intervallic pattern, an individual harmonic coloring, and a greater degree of built-in dissonance than the key of C major (in basic meantone the increase of dissonant relationship can be measured by the increase of sharps or flats in the key-signature). Thus each key possessed a distinctive key-coloration and harmonic tension, and by common agreement was supposed to exemplify a distinct type of emotion, governing in part the means of expressive figuration to be used with it. This notion that each key speaks for a particular emotion is still held by many persons who are unaware that the presumed individual emotionality of the key disappeared with the end of meantone tuning and has not existed in European music for 150 years. In equal temperament the coloration and harmonic tension are the same for every key.

The art of seventeenth-century keyboard music is therefore not to be found in its sense of formal particularity, however interesting this may be, but in its detail, the representative or expressive content of each passage. It is not "what the music does to me" but what I find there. Instead of concerning itself with structural movements designed to succeed one another in larger forms, the seventeenth-century art is a craftsmanship of units. In some of François Couperin's keyboard *Orders* we encounter groups of

10

movements or occasional entire suites presented together as a deliberate sequence of events. J. S. Bach was perhaps the first to give to larger organizational grouping, such as suite or partita, an integral validity not less than that of its units, imparting to each movement a clear definition and relationship among its fellows.

In Italy Girolamo Frescobaldi had expanded the older indigenous instrumental forms used by lute, organ, and harpsichord into *canzonas, capriccios, toccatas,* and *ricercars,* loose-joined as the Spanish fantasy but with each section more tightly worked by fugal or canonic imitations, or re-entries of the theme. The *ricercar* was originally the free lute-prelude to a song. The *canzona* came from a French source, the vocal *chanson.* The *toccata* is a touch-piece intended for rapid playing. The *capriccio* is a free prelude; Frescobaldi expanded it into a short succession of variations.

Living at the center of the Roman world, Frescobaldi exerted wide influence. He was a famous organ virtuoso, no less skilled in playing and writing for the harpsichord. Much of his work is playable on either instrument, but his best-known compositions, the *Fiori Musicali,* are for organ. This is a collection of liturgical pieces of mystical character, to be used instead of vocal music in accompanying portions of the Mass. The music is to be heard, therefore, not directly but peripherally, a criterion we customarily forget when listening to devotional music as if it were made to be itself the object of primary attention, like a piano concerto.

Though Frescobaldi prefaced the *Fiori Musicali* with careful directions for playing, proper realization of his music remains today as mysterious as it is tempting. Neither expansive nor naturally melodious, it requires in playing an elaboration of embellishment we do not know surely how to give it. (No reason for not trying!) Even in plain reproduction it shows an austere authority and a technical sophistication as rich as that of the contemporary Italian madrigal, from which it derives some of its harmonic waywardness.

When John Bull fled from England to Holland, he formed there a close friendship with the Dutch composer Jan Sweelinck, son of a Dutch organist and his exact contemporary in age. Under the influence of Sweelinck the English composer wrote organ compositions in a more developed counterpoint than he had previously attempted. His own virtuoso skill may have opened up Sweelinck's more methodical workmanship into the great fantasies and fugues, that noble art of organ composition which, spreading across Europe for a century, culminated in the work of Buxtehude and J. S. Bach.

▶ Nobody can define exactly the strict form of the *fugue*, although strict rules for it abound. J. S. Bach confined his rules to his practice, and that no strict rules confine. Most simply, a fugue is an example of what Bach called the *art of fugue*, an art he expounded characteristically by a large, closely organized composition made up of a variety of exemplary fugues and several canons. We shall do better to follow his example by speaking not of a fugue but of *fugue*.

Fugue consists of thematic imitation in several voices, regulated by the succession of the entries. When the thematic material is stretched over a longer time, it is said to be in *augmentation;* when shortened in time and quickened, it is in *diminution*. Augmentation in one voice may companion diminution in another voice. When the returns or re-entries of the thematic material occur more rapidly and pile up across the several voices, the effect is called *stretto*. Episodes of related or new material may be inserted between sections of thematic material. Larger fugues combine several or all of these devices.

Fugues of very strict design, in which the thematic material enters continually according to a specified intervallic plan, are called *canonic* or *canons*. Puzzle canons may be written giving only the thematic material and sometimes a clue to what is to be done with it. In fugues and canons the thematic material may be presented forwards, backwards, upside down, or upside down and backwards. These combinations can be fascinating intellectual exercises. Composers have written for their amusement strict canons which by their shape or movement interpret or illustrate verbal texts, as jokes, compliments, epigrams, and for the abstract pleasure of manipulating technical devices and intervallic relationships, often with little or no regard for the actual sound of the music, if performed. But some of the most beautiful smaller compositions by Bach, Mozart, Schoenberg, and Stravinsky are in strict canon.

By the multiplicity of recognitions which the mind catches rather than the ear distinguishes, complex fugues can be music of an excitement unequaled by any other form. Such multiplex fuguing heightens the drama in Beethoven's compositions of the last period. It was revived by Schoenberg and is behind the theory of present-day *tone-row* or *serial* composing.

The fugue grew from the marriage of a rather brittle Latin style to a buxom and expansive Northern European idiom. The Italian style laid down the household regulations, and the Northern composer enlarged upon them as he pleased. The strict Italian style concluded, after two centuries, in the textbook fugues by Clementi and Cherubini. The German idiomatic fugue swept on through Bach, Handel, and Beethoven to Hindemith and Schoenberg.

Fugues can be written in brief space or at great length. Larger fugues are often in two, three, or four parts, each part having a distinct theme; the successive themes often combine towards the end. Fugues may be in as few as two voices or in as many as the composer believes the performer can manage, usually not more than six.

Germany entered modern music with the compositions by Samuel Scheidt, a pupil of Sweelinck. Scheidt's *Tabulatura Nova* looks back to the *Tabulaturen* of Arnolt Schlick. Scheidt inaugurated the habits which would prevail in Germanic organ music during the next century. He established that distinctive Germanic form, the *chorale prelude*.

The oldest type of chorale prelude, represented by the *cantus firmus* compositions of Schlick or the preludes on a psalm-tune of Cabezón, embellished a fixed liturgical melody. In England a type of the organ fantasy called an *In Nomine* or *Innomey* was always composed around the one melody of a Gregorian *Gloria tibi*. In German Protestant usage a Lutheran hymn (*chorale*) usually replaced the older Gregorian melody, though J. S. Bach used both.

Scheidt developed a new form of closely organized chorale prelude, with expressive figuration to convey the meaning of the hymn text. Johann Pachelbel, who was born a year before the death of Scheidt, elaborated each successive line of the hymn in imitative or fugal style, a method favored by J. S. Bach, whose last chorale prelude, *Vor deinen Thron*, shows the form in marvelous purity.

Frescobaldi's chief pupil, Johann Jacob Froberger, a German, carried the Italian style to Germany, where he set in motion an Italianate tradition paralleling the German tradition of Scheidt; these two combining soon made German organ music the richest and most varied in Europe. A considerable amount of this German organ literature has been preserved, giving historical repute to isolated provincial organists of talent who might otherwise have been forgotten. Their compositions, however indifferently performed, remain a staple of the present-day organ recital. Any collection of their works, as well as the organ works by J. S. Bach, includes attractive compositions for manuals only, without pedals, able to be read with pleasure at the piano.

Froberger's art brings together the Italian figurative *affect* with a typical Germanic *expressionism*. Some of his occasional pieces are intended to convey the emotion of a particular experience, for instance his *Complaint Written in London to Overcome Melancholy*. He was among the first to compose relatively formal suites of dances, in the French style, using what was to become the standard arrangement of *allemande, courante, saraband,* and *gigue*. His compositions are especially well adapted to the clavichord, though he undoubtedly performed them also on harpsichord and organ.

The French taste for small dances, like those in the Attaignant collections, was taken up by a school of courtly lutenists, who boasted of a "secret art." Secret arts had sprung up from time to time in European painting as well as music. They had their origin in a religious or professional exclusiveness, having a language of symbols and figures which conveyed its meaning only to initiates. The painting of Hieronymus Bosch is supposed to convey the symbolism of the Adamites, who met secretly in the nude to celebrate the innocence of Eden. A secret art of musical expression grew up among the Netherlands polyphonists.

The secret art of French lute-playing may have been the new style of decorative embellishment, with narrative and symbolic references, which became the habit of subsequent French clavecinists from Chambonnières to Rameau. Denys Gaultier was the principal lutenist in this style; his *Tombeaux* or elegies in honor of deceased persons undoubtedly influenced the melancholy keyboard pieces by Froberger. The collections of dances decorated by these composers in their special manner originated the French type of the suite. The experimental lute-tunings they invented, including a "sharp" and a "flat" tuning, contributed to the use of similar sharp and flat meantone tunings of the harpsichord. This skill, overlooked by historians, imparts to the French clavecin music a variety of key-colorations extending beyond the eight keys to which music in meantone is limited by any one tuning.

Jacques Champion de Chambonnières was the first French composer to carry over to the keyboard the secret style of the French lutenists. His compositions, like those of Frescobaldi, are more admirable for their evident sophistication than easily approachable as music. Among his pupils were two composers of equal eminence, Jean-Henri d'Anglebert and Louis Couperin, uncle of François Couperin. Only a few isolated compositions by these composers are to be found outside the almost inaccessible complete editions of their works. Their music has a wonderfully sweet gravity and a courtly eloquence, more impersonal in style than that of François Couperin. Their works should be at least as well known as those by the contemporary German organists which fill up so much space in keyboard collections. To read their music requires study and skill in playing the carefully notated ornaments, which alter the melodic shape and character of the phrase.

Modern harpsichord-players generally dismiss as local eccentricity the carefully notated rhythmic detail of the seventeenth- and eighteenth-century keyboard music. They should instead observe and compare the distinctive notational means used by Chambonnières, d'Anglebert, the Couperins, and Dandrieu, among others, to convey the exact intended nuance of every phrase. Players indoctrinated to revering the blocklike accumulations of sonata-form structural composition do not esteem with an equal appreciation an art concerned entirely with the inworking of its texture.

Musicians today seldom do more than comment on the rhythmic distinctions between seventeenth-century French and Italian habits of reading music, though Frescobaldi and François Couperin in their written instructions to the player emphasize these differences. The Italians played in a relatively strict "falling" rhythm, the French in a markedly altered "rising" rhythm. Such expressively altered rhythms were used and notated with varying degrees of efficiency well into the nineteenth century (for example, in the *Carnaval* by Schumann).

The keyboard player today has become so habituated to playing notes only as they are printed and only those notes which are printed that he seems scarcely able to imagine that music could at any time have been played otherwise.

The connection between the relatively unembellished Italian style, which left much of the music to be improvised by the player, and the more completely notated French style is to be found in such compositions as d'Anglebert's unbarred Preludes, keyboard overtures in a nonorchestral style related to organ preluding. Such preluding, ascribed to the earlier North German organists, was very likely a habit throughout Europe, commonly improvised but not often written down.

D'Anglebert devised his own notation for embellishments, in some ways more complete and precise even than that of François Couperin. The table of *Marques d'agrément et leur signification* accompanying his compositions delineates the shape and use of these ornamental indications so exactly that no one should have serious difficulty learning to read and perform them. But I must warn again that such embellishments or ornaments—the French word *agréments* indicates their conventional nature—are not to be applied to the music but grow out of it; they phrase, color, distinguish, and give emphasis. And because the composer has so exactly defined and delineated the use of them (though he nowhere explains, as Couperin did, the alterations of rhythm without which they sound merely stilted), a careful study of d'Anglebert's embellishments and their *application,* to use another French term of the period, in and as a part of the melodic phrase, will provide an illustrative comparison with the significance of similar ornaments as used by Couperin.

The music of d'Anglebert has a grand, sonorous gravity, still retaining the deliberate indeterminacy of the postmodal harmony between major and minor. In Rameau's keyboard writing, except the harmony, there is as much of d'Anglebert as of Couperin. Rameau revives in a few examples the free, unbarred preluding.

François Couperin, member of a distinguished musical family scarcely less numerous than the Bachs, was called among his contemporaries "the Great." He succeeded to his father's Paris church position as organist, which was held for him until he was old enough to assume it. He was not one of those who experience the vagaries of fortune for the sake of their art. While retaining his official post as organist, he became a favorite harpsichordist at the court of Louis XIV, sharing musical honors with his elder contemporary Jean-Baptiste Lully, an Italian, who directed the court orchestra of violins. Lully wrote some excellent keyboard music, besides becoming the first mass producer of operas and ballets. These two composers, as members of the French court which set the style of monarchy in its relation to the arts for the century that ended with the French Revolution, definitively established the high central era of modern music, in which the orchestra and the secular keyboard predominate above all other means.

Even more than Frescobaldi, Sweelinck, and Scheidt, François Couperin influenced the entire musical habit of Europe. The admiring imitation of his art was often superficial and clumsy, but it imparted to the music of J. S. Bach that cultivation of taste and fine discrimination in means which distinguish his keyboard craftsmanship from that of his more narrowly German and Italian contemporaries.

All roads through seventeenth-century music lead ultimately to J. S. Bach. The final road is by way of the North Germans, from the free preluding of the early North German organists to the mighty toccatas and fugues by Dietrich Buxtehude.

In England a few small but precious keyboard compositions by Henry Purcell and the learned but provincial writings of John Blow revived but did not restore the earlier individuality of English keyboard art. From that time until the present day, with the solitary exception of George Frideric Handel, a German, whose keyboard writing shows an occasional awareness of the departed English tradition, there have been no better keyboard composers in England than the three generations of the Wesley family: Charles Wesley, the hymn-writer, his son Samuel Wesley, and his grandson, without benefit of marriage, Samuel Sebastian Wesley, both composers and successively the best organists of England. Samuel was one of the first composers outside Germany to acclaim and perform the keyboard writings by J. S. Bach, in honor of whom he named his son Sebastian.

The Amateur today, making the grand tour of seventeenth-century keyboard composition, is hampered by the false tonal registration of our invariable tuning in equal temperament, by the technical difficulty of performing this music at the piano, by the facile incoherence of the modern organ, by his lack of experience in correct organ and harpsichord registration, by his inability to approximate the rich technical subtleties of the clavichord. For this art of extraordinary sound he must substitute the relatively toneless interpretations of modern keyboard playing. Instead of hearing the music in proper surroundings, he listens to it in oversize concert halls and through the hole-in-space of the loudspeaker, which has, for organ music, no acoustics at all. He receives it in styleless display versions, every nuance of a vastly varied idiom reduced to a common superficial virtuosity, with scarcely a hint of the vital rhythms and the fluency of habitual embellishment that governed the tastes of performer and composer during this long period.

The true Amateur's best recourse is to play the music himself, adding to it all the resources of an informed imagination. He can, if he will, obtain a harpsichord and train himself to tune it correctly in meantone. A graceful spinet with one set of strings will suffice for most readers. It is one of the smaller and less expensive of the keyboard instruments, easy to maintain and to tune.

13

THE EIGHTEENTH
CENTURY

Before starting on the eighteenth century, let us disabuse ourselves of any false notion of what is called "originality." A fully
creative artist makes the best of whatever means he has, however limited. Using no more, he can break through to a practice
not before thought of, as young Charles Ives composed radical
psalm-settings of no more than simple arpeggios and triads.

During the seventeenth century the course of music-making
had been heading, however unconscious of the future, towards
the music of Johann Sebastian Bach. For a hundred years every
serious composer had been doing the best he could with the
means he had to make one or another kind of new music. All
directions and kinds came to synthesis in the accumulative craftsmanship of Bach.

After the death of Bach in 1750, at the exact mid-point of the
three-hundred-year period of modern music, the course of music-
making changed completely. While Bach was still living, the new
direction of music-making had appeared in the compositions of
his son Carl Philipp Emanuel and of Domenico Scarlatti; the new
style approached tentative synthesis in the early work of Franz
Joseph Haydn. When Haydn was about halfway through his
long career, young Mozart brought together the entire creative
musical art of Europe into a concentrate so powerful and pure
that, even in the presence of Haydn, it seemed a fresh creation.
Mozart learned from Haydn, then Haydn learned from Mozart;

after Mozart's death Haydn carried forward his experimental crafting towards the contrary romanticism of the nineteenth century. This is the classical period of modern music; Beethoven comes at the end of it.

Beethoven carried forward the arts of seventeenth- and eighteenth-century music, the whole of them, to a final synthesis. Schubert, Weber, Chopin, and Liszt, using only a part of all that had been learned during the high period from Bach to Beethoven, each created a separate but partial synthesis.

After that, the course of music-making which had opened approximately with the year 1600 began seriously to disintegrate. The frayed, disorganized partiality of Liszt, immensely gifted but incomplete, the reconstructive classical labors by Brahms, originated the principal styles of composition of the twentieth century.

Through all this time originality has never ceased, but the breakthrough of individual originality has been less productive and significant than the originality of synthesis.

For our historical purposes the seventeenth century began approximately with the year 1600 and continued until the death of J. S. Bach in 1750. The eighteenth century began with the early maturity of Bach and ended with the death of Beethoven in 1827. The first composer to doff the eighteenth century and put on the nineteenth was Schubert, who died two years after Beethoven. The nineteenth century did not begin anywhere at all; it was a consequence of the many breakthroughs of the lesser individual originality which companioned the synthesizing originality of the greater eighteenth-century masters.

Dates get in the way, but we have to drop a plotting-point here and there to keep the situation in focus.

Music of the sixteenth century had been an art of the people, of their assembling in churches, their private gathering in groups to make music together, and their novel passion for dancing.

In an age of the popularity of sermons, seventeenth-century style aped the preacher. The popular art of music was being replaced by the new formal art of entertainment centering in the courts. The wind instruments of the sixteenth century were giving way to the string orchestra. The equal participation of voices and instruments in madrigal suddenly vanished, to be replaced by the solo voice or solo instrument accompanying or imitating the dramatic voice. In the theater, declamation took the place of speaking action. A decayed appearance of the grand posturing of that day survives in operatic acting to the present time. The seventeenth century was the great age of the popularity of opera, which continued through the eighteenth century and declined into the high-toned bourgeois display of the nineteenth-century opera house.

By the end of the seventeenth century a new synthesis was already in formation. Wind instruments were being reintroduced into the orchestra. Popular opera was creating a new art of mixed acting and declamation, spiced with popular song; operas grew reputations overnight, like our musical comedies, and disappeared. Solo instrumental music was imitating aria, was encroaching upon the orchestra, was ingratiating itself again into domestic living in a new art of chamber music. The aria is itself a reproduction of the new extramusical skills of musical instruments. The art of singing freely, flexibly, and over an unnaturally wide range, elaborating cadences with the impersonal dexterity of an instrument, is called *bel canto* (beautiful song). It is the principal directive force behind Italian music between 1600 and the later nineteenth century. During the seventeenth and eighteenth centuries the Italian music was the most fashionable; its authority continued preponderant throughout Europe until the later lifetime of Richard Wagner.

Instrumental accompaniment, having transmitted its equality with the voice into the new separate arts of the solo keyboard and the orchestra, withdrew into monody, filling out the harmonies for which the solo voice or instrument supplied the chief part. But skills lost in the development of a vital culture are quickly replaced and themselves generate new skills. While the new instrumental art was luxuriating in counterpoint, the monodic accompaniment was moving, especially in Italy, towards the chordal structure of the modern sonata. The type of accompaniment in broken chords which bears the name of Domenico Alberti, the *Alberti bass*, is the formula around which Bach's sons and their contemporaries wrote instrumental movements that are essentially without counterpoint, the right hand playing melody, the left hand its accompaniment.

Thirty years ago it was a critical commonplace to deprecate Mozart's piano sonatas because of their "Alberti basses." Nowadays one scarcely notices them; we hear the sonatas in more detail and know how Mozart constantly altered and developed the Alberti principle. In listening to or reading music of this period, we should chasten our overvaluation of originality by observing how much of the written notation is as conventional as the Alberti bass; the real originality was to do the utmost with the convention, not to do without it. Beethoven, like Michelangelo, stretches the elasticity of the convention to extreme dimensions: some part afterwards snaps back; the remainder has been either broken or distorted.

In the sixteenth century, dancing had broken free of the centuries-long disapproval of the Church. Everybody danced, and the dance originated a new type of formal music. During the seventeenth century these dances grew more self-contained, and their articulation as music was formalized in movements not intended for dancing and retaining only the metrical order of the dance. (This had happened in England, with the pavan and galliard.) By the eighteenth century these dance movements had grouped in formal sequences, almost without reference to their dance origins, to become *suites, partitas,* and *sonatas.*

Keep in mind, however, that the contemporary composer and his listeners were far more aware than we are of the dance measure in the abstract movement, of the ground or tune that was varied, of the hymn at the heart of the chorale prelude. When we play a chaconne or a saraband we should let our feelings ride not solely on the grand declamation but on a deliberate retention of the muscular rhythm of the dance. It is like riding a horse instead of driving a car in a procession; you can feel the muscular movement under the skin. With this feeling, the muscular dance measure should be heard in every variation of the rhythm.

These various styles commingled in the realization of a new type of accompaniment, the *continuo* or *figured bass,* consisting of a single line of written bass notes sometimes accompanied by numbers indicating the desired chordal harmonies. Reading these indications an unskilled player could strum a simple accompaniment in plain chords; a skilled performer would weave around them an improvisation of broken chords and counterpoint, echoing and responding to the solo, rich and elaborate as an orchestration. Mozart's left-hand accompaniments and Handel's long and demonstrative chaconnes exemplify how much could be done with continuo figuration.

Interpenetrating these styles, the now highly developed figurative language of the *affections* conveyed an unprecedented freshness and variety of nonverbal meaning. Music was learning to speak for itself without its traditional dependence on song or liturgy, to become what we now too easily presume all music to be: a sensuous, formalized speech of the emotions.

Musical meaning in the past had implied or required words, or birdsong, or such descriptive devices as the characteristic intervals of the huntsman's horn; it had needed to be verbalized or representative. But now the musical meaning existed without these obvious references; it was even applied to words to give them significance, as Bach composed theology around the trite cantata texts written by Picander. Meaning appeared in the conjunctions of figures, the relationship of keys, the suggestiveness of abstract devices which could dispense with referential description, which, like Bach's *Inventions* and exemplary pieces, could embody a textbook. Meaning was dramatized by chromaticism, by unexpected accents and entrances, by degrees of dissonance, and by the progress and recession of harmonic modulation. From d'Anglebert and Couperin through Beethoven the breathing articulation of silence has significance. The distinctive intervallic patterns of each key in meantone tuning imparted an individual character and emotional voice, changing mood and color with each modulation.

The choral polyphonies of Vittoria, Palestrina, and Byrd confer a mystical grandeur upon the words of the liturgy. The organ *Elevations* by Frescobaldi (from the *Fiori Musicali*) convey the transcendental atmosphere at the raising of the Host. Bach's counterpoint meditates on and explains the sacred text, as some of the chorale preludes represent the meaning of the successive verses or stanzas of the hymn. This overt response to the presence of certain words in the text had originated among the madrigalists and was vividly present to the morbid sensibility of Gesualdo. In that case the composer responded to the presence of the words; he did not, as Bach did, set the words forth within a clear ambience of meaning.

During the nineteenth and twentieth centuries the two conflicting and oftentimes mingling responses of music to verbal meaning and of poetry to music became romantic, until in much poetry a musical suggestiveness took the place of a meaningful literary order. The concept of musical meaning did not stop within the scope of words but spread across the esthetic landscape, until Vasily Kandinsky, painting the colored forms of music as he conceived them, released visual art into conceptual analogies of abstraction.

Most persons believe that the eighteenth-century period of Bach through Beethoven was the high period of the world's music-making; within the globular perspective of the three hundred years of modern music they are right. But we should be aware that this was a very special era, brought about by particular conditions, to which we cannot go back. Art grows by an evolutionary process in which man participates and genius guides only a little. Schoenberg, in his last public address, said of the method of composing with twelve tones, that it was waiting to be discovered and that at least a half-dozen other composers might have come to it as readily. Art continues to evolve even when a conservative generation tries to wind it backwards.

If J. S. Bach was a genius, so were his three sons who became eminent: Wilhelm Friedemann, whose talent, however interesting in his own work, had no future; Carl Philipp Emanuel, who gave to keyboard form and playing-style the decisive direction that would continue through Haydn, Beethoven, and Chopin; and Philipp Emanuel's pupil, the youngest of the Bach sons, Johann Christian, who went on to study with Padre Giambattista Martini, the Franciscan monk and composer who was the most eminent teacher of the Italian tradition. For a century C. P. E. Bach and J. C. Bach were the composers whom one meant if one said "Bach." In England, Mozart at the age of eight sat on Johann Christian's knee, playing with him alternate passages at the keyboard. At that time, and again when they met years later in Paris, Mozart learned from him the suave formal elegance in the Italian manner which distinguishes Mozart's keyboard composing from the master craftsman's idiom of Haydn. The opening of Mozart's B flat Piano Sonata (K. 333), composed in Paris near the time of their rencontre, refers to the opening of J. C. Bach's Piano Sonata, one of his finest, in the same key.

Every true Amateur should know well the two books of keyboard sonatas by J. C. Bach, that reach forward to Schubert, and the eighteen exemplary pieces (six Sonatas and a Fantasy in improvisatory style) which C. P. E. Bach wrote to accompany his book, *The True Art of Playing Keyboard Instruments.*

Looking backwards, we see only the brighter luminaries and their productions, forgetting the initial impetus, the breakthrough, caused by other genius which was, on the contemporary scene, the more original. Indeed, our whole notion of originality is a modern conception applied to rather than inherent in the act of creation. Beethoven when young did not hesitate to steal from Clementi, and in later years to emulate Rossini and Cherubini.

The definitive eighteenth-century composer is neither Bach nor Beethoven but Mozart; in his own time it was Haydn. Learning almost entirely from his immediate contemporaries, Mozart transmuted everything he learned to convey it back to his contemporaries in a refinement of style that could not be improved upon. The highest development of eighteenth-century refined formality is the concerto for solo instrument with orchestra, from Vivaldi through Mozart. In Mozart's music the formality of the concerto presides over that of all other forms, as characteristic of the solo sonata as of the operatic aria.

Unlike Mozart, Beethoven did not transmute the styles he borrowed but instead used them to build with. From J. S. Bach came his practical awareness of counterpoint as a means of concentration and his inherent tendency to fugue and dissonance. From Handel he learned the rich eloquence of simple, sonorous harmony in chordal textures. He borrowed from C. P. E. Bach—and this is not sufficiently acknowledged—the unprecedented range and shock of dynamic contrast, the free play in the top octave of the contemporary keyboard, and the decisive shaping of figurative thematic units, which are to be found in the "German" Bach's compositions for the large clavichord, written during his later years in Hamburg, but not in any keyboard writing by Haydn, Mozart, or Clementi (see particularly the six volumes of C. P. E. Bach's *Sonatas, Free Fantasies, and Rondos*). He learned from Haydn the analytic structure of theme and movement and from Mozart something of his unique thematic and melodic freedom and elegance. To complete these structural means, Beethoven expanded upon the scales "in sixths and octaves" against which Mozart so strenuously protested, to make of them the structural members, the girders of varying harmonic thickness, that support the increasing length and weight of his sonata movements.

The greater complexity of Beethoven, commingling these contrasting styles and means, in prophetic enthusiasm broke through the eighteenth-century clarity of the movement and of the relations among movements. Masterpieces which now seem to us conventional began an erosion of formal style that the nineteenth-century composers of symphony and sonata were helpless to prevent. In Beethoven's later conception a variation movement may be also fugal, include aspects of the rondo, and still be inlaid within the broader niceties and freedom of what is called "allegro," or "first-movement," or "sonata-allegro" or "sonata" form, for example the choral finale of Beethoven's Ninth Symphony.

▶ Around *sonata form,* to use the most practical title, musical scholarship has woven its most space-filling fantasies. A fugal subject, no matter how far it travels or how often it changes position, remains essentially a unit. A sonata subject exists by alternation with something else, which may be, at the least, only itself in a new setting. Sonata form is the outcome of simple modulation, having only the very general rule that what begins shall alternate with something else, usually but not always in a different key (*exposition*); that these two may then develop or explore or work out their differences in a play of harmonic drama (*development*) until the return of the opening (*recapitulation*); after which the movement ends, unless the impetus or inward necessity of the drama requires a supplementary argument, formal peroration, or overflow of energy to bring it to a close (*coda*). Within this general formulative outline a composer can include anything he pleases.

The form of a sonata, which is distinct from sonata form, may be in one, two, three, four, or five movements, not normally more. The derivation of sonata from suite is thereby evident. The normal first movement is a sonata-allegro, the second a slow movement often patterned on an aria, the third a minuet or rondo. A four-movement form has both a minuet and a rondo. A fifth movement is normally some type of interlude. A theme and variations may take the place of any one of these movements.

11

Extension of the alternating form to several recurrences with some variation but no real development produced the French *rondeau,* cousin to the English *round,* and eventually the *rondo,* the most common final sonata movement. The alternating convention establishes the basic *allegro-adagio-allegro* succession of movements in sonata and concerto. It inhabits the form of the *minuet* or *minuet with trio,* which, learning playfully to wag its tail, becomes a *scherzo.*

In eighteenth-century society and music the minuet turns up everywhere. Mozart invented a game for composing minuets by throw of dice. Minuets for dancing were composed by the thousands, being replaced in the nineteenth century by the *waltz,* which however found no place in the sonata. The minuet is today the one movement that is usually played as it should be, with all indicated repeats.

When the subject material of a sonata, large or small, is of the structural-analytical type, a figure able to be taken apart and recombined, the sonata-form movement need not be large and may consist of episodes in continuity, each enjoyable for itself, without the cumulative effect which, during the century after Beethoven, was felt necessary to convey "emotion"—lacking which, in critical opinion, "great form" had not been achieved. The Italian or German sonata in one, two, or three movements, in the work of Domenico Scarlatti, or C. P. E. Bach, or J. C. Bach, or so late as the two-movement Piano Sonata opus 54 by Beethoven, exists for itself in its own terms and can convey quite enough feeling, when performed with conviction in a correct style, to be a complete and satisfying work of art. A flower arrangement has its own tradition of beauty and need not be compared with an apocalypse by Rubens. A responsive imagination may take more pleasure in the flower arrangement than in the apocalypse.

As the episodes in a sonata movement become climactic and the continuity a dramatically conceived whole, one figure or tune may begin repeating, extending, or unwinding itself, binding together in larger proportional relationships the contrasting aspects of the drama. This type of sonata form, as an elementary display movement, is as old as the episodic type and appears in the work of the same composers.

With this type of movement there is a likelihood that the extending figure may have or take on the characteristics of a fugal subject, or that the modulations of the sonata without climax will cease to obey but instead will govern the accumulation of episodes to climax. When both of these are happening at the same time, the capacity of the movement for rhetorical flourish, as in a sonata by Clementi, will be transformed into unifying drama, as in the three sonatas of Beethoven's opus 2. In such circumstances there is no kind of formal action that a sonata movement cannot accommodate.

In the finale of the so-called *Moonlight Sonata*, opus 27:2, the accompanying figure, starting as an Alberti bass, almost at once takes on a fugal character, a continuous urgency against which the sonata episodes are tossed only to be swept away. This persistent interpenetrating of one idea into every aspect of the musical structure is the vital principle of fugue. Whether the consequent movement is in sonata form, or rondo, or outright fugue as in the finale of the *Hammerklavier Sonata,* opus 106, or fugue with alternating episodes as in the final movement of the Sonata opus 110, or variation style, the unitary fugal sweep overrides the analytical distinctions of strict sonata form, a little less in the variation finale of opus 109 and much more in the variation finale of opus 111; and the result is a polyphonic multiple of overlying forms, integrally composite but not ambiguous.

Beethoven's last sonata, opus 111, contains in both movements the essentials of sonata form; the first movement includes fantasy, fugue, and a march; the second movement is also a theme and variations; but the driving unitary energy of both movements is of the character of fugue. Compare this variation movement with the digestively analytical *Diabelli Variations*, which gives no hint of sonata form, is but subordinately fugal, and could not conceivably be a sonata movement.

Such an achievement can have no real descendants but only consequents. Schubert, failing the counterpoint, imparts the character of fugue to his enormously extended and reiterated final rondos. Whereas Brahms, possessing the counterpoint, fails to achieve the unitary driving urgency of fugue.

Textbooks and treatises are crammed with information on how all these things were done, and the tricks of them are still solemnly taught as the art of composing music. We may read the books with profit and receive the teaching usefully, if we keep in mind that these explanations are no more pertinent to the working of live musical creation than anthropology to the formation of the living cultures of mankind. The skills of explanation have little to do with the habits of creation. Musical pedantry can no more create a living music than books of history can create a civilization. Rules and categories of art are evasions of exceptions. We know enough if we know the general principles and draw individual conclusions about individual works. Idiomatic habit develops in each application its controlling rules, so that error or myth takes on the creative authority of truth; no rules can supplant or revive idiomatic habit.

Alongside the mainstream of eighteenth-century musical creation the lesser composers revolve in historic eddies before returning their separate currents to the mainstream. In modern musical history the German composers of the eighteenth century are shown as the mainstream. At the time, the Italian tradition, Alessandro Scarlatti to Padre Martini to Gioacchino Rossini, was by far the more fashionable, popular, and authoritative. Cynosure of the Italian tradition was Alessandro Scarlatti, a master composer so decisively cut off from us by change of musical fashion that we are scarcely able to approach him.

Alessandro Scarlatti died seven years before the birth of Haydn and twenty-five years before the death of J. S. Bach. Among his numerous compositions are nearly as many exquisitely poetic cantatas for solo voice as there are keyboard sonatas by his son Domenico. Alessandro Scarlatti wrote a considerable body of keyboard music, most of it seemingly empty and half-composed, skeletal white-note compositions, intended to be filled out by an improvised variant performance at each reading. German and French composers wrote out such harmonious designs with most, though by no means all, of the subsidiary notes, plus the signs of embellishment. Yet the framework is so like that a properly improvised reading of an aria for keyboard by Alessandro Scarlatti might persuade the hearer that he is listening to an unknown composition by Bach or by some lesser German master. In reading such music, the player should recognize that a stand of open chords in white notes is to be elaborated into a pattern of arpeggiation, that a stiff succession of whole-notes, half-notes, and a few quarter-notes is to be inflected and embellished according to the taste and experience of the performer, with many more notes than are written. Bach's *Italian Concerto* and the *Aria* of Handel's Suite in D minor, written out as Handel played it, are examples; there are many others.

Ability to read and fill out such compositions at sight or to improvise a continuo accompaniment on a figured bass were the real tests of eighteenth-century musicianship. All of J. S. and C. P. E. Bach's and Handel's secular keyboard music is intended to serve as teaching material for these skills. The art is nearly lost to us, able to be rediscovered only by careful application and practice, though written explanations and examples by composers of the time exist to tell us how these things should be done. With the increasing dependence of performers on fully notated composition, the earlier skills were forgotten. No scope for them remained but the *cadence* on a terminal measure—seldom heard today but in process of revival—and its more elaborate variant, the *cadenza*. By the end of the eighteenth century, both cadence and cadenza were being precomposed by Haydn, Mozart, Clementi, Beethoven, and Hummel.

Thus the toccatas and other keyboard compositions by Alessandro Scarlatti have gone out of use. There remains one composition, the *Toccata alla stesa*, sufficiently written out by the composer to be read from the notes, though one must be prepared to amend it by some elaborative passages, as one must do to play many works by Johann Pachelbel or Handel. It begins with a strongly articulated toccata, leading directly into an accompanied fugue (a fugue plus an Alberti bass), followed by thirty variations on a popular air of the period, the Folia. (Over a hundred sets of variations on the Folia are in the literature, by composers from d'Anglebert to C. P. E. Bach to Rachmaninoff.)

Domenico Scarlatti, son of Alessandro, went to Spain, where he became the principal court composer of keyboard music. Instead of carrying on his father's broad range of composition, including operas and cantatas, he confined his chief efforts to writing keyboard exercises after the style of Italian single-movement sonatas. These exercises, which we now call sonatas, were composed for the pleasure of Queen Maria Barbara, who must have been skilled with her fingers to have played them. It may be because she lacked the musicianly skills to match her digital ability that Domenico Scarlatti abandoned the Italian skeletal notation and wrote out all the notes, leaving little to be filled in from the convention. So doing, he freed himself from the familiar habits of Italian figuration, developing a keyboard style of great originality that spread across Europe. The speed, facility, and tunefulness of his keyboard writing provoked increasing attention to the technical skills of playing rapidly with ease.

We are wrong to think of Domenico Scarlatti as a superficial composer. Like John Bull before him and Franz Liszt after him, he aroused by his music a new interest in performing techniques, but his art, though limited, is less exploratory and more consistent than that of Bull or Liszt. He was among the first to liberate keyboard music from the influence of continuo-playing.

Scarlatti warmed his sonatas with imitations of the guitar and reflections of Italian and Spanish vocal and instrumental music. A younger Spanish composer, organist, and theoretician, Father Antonio Soler, wrote organ and harpsichord pieces in similar style. Soler was not Scarlatti's pupil, and the question of influence between them is less meaningful than an appreciation of their common stature. One should also mention here the keyboard works by their Portuguese contemporary Carlos de Seixas.

Our knowledge and appreciation of the keyboard music by George Frideric Handel, and our ability to perform it, are limited by our lack of competence to read and properly fill out a continuo part. Even more in his operas and oratorios, his instrumental sonatas and concertos, the expanding of the continuo and the filling out of white-note skeletal notation has been left to the initiative of the player. We cannot hear his operas and arias or his instrumental sonatas in their proper idiom until keyboard players will train themselves to restore the art of continuo-playing to some measure of its former skillfulness.

The last of the French masters of the clavecin, Jean-Philippe Rameau, composed in chorded or vertical harmonic idiom, while retaining the manner of the earlier French keyboard composers in embellishing the melodic line. For this reason his keyboard pieces suffer less by modern performance and are played more often than the works of the earlier clavecinists, though they are no less difficult. Rameau's treatise on harmony and his proposals for the inversion of the chord prepared the way for the disintegration of thoroughbass and gave theoretical justification to the progressively more extreme harmonic practices of nineteenth-century composers.

Throughout the seventeenth and eighteenth centuries the harpsichord sat at the center of the orchestra and of nearly all chamber music and vocal ensembles, making up for the deficiency of instruments by elaboration of the bass continuo. Apart from theoretical knowledge, much of the skill of continuo-playing consists in knowing when to play more lightly or more heavily, when to supplement or replace an instrument, how to control rhythm and harmony in an ensemble and overcome mistakes, when to use chords and when single notes and how to disperse them rhythmically, and when not to play at all.

Though the influence of the thoroughbass habit of erecting harmony upon the bass line of the composition remained in effect as the root of formal harmonic theory, the removal of the keyboard instrument from the orchestra quickened the drift, beginning with Berlioz and Liszt, towards harmonic habits which tended to treat harmony as if it were as pliable as paint.

Beginning with d'Anglebert and François Couperin, the harpsichord as a solo instrument, especially in France, began imitating the full harmony and coloristic clangor of the orchestral overture at the start of opera and ballet, as an alternative to the refined play of rhythmically differentiated melody across time and silence which was the legacy of the lutenists. Bach's several *Overtures in French Style* for harpsichord are a model.

The older, refined style survived among the German players of the clavichord, joining with the more outwardly emotional, expressionist legacy of Froberger to create the distinctively German manner of performing sonatas and dramatically lyrical independent movements exemplified by the clavichord compositions of C. P. E. Bach. The further transition of this style from the large German clavichord to the early piano occurred quite rapidly. Though lacking the infinite variability of the clavichord, the earlier pianos kept some of the tone quality, with greater volume,

increased dynamic projection, and dramatic contrast in the distinction between *forte* and *piano*.

The first name of the new instrument, *fortepiano*, indicates that
the increase of volume was a welcome improvement; the subsequent reversal of the name to *pianoforte* takes for granted the increase of volume and places emphasis on the refinement inherited
from the clavichord. These refinements appear throughout the
keyboard compositions by Haydn, Beethoven, and Chopin and influence the dotted rhythms of Schumann.

Performers from C. P. E. Bach to Chopin were accustomed to
performing the same compositions alternatively on harpsichord,
clavichord, or piano, and occasionally on the organ. One can
sometimes deduce by study of a composition for which instrument it was meant. It is reasonable to presume that a good player
altered his style of performance with the instrument. The harpsichord style is more florid; the clavichord style is smaller, more
finely pointed; the piano style makes emphatic the *forte-piano*
contrast and the projection of individual tones. The piano pedal
was beginning to make itself noticed.

In three numbers of the fourth book of the collected piano
sonatas by Haydn (Peters edition) one can trace the developing
of his keyboard style from clavichord to piano. Number 37 in G
major, composed in 1766, is plainly for the clavichord. Number
39 in D, composed ten years later in 1776, suggests by the octave
passages in the finale a large clavichord or piano. The finale of
Number 38, also in D, written in England, shows evidence of the
new English fortepiano which made possible Beethoven's heavier
dynamics. Number 47 in C major, in the fourth book, contains
instruction that in two places the pedal is to be held down for
the playing of a succession of notes, without pedaling distinction.

Reading the works of this period, we are so habituated to
wrong modern practice that it is hard for us, imaginatively, to set
it right. It was in defense of the older and more learned tradition
that Mozart critically denounced the more modern playing of
Clementi.

In the older style the melody is continually varied, and the
variants, by rhythm, embellishment, and silence, are in general
quite clearly marked for anyone who will learn to read accurately the composer's indications. The effort to revive a similar
finely articulated style in twentieth-century composing is a prin-

cipal cause of the constant changes in time-signatures and the notational intricacies which set up a visual barrier between music and reader. In the older style, realization of these subtleties belonged to the performer, who was expected to alter his realization at each reading; whereas the modern inflexible notation allows the performer no more privilege than to reproduce the notes exactly as written.

14

THE NINETEENTH
CENTURY

The year 1800 marks the beginning of modern practice in piano
design and the rebuilding in their present shape of the older
violins. At the same time François Tourte was inventing the new
violin bow which bears his name. These adjustments and inventions increased the volume of instrumental tone at the cost of its
flexibility. The modern piano is a less flexible instrument than
the clavichord, though it can make itself amply heard in a large
hall where a clavichord would be inaudible. The modern violin
and bow redouble the volume of the instrument but impair a
proper reading of Bach's compositions for solo violin. The modern piano blocked for a century proper realization of any music
written before 1800.

The nineteenth century is the period of the grand piano, the
large orchestra, the oversize organ, the vasty opera house. Music
was ceasing to be a personal art. Beethoven improvised variations
and composed sonatas to be read by other players; he performed
in public only his concertos. Schubert played the piano and accompanied but did not perform as a concert artist. Hummel,
Mendelssohn, Field, Chopin, and Liszt won renown as professional performers.

For the retreating amateur there was a proliferation of small
piano pieces to be read in the parlor. The serious amateur did
the best he was able to imitate a professional performance, an
incorrect stance in which serious amateurs have been propping

themselves or being propped by their teachers ever since. All music of consequence was directed, as it still is, to the public audience, where the amateur was supposed to present himself as an appreciative listener. During the twentieth century the division between amateur and professional has become still more stringent.

In spite of the larger forms and formulas of nineteenth-century musical composition, and the originality of some of its composers, the underlying pattern of musical permissiveness grew narrower than in the eighteenth century. Audiences, theorists, and their critics turned to the music of the past as they understood it, holding it up as a model—usually a falsified model—for music of the present. Goethe venerated the music of dead Mozart but did not respond to compositions respectfully sent him by living Beethoven and Schubert, though these were the now famous settings of his songs.

The cult of the dead composer at the cost of the live one appeared when Italian theorists turned back to Palestrina to derive the rules of formal counterpoint, when English devotees of Handel organized annual festivals to perform his music. Until that time nearly all performed music had been contemporary music, often written for the occasion. So began the war of intolerance between music of the past and music of the present, between classic and contemporary music, which is interpreted today as a "lack of communication" between living composers and their public.

In comparison with the high order of the eighteenth century, the disintegration of what I have called modern music during the nineteenth century was rapid and soon became irreversible. During the seventeenth century all roads lead to Bach; during the nineteenth century, to Schoenberg.

Two systems of harmony and of linear working existed side by side in European music: the Italian method of filling out a notated shorthand by means of relatively standard figures harmonically anchored to the principal notes of the chord; and the German method of working out the parts in such a way that the vertical relationships are compromised by devices which divert from the resolution of the chord.

Palestrina in the sixteenth century restored Italian polyphony to clear harmony and unambiguous linear relationships, instead of the complicated, intellectually inventive part-writing of the fifteenth-century Flemings. Italian music schools during the eighteenth century educated professional musicians in the formal counterpoint that Beethoven never got around to learning and that Schubert regretted he had not had time to study. (I am told that Schoenberg, too, once regretted, in a lecture, that he had never mastered the conveniences of formal counterpoint.)

The Italian teachers rested their authority on the practices of such conservative polyphonists as Palestrina, interpreting these practices in a harmony no longer founded on just intonation. By choosing the way of Palestrina, these scholars made unintelligible the very different potentiality of Gesualdo. They asserted the priority of concord over discord, but defined form in narrowing terms of a vertical consonance that was not concordance.

In the same way, musicologists still describe all harmonic habits during the long history of European music in the language of nineteenth-century musical technology; the present-day performer interprets all harmony throughout the music of these centuries as if it had been composed only in vertical harmony and exact temporal relationship. Experts who reject an orchestral transcription of a Bach organ composition do not cavil at a performance in equal temperament, with false harmonic chording, of a fifteenth-century work intended to exploit the sonorous perfect fifths and discriminatively dissonant thirds of the Pythagorean temperament. To presume that all sailing captains went to sea speaking the language of steam may flatter a few steamship captains; it will not increase our knowledge of the millennia of sail.

The monument of this Italian harmony is the four-volume collection of keyboard examples composed by Muzio Clementi, his *Gradus ad Parnassum*. At a time when knowledge of J. S. Bach's major compositions was the private possession of a few composers in Vienna and Samuel Wesley in England, Clementi's *Gradus*, supplemented by other teachings of the Italian school, including Cherubini on the writing of fugues, was freezing in now forgotten music the Italian harmony, from which scholastic theory has not yet broken away. The *Gradus* is the testimonial of an art that was expected to succeed but failed. Clementi could not stretch the Italian rules to meet the German idiosyncratic challenge of Mozart or Beethoven.

In middle life Clementi withdrew from public performing,

padding the doors and windows of his room so that he would not be overheard when he played the piano. The only surviving movements from his mature orchestral works, which he seems to have destroyed, are found in piano transcription in the *Gradus*. We may judge how incapable Clementi was to challenge the primacy of Beethoven by reading what is perhaps the finest of his piano sonatas, in G, opus 40:1, with its strongly stated but rhythmically inert first movement, its scherzo skipping in scholastic two-part canon, its big, dull *presto* finale. Placed among these, the *Adagio: molto sostenuto e cantabile* gloriously justifies Clementi's preoccupation with *bel canto* operatic song. Beethoven's Piano Sonata in G, opus 31:1, parodies the *bel canto* style. Clementi, reading the slow movement of this sonata, must have felt as though he were being swallowed by a boa constrictor. Schubert, seemingly unaware of the carnivorously digestive humor, took this Beethoven sonata for a model.

The Italian tradition, with its simple accompaniments and ornate melody in the *bel canto* style, brought to birth a flock of small progeny, among them Mendelssohn's *Songs Without Words*, the *Nocturnes* by John Field (imitated by Chopin and Liszt), and the sonatas by Carl Maria von Weber. In the larger frame of the German sonata the style failed repeatedly. Mendelssohn's piano sonatas and concertos, in a style no better than Clementi's, succeed by noisy insistence on their occasional virtues.

John Field, a pupil of Clementi, played as a boy before Haydn in London. He went with Clementi to Russia and remained there, returning to Europe from time to time to perform his sonatas and concertos. Though less capable than Clementi as a composer, he seems to have been the more attractive pianist; his compositions, especially his *Nocturnes*, exhibit the elegance of his pianistic skill. In Russia he became successful as a teacher, having the composer Michael Glinka among his pupils. His idiomatically relaxed, aristocratic, but uninventive manner of playing, the style described as a "string of pearls," concerned more with tone and a relaxed fluency than with rhythm, remains the tradition of Russian keyboard art to the present day.

The Italianate Russian harmony, though periodically diverted by new fashionable styles from Europe, continued to reject Germanic "formalism" in favor of showy and relatively unambiguous pattern-making, designed, in keyboard music, to show off the

fingers. This habit of musical thinking is now "official," being enforced by fiat of the Soviet government against every "dangerous"
deviation; it is welcomed with equal enthusiasm by the Western
"bourgeois" listener, who prefers it to the native musical idiom of
any other Western culture—he would rather be right than
prescient.

The purpose of the Italianate harmony is to enrich the sonority
by dwelling on the compatible tones of a key. The less compatible
tones are reduced to subordinate positions, where they either do
not influence the harmony at all or else brighten it by an
acciaccatura (a dissonant tone that is sounded with a concord
and immediately released) or by an *appoggiatura* (a dissonant
tone, the movement of which into the harmony is delayed just
long enough to emphasize the happy resolution to a consonance).

French music, from its earliest history, has been more concerned with the rhythmic subtlety, or poetry, of the line than
with the sonority of the harmony. This interest reappeared highly
developed in the compositions by the seventeenth- and eighteenth-century clavecinists.

German music borrowed the Italian harmony but explored the
French interest in the working of the line. J. S. Bach, who learned
from Couperin as well as from the Italians and the elder Germans, allowed the working of the line to expand its more dissonant potentialities. Schoenberg notes "that J. S. Bach in many
'Introductions,' for example, and especially such pieces or parts
labelled 'Fantasia' prefers a disposition of the harmonic structure
which neither in its entirety nor even in its detail can be easily
referred to a key." ("Problems of Harmony," from *Modern Music,
A Quarterly Review,* May-June 1934) Such built-in dissonance
became the directing energy of German contrapuntal harmony,
particularly in the sonata.

This built-in dissonance expanded during the nineteenth century towards key-chromaticism, presuming a hierarchy of relatively significant connections between any one of the twelve notes
in the octave and the principal note of a particular key. (This relationship is called, for lack of a more explicit term, *tonality*.)
When harmony had been stretched beyond acoustical relationship to any key, the distinction between consonance and dissonance and among relative degrees of dissonance lost sharpness

and ceased to be efficient or dramatic. (This lack of relationship has been called, with similar inaccuracy, *atonality*.)

The contradictory German and Italian traditions, gradually released from the common guidance of thoroughbass, were rationalized by nineteenth-century theorists to explain every sort of music. The rationalized theoretical systems and their rules, stricter than the habits of composers who are appealed to as authority for them, have governed all educated music-making to the present day.

The nineteenth-century composer, believing all these incompatibles to be undifferentiatedly the musical tradition, tried to make them work somehow together. Carl Czerny, a pupil of Beethoven, edited for publication the 48 Preludes and Fugues of Bach's *Well-Tempered Clavier*. The fingerings and expressive markings are supposed to illustrate Beethoven's manner of reading them. Czerny, the teacher of Liszt, mounted to fame upon his innumerable finger-studies in the Italianate harmony and figuration, the technical foundation of nineteenth-century keyboard virtuosity. The virtuoso preference for fleet-fingered displays of keyboard coloration at the expense of dynamic interest begins in Czerny's exercises. This style almost automatically excluded performance of the greater Germanic keyboard literature. The famous teacher Theodore Leschetizky, who studied with Czerny, transmitted this keyboard style into the twentieth century. The greater virtuoso pianists adapted at least the major keyboard works by Bach and Beethoven; they adapted, converted, and incorporated these works into their editions, to the still greater confusion of musical understanding.

Frédéric Chopin translated the linear working and precise embellishments of C. P. E. Bach into the the simpler harmony of Clementi and Czerny. He developed the typical nineteenth-century species of semitonal dissonance that became, in the workmanship of Liszt and Wagner, the ability to use all the tones of the octave as a part of any key. Imitation of Chopin released a small torrent of emotional display-pieces, resembling the fragmentary keyboard literature of the seventeenth century but retaining scarcely a vestige of Chopin's musical intelligence.

Chopin was not, as he believed and many after him, the first to write for the piano in the idiom of the piano. "When writing for the piano," Chopin wrote, "[Beethoven] sometimes forgets that it is not an orchestra. . . . I myself best understand the piano. . . ." But some of Chopin's compositions will go very well on the harpsichord, while few pieces by Beethoven will do so. Beethoven's keyboard style, though influenced in detail by the clavichord idiom, is solidly pianistic, even in his smallest minuets. Chopin played the piano as if it were a clavichord, so softly that he could scarcely be heard in a large hall. It was not Chopin but his friends Liszt and Kalkbrenner who established the virtuosic, demonstrative manner of playing Chopin's music.

In the Germanic system, modulation ranged ever more widely into contrapuntal relationships never before formalized within tonality. German composers and scholars argued the clearer Italian practice, while trying to expand it to the gigantic scale of Beethoven's Ninth Symphony. The consequence was Wagner, who accomplished the impossible so neatly, without benefit of technical education or skill in playing an instrument, that he had won the popular ear and the devotion of a world-wide audience before any theorist could explain what was happening.

With Wagnerism the nonplaying amateur could involve himself for the first time in critical mysteries, substituting the moral fairy tale told in characteristic thematic *motives* for the musical explanation. Musical criticism gained an enlarged vocabulary, as undemanding and inflated as the Wagnerian time-scale, which does not exhaust listeners by its length because it offers so few passages requiring concentrated attention. The most elaborate Wagnerian polyphonies strum along on harmonies which seem trite and almost absurd in piano reduction. Behind *Parsifal* there is as much of *La Sonnambula* as of sanctity.

The Austrian critic Edward Hanslick fought a losing battle in opposing Wagnerism, but he fought for a good reason. Well aware of Wagner's virtues, he opposed the excesses of Wagnerism that were persuading music, as he understood it, to destruction. He could not be expected to foresee that another informally trained amateur, Arnold Schoenberg, by drawing the right conclusions from Wagner's excesses and forcing these to combine with the radically conservative "tiny-work" for which Brahms was severely criticized, would precipitate the principal element of twentieth-century music, the emancipated dissonance.

We have no information concerning the habits of tuning preferred by composers, professional musicians, and amateurs for the different types of music written between 1750 and 1850. Well-tempered tuning was invented during the first half of the eighteenth century. The English manufacturers were still tuning new Broadwood pianos to meantone as late as 1850. The first clear evidence of a predominance of equal temperament appears in a new preference for extreme keys outside the customary range of meantone.

Different degrees of sharp and flat tuning in meantone account for the occasional movements in extreme keys by François Couperin. Wesley Kuhnle demonstrated that a sharp meantone having the C natural, the starting note of the tuning cycle, returned to a B sharp, and an F double sharp and a G on the two different registers of a harpsichord, gloriously "explains" by the coloring of the modulations the built-in color-registration of J. S. Bach's great Toccata in F sharp minor. Like the *Italian Concerto*, the *Chromatic Fantasy*, and the *French Overture* for keyboard, it is a demonstration piece, a stained-glass demonstration of the now forgotten art of variable instrumental tuning.

Similar methods will "explain" some at least of the sonatas with extreme key-changes by Domenico Scarlatti and such other composers as Haydn. Such "new music" experiments in variable tuning went beyond the capacity of the ordinary player, who preferred to keep his instrument in one accustomed tuning.

Since professional tuners were uncommon until the nineteenth century, the ordinary householder preferred a simple meantone, which can be tuned quickly and verified for accuracy by the successive beatless major thirds. When Mozart or the young Beethoven improvised on an instrument away from home, we may presume that he did so usually on an instrument tuned to meantone. So we find that all of Mozart's keyboard variations and the earlier sets by Beethoven gain by performance in a meantone tuning. Similar evidence indicates that they preferred a well-tempered tuning for their own instruments, on which they composed their sonatas and concertos. The final change from well-tempered to equal temperament in Beethoven's composing occurred probably between 1799 and 1805, at the latest shortly after the writing of the *Waldstein Sonata*, opus 53, the opening modulation of which would seem to indicate a well-tempered tuning. The new equal temperament and its strumming style, which

12

Beethoven parodied in his *Funeral March Sonata,* opus 26, soon afterwards became the natural language of his instrument.

Such guesses are not history. They indicate only how sedulously scholars have not studied one factual aspect of the classical European keyboard literature which is of far greater practical significance, for the study of harmony and correct keyboard practice, than the entire corpus of scholarly speculation about each composer's love affairs.

The elder German composers strummed occasionally, in the accompaniment but not usually in both hands; their art began in the contrapuntal realization of a figured bass. Their meantone tuning did not encourage playing in full chords, and their music sounds best when spread linearly with broken chords, arpeggios, and acciaccaturas, when the intellectual pleasure of the dissonance is touched upon and the embellishment drawn out with grace.

One of the first reactions to the appearance of vertical harmony in chords, however, was to repeat the same chord over and over like a drumbeat, for example in battle pieces. The emotional affect of this type of simple harmonizing spread to the string accompaniments of Italian instrumental concertos. Domenico Scarlatti added to this the throbbing rhythms of the guitar. Beethoven strummed to underline a key or bring leviathan to a full stop. An example of what we may call Schubertian strumming is the howling parody in the middle of Beethoven's *Eroica Variations,* opus 33, for piano. Humorless virtuosos were soon strumming Beethoven's *Funeral March Sonata* and Schubert's *Wanderer Fantasy* with an equal seriousness.

When Beethoven went over from well-tempered tuning to equal temperament, he countered the resulting lack of affective variety in the modulations by an increase of tough dissonances in the counterpoint. He was still thinking in these widening chromatic relationships the precise and intricate language of the past.

Schubert came late enough to encounter the piano tuned in equal temperament. One could play on it full chords with both hands in any key, and so one strummed. Formal counterpoint was already becoming the dead art of manipulations which Schubert died wishing he had learned. Yet his basses move, like Chopin's, with contrapuntal finality, as Liszt's do not.

With such full, rich harmonies in both hands now possible, and the piano as an instrument begging to throb out in full chords, Schubert strummed and modified the art of strumming, found melodies in pure resonance, and created, in enthusiasm, a radically fresh harmonious-melodious art. He did not throw aside the past; he borrowed from it an amount of exemplary information, which he used. His gifts, prodigious as Mozart's but less disciplined, matured so rapidly he was spared any education he did not seek. He experimented assiduously, impelled by the need to make his big new harmonious melodies progress somewhere, his enriched vertical harmonic framework structurally succeed.

His gift of melody was so complete as to be in reality a new harmonic invention, an art with reference to the past but without a past. His abundance of melody and full chordal harmonies did not allow him to continue directly the line of contrapuntal invention from the clavichord.

Schubert preceded Liszt in transforming accompaniment into a pianistic orchestration. He made of his accompaniments an emotionally charged atmosphere, an enlarged melodious landscape, through which the principal melody pursues its way. Instead of counterpointing the melody, he kept it whole; he did not expand on the melodic fragments.

The inheritance of Germanic music from Schubert, gradually apprehended, created problems not conceived by Beethoven, a destructive aberration that could be only compromised but never mastered by his successors, who tried to mingle it within that other art of dramatic-intellectual counterpoint which culminated in Beethoven's last works. Brahms, especially, divided his skill between the effort to engross melodies like Schubert's and the imposition of a classic contrapuntal discipline. The struggle was finally resolved, though not wholly, by Schoenberg, who married the full-bodied melody to counterpoint at the cost of harmonic innocence.

Because they could not explain Schubert, the German theorists dropped his accomplishments to a lower level of their scholastic hierarchy and tried to make up the difference by adoring sentiment. Schubert's keyboard art went into eclipse, until it reappeared, with Mozart's, in the 1930s.

If the break between the eighteenth and nineteenth centuries is most marked by the decisive originality of Schubert, the continuity of tradition between the eighteenth and twentieth centuries was carried forward through the workmanship of Franz Liszt.

This amazing personality, whose life spans the nineteenth century from Beethoven to Debussy, has been made the scapegoat of the second-rate. Yet his art forms the continental divide between the high period of modern music and the twentieth century. What is called *romantic* in music may be highly emotionalized composition in clavichord style, from Froberger through C. P. E. Bach into Chopin and Schumann; or it may be literary, as in Schubert's *Wanderer Fantasy* or a Berlioz tone poem; or operatic, as in the *bel canto* movements by Clementi and Field; or brilliant on the surface, like many well-ordered compositions by Weber and Hummel; or prevailingly lyrical, like Field's and Chopin's *Nocturnes;* or essentially songlike, melody and accompaniment, however elaborated. Liszt combined in his unequal and unlike compositions all these romantic forms, styles, mannerisms, gestures, and appearances, while preserving a thorough knowledge of classical organization when he wished to apply it, usually to unsuitable material.

Liszt's Piano Sonata in B minor stands isolated as the most successful formal organization of the nineteenth-century stylistic conglomerate. By sheer determination, and without innate need in the material, he spread the single-movement sonata form over an entire large sonata, somewhat in the manner of Schubert's *Wanderer Fantasy,* without breaks to distinguish movements. (Schoenberg did the same even more largely in his First Quartet, imitating Liszt, but with distinct, separated movements.) The idiom of Liszt's Sonata reaches forward to the piano sonata and concertos of Béla Bartók.

Liszt cut loose harmony from the control of thoroughbass, precipitating *impressionism* and the notions of formulative and thematic *originality,* the belief that a composer can, of his deliberate wish, invent a form. Experimenting with classical proportions Liszt evolved the Big Work with recurrent theme, the Big Work in a single movement, and other coagulate, eclectic forms.

By teaching the pianist to imitate an orchestra, he translated the *tone poem* into pianistic terms. His romanticized imitations of Hungarian folk music and the sound of the hammer-beaten *cembalom,* though less genuine than Chopin's compositions in Polish folk style, stirred up an unprecedented musical nationalism. Bedřich Smetana and Antonin Dvořák wrote in the language of Bohemia; Modest Mussorgsky conceived a native Russian music; Charles Ives drew together the American commonplace of hymns, ragtime, popular melody, and patriotic tune. In every country some composer of better or worse quality found a voice in the speech of his environment, if only by such indirect reference as the nature sketches of Grieg and Edward MacDowell. Other composers, by nationalistic analogy, put on a folk habit not their own, Brahms composing Hungarian dances, Dvořák a *New World Symphony* with American Negro tunes, and Ferruccio Busoni an *Indian Fantasy* for piano and orchestra on American Indian themes.

This is no more than a partial reckoning of Liszt's contributions to the originality and the often pretentious individualism of subsequent composing styles. Because of this diverse capacity he produced few first-rate compositions, but his twentieth-century inheritors are unwise when they deny his influence. Liszt transformed the art of music during his own lifetime.

Liszt was the first composer-conductor to devote a part of his gifts to propagating the works of his predecessors and contemporaries; the first to direct selective attention to the older musical literature and to bring a part of this literature into common usage by transcribing it for piano. A supreme musical aristocrat, he was responsible and selfless in furthering, without thought of personal advantage, the broadest scope of his art. He consummated the virtuoso skills of public piano-playing and taught them, in the manner of a *grand seigneur,* to more than two generations of disciples. The best of these disciples, keyboard masters like Carl Tausig and Hans von Bülow, memorized and performed the entire classical and romantic piano repertoire, editing it to their taste, in pious conviction that all music of whatever period should be made contemporary with their own—a project of pious misunderstanding which may be thought to have reached cataclysm in the era of the phonograph record.

During the nineteenth century Beethoven's symphonies circulated more widely in piano transcription than by orchestral performance, but his mountainous accomplishment stood in every creative view. Chopin wisely did not emulate him. Mendelssohn, a naturally lyric composer, coarsened his art when he tried to make it "absolute" and large. Schubert conceived largely even when he wrote on the smallest scale; his limited means became miraculously capable of every demand he made on them.

Robert Schumann, an eclectic but positive critic of all that he admired, infused his warm personality into his themes and smaller songlike compositions; he filled out his larger compositions by technical devices incapable of living growth. His best music survives in the appreciation of that public which knows a good thing when it hears it but is able to listen only by short snatches. His friends Liszt and Johannes Brahms, and his wife, the famous pianist Clara Schumann, popularized his music so well that even today it is performed more often than it intrinsically deserves. His talent, in similar range, resembles that of Giles Farnaby.

It is as natural to speak of Brahms by his given name, Johannes, as it is impossible to speak of him as John. His art exists by a similar inflation. Though he was a devoted friend and admirer of Schumann, he began his career by composing a Piano Sonata, opus 1, in imitation of Beethoven's *Hammerklavier Sonata;* the best movement is the least pretentious, in the style of an old German *minnelied.* Brahms found his natural vein as a composer for piano by writing groups of intermezzos and caprices, single-movement sketches in a style heavier than Schumann's; in my opinion these are pleasanter to hear than to read. He enveloped rich melodic ideas in thick sauces of admirably individualized counterpoint, but his melodic gift and the skilled "tiny-work" in which he wrapped it seldom become one conception. For this reason his two great piano concertos are orchestral rather than soloistic; the piano part does not retain the independence from the orchestra that is the real character of the solo concerto in Mozart or Beethoven. The architecture of his larger conceptions resembles modern imitation Gothic, a steel frame supporting the decorative stone. His skill makes up by sculptural mass what it lacks in natural contour and in color.

The conception of large, abstract, "absolute" music as a type of tragic drama became current at this period. Bach's *Chaconne* for solo violin, extracted from its Partita, and Beethoven's *Sonata Appassionata* and Fifth and Ninth Symphonies were equated with the tragedies of Aeschylus, Sophocles, and Shakespeare. European tragedy had been in the French and Italian manner, derived from Seneca, a pathetic declamation suitable to the emotion

rather than expressing individual character. The romantic rediscovery of Shakespeare reversed the tragic emphasis from the
general to the individual. Beethoven's Heiligenstadt Testament,
revealing the tragic discovery of his deafness, imparted to his
music, in the minds of its devotees, this new sense of personal
tragedy expressed as absolute music. But Beethoven's comedy
and customarily aggressive finale counter the resignation of the
slow movement.

German romantic-sentimental idealism, the heart of its new
song-literature as typified by the song-cycles of Schubert and
Schumann, concerned itself intimately with defeat in love, the
heartbreaks and failure of living, and death, in the presence of
nature's beauty. Schubert's last keyboard compositions, the three
posthumous sonatas, as well as the G major Quartet and the C
major Quintet, convey his awareness of impending death in a
musical speech both intimate and largely tragic. He dies not like
a Shakespearean hero-villain in the face of life, but passing
through life. The tragic assertion is succeeded by an exquisite
awareness of tragic beauty; his scherzo is the joy and play of
being; his finale, a psychological fugue across fields of flowers.

For Brahms the aggressive mood seemed necessary to great-
ness, perhaps because he was not by nature aggressive. In his
larger works he labors mightily to affirm life. His private living
was doubtful and withdrawn. His pious mind attempted to compose an affirmation which would suffice for his belief. An emotionally perplexed thinker, he sought precise theories and believed
in them as proofs. The *German Requiem* substitutes for the
liturgy a text of his own assembling. His most moving compositions, the Clarinet Quintet and the *Four Serious Songs*, like the
earlier Horn Trio and *Alto Rhapsody*, convey his sense of personal finality.

In the same way that Mark Twain compromised writings which
displeased his wife and friends, Brahms backed out of daring in-
novations at the insistence of Clara Schumann and his friend the
violinist Joseph Joachim. But the implication of these adventures
became, more than the Wagnerian largesse, the inworking source
of twentieth-century creative radicalism.

At the height of his pianistic creativeness Brahms wrote several
sets of keyboard variations, among them the ponderous *Variations
on a Theme of Handel,* with its heavily harmonized, thumping

fugue, and the more flowing *Variations on a Theme of Paganini.* Though Brahms knew and played Beethoven's *Diabelli Variations,* he preferred for his model the popular 32 Variations in C minor, composed during 1806 in the new fashion of display passage-work and strumming—a composition Beethoven came to detest equally with his Septet because of their undeserved popularity in comparison with his better work. The 32 Variations crystallized what was to become the new pianistic idiom of the nineteenth century, the display style of Clementi, which Mozart decried. Brahms indeed conceived his *Paganini Variations* under the title *Studies for Pianoforte;* formally they do not end but cease.

(It is interesting to note that, with our own popular preference for Beethoven's idiosyncratic later idiom, the C minor Variations have disappeared from the place they so long held in the pianistic repertoire—rather unjustly, since they are among the first and best of their kind. They are also not without a measure of Beethoven's fun, for example the scales of the eighteenth variation; but they are customarily played without humor.)

The disintegration of the classical style is nowhere more evident than in the incapacity of nineteenth-century composers after Beethoven to write keyboard variations. (I mean theme and variations as a self-sustaining composition, not as a movement in a larger composition; nineteenth-century composers wrote the latter type more successfully.) The general style is that of Mendelssohn's *Variations sérieuses,* a lyrical series of prevailingly chordal inventions in finger-exercise style, after Beethoven's C minor model, around a theme which does not alter or progress. The succession of ideas no longer adds up to a clear system of development and contrast with a decisive ending. A richer work, the melodious *Variations on a Theme of Anselm Huttenbrenner* by Schubert, is unjustly neglected by pianists.

Brahms helped to edit the complete *Orders* for keyboard by François Couperin, a model of its kind and a reproach to the French, whose standard complete edition of Couperin is in effect a nineteenth-century translation. He owned several manuscripts of works by Domenico Scarlatti. He borrowed for his keyboard music and piano concertos passages and devices from these earlier keyboard techniques, so inworking them within the heavier counterpoint of his own style that they remain relatively unnoticed.

From Couperin to Rameau to Berlioz and eventually to Debussy, the course of French musical idiom has been devious but consistent, an intellectual impressionism, the eye within the ear. From Lully to Piccini to Cherubini to Verdi, visiting Italian composers have shared in the fashioning of French operatic styles. Gluck, Chopin, Liszt, and Stravinsky, adopted by French taste, have contributed each a unique orientation. In the nineteenth century the influences of Beethoven and Wagner threatened an esthetic conquest.

Against the prevailing Wagnerism three French composers, Claude Debussy, Maurice Ravel, and Erik Satie, led the counterattack of the French idiom. From Rameau to Debussy there had been no French keyboard music of importance, though some pianists, among them Busoni, have found virtue in the keyboard writing of Camille Saint-Saëns. Debussy revived the distinctively French idiom, poetically organized and pictorially colored. Abandoning narrative, abstract drama, and formal conventionality, Debussy reproduced the tone of contemporary French poetry and painting, the appreciation of light, color, and visionary imagination for their own sake, preferring atmosphere to representation, the indicative symbol instead of the whole scene. Putting aside traditional harmony and counterpoint, he took for his own use the *whole-tone scale*, without semitones, to obtain a panchromatic plasticity of color, the melody always within the coloration of the chord. In his great songs, his piano and instrumental pieces, his operatic and choral works, the form is continuously invented, until even the harmonic coloration of the chord ceases to govern the keyless plasticity of tone. Within this medium Debussy restored the rhythmic subtlety of line which had been a chief characteristic of the French idiom. Debussy's art intuits an essence of musicianship without a structural body or a message.

Debussy's antistructural composition, dismissed by contemporary formalists as without substance if not incompetent, ended the sway of nineteenth-century giantism. All music after him had to reckon as much with the over-all clarity of its texture as with the working out of pompous or motivic themes.

Maurice Ravel, a lesser but quite independent composer, converted the later impressionism of Liszt, which Debussy reflected, to a new clarity of outline, aware of both Couperin and Debussy, inventing his own keyboard virtuosity, tenuous and without obvious display. He is the last of the nineteenth-century keyboard masters who stem from Czerny, as Béla Bartók is the first keyboard master of the twentieth century.

While these two idiomatically French composers were undermining the ramparts of the German tradition, Erik Satie turned his back on it, encouraging his few followers to exploit simple musical designs which eschew all traditional working, provoking solemn antagonism by parodistic and seemingly foolish whimsies. The purity of his skill, apart from the whimsicality, gave to younger twentieth-century composers a new faith that music could be rethought from its beginnings. His distortions of musical practice and theory added a twist of defiance. An isolated artist, who seemingly aspired to nothing, he is the forerunner and hero of those twentieth-century originals who continually begin fresh, in disregard of any tradition. His peculiarity has become the honored criterion of a mid-twentieth-century radical academicism. His dress, his manner, his *petit-point* pedantry, his studies all show him to have been at heart the academician he parodied. His esthetic-philosophical guidance, a matter of attitude rather than expression, commingling dadaistic fun with inward seriousness, helped release twentieth-century music to still unknown destinies.

15

THE TWENTIETH
CENTURY

The twentieth century begins emerging from the nineteenth century around the year 1885. Apart from innumerable manifestos and dead-end "new directions," the evolution of music into and through the twentieth century has been a definite, almost a precise development. During this century following the disintegration of modern music, the period of vertical harmony and key-tonal relationship, those composers who have tried to control the future or preserve the past by reorganizing musical theory have almost unanimously failed, whereas the composers who have worked out their experimental ideas in music, whether or not afterwards explaining them in theory, have more commonly, though belatedly, succeeded.

Five distinct streams of music mingle in the twentieth-century keyboard art: the French, the Russian, the German, the inheritance of Liszt, and American experimentalism.

In France, Debussy and Satie broke with musical tradition but not with the historic nature of the French idiom. The work of their French contemporaries who imitated German styles has in large part perished. Darius Milhaud writes, apart from a few gigantesque works, rather simply in a style naturally French, though he has borrowed from South American idiom. The idiosyncratic contrapuntal independence of Berlioz and César Franck reappears among the crowded literary references, sound-effects, imitations of nature, and technical experiments of the composer-organist Olivier Messiaen.

Paralleling this development, a continuity of more formally linear writing, calm, cool if not a trifle cold, with an equally French satisfaction in its self-sufficiency, leads from Gabriel Fauré, teacher of Ravel, through Ravel and its last master, Francis Poulenc, all excellent pianists.

Erik Satie, whose persuasion and encouragement brought out the impressionistic poeticism, the plastic, delicate coloring, and the simple outlines of Debussy and Ravel, returned to composing after an interval to become the interior guide of a new French generation. In one sentence Satie restated the character of the French idiom: "Do not forget that the melody is the Idea, the contour just as much as it is the form and content of a work." And: "Music grammar is neither more nor less than a grammar."

In his later works Satie composed by discontinuous nodes of idea, fragments standing apart like pieces of furniture, music which refuses to assert itself, to be the voice of an emotion. His art became its own manifesto, its commentary noted by verbal irrelevancies in the margins, an art making no effort to be popular or, on occasion, playable. Satie's ostentatiously unambitious but sure skill coupled with the slight but superlatively competent draftsmanship of Anton Webern revolutionized twentieth-century musical esthetics, in each dictionary signification. *Esthetics: The branch of philosophy dealing with the beautiful, chiefly with respect to theories of its essential character, tests by which it may be judged, and its relation to the human mind; also, the branch of psychology treating of the sensations and emotions evoked by the fine arts and belles-lettres.* [*Webster's New International Dictionary,* Second Edition])

The preface to the collection of twenty short pieces, *Sports et divertissements,* published in a facsimile of Satie's beautifully precise calligraphy and notation, begins: "This publication is made up of two artistic elements: design, music." *Socrate,* his concise setting of three texts from Plato in French, is for those who love him the summation of his art. I prefer the setting with piano to the performance version with several instruments. (My long appreciation of Satie has sharpened to renewed focus after reading the chapters about him in Roger Shattuck's introduction to the twentieth century in France, *The Banquet Years.*)

Pierre Boulez exploits an academician's knowledge of music in a style which has reference to Satie, Messiaen, and Webern but is more anchored in the amorphous atonality of Debussy's late orchestral compositions. He elaborates a musical line very much in his own taste, subordinating any hint of melody or color to the formal articulation of an exact design. His compositions for piano go beyond the capacity of the piano as a sound-medium to realize them; they cannot be read but must be worked out for a performance. He fails like Mendelssohn when he attempts to write beyond his lyrical reach. A superb conductor of romantic music, he thinks eloquently by the phrase; as composer he substitutes for the romantic continuity of successive phrases an enforced pattern of sound-references that will not sustain his music at length.

In French music of the mid-twentieth century the discontinuity practised by Satie in later compositions has become a fashion, an omnidirectional continuum like a sixteenth-century madrigal, with discrete purpose but no external shape.

Throughout twentieth-century music one must be careful to disentangle any theory from its practice. The theory will be sometimes a more interesting invention than the musical resultant.

French esthetic theory has a literary flair, exclusive, nationalistic, moralistic, with heroes and villains and as goal an apotheosis, the final process so individual that only one can do it. At the head of the modern French critical-creative pantheon stand those two uncompromisingly rational unreasonables, Poe and Baudelaire. Poe's fictive and (as we see it) fruitless pragmatism, translated by the art of Baudelaire, is the genius of modern French creative criticism. For the artist in France, to create is to be a critic, an utterer of epigrams, a polemicist. The theory is divisive, the polemic salesmanship, the effect commercial, hidden behind an existential conviction of uniqueness, a self-dramatizing anarchism that helps to explain the very French, infectious, theory of the absurd.

The Russian composer is, by contrast, without theories. From Field to Prokofieff and Kabalevsky, Russian composing has not essentially progressed or changed its conviction that keyboard art is intended to show off the piano, with all possible niceties of gradation, upward and downward, at the keyboard. The harmony remains that of the Italianate theory and Clementi, modified but not altered by Liszt. Chromatic passages embellish the harmony but do not subvert it; more than one key at a time (*polytonality*) is acceptable so long as the conflict is between opposing diatonic keys.

Within these limitations Anton Rubinstein, Tchaikovsky, Rachmaninoff, Prokofieff, Shostakovich, and the other Russian composer-pianists have written their concertos and incidental piano compositions. Under the present government no serious deviation from this archaic stylistic formula is permitted. The ample, upholstered concertos, with their simple, effective, sentimental melodies, compete, in the public ear, with the major classics more successfully than any other twentieth-century music. The best of them, Sergei Rachmaninoff's Third Piano Concerto, suffers constant deformation at the hands of pianists incapable of realizing its suave aristocracy. The weakness of the Russian keyboard style is evident in the solo pieces, and it is here that the few nonconforming pianist-composers have made their mark. Modest Mussorgsky's *Pictures at an Exhibition* and his songs with piano have a breadth and personality which shame the persistent Russian archaism; though more widely performed in orchestral arrangement, the *Pictures* are heard best when played at the piano.

The piano compositions by Igor Stravinsky emphasize the eclectic archaism of their Russian origin but do so in strictly non-Russian style. The Sonatas for piano solo and two pianos might have been written in the lifetime of Clementi; the Concerto for two solo pianos abundantly exhibits Stravinsky's intimate reappraisal of the art of Beethoven. Stravinsky's sophisticated taste has been disciplined by the French linear tradition; his firm writing avoids the superabundance of mere passage-work which mars the Russian piano concerto, even in the work of Prokofieff, who tries to imitate him. For this reason Stravinsky's Concerto for piano and winds and his *Capriccio* for piano and orchestra have never enjoyed the popular success of their otiose Russian rivals. His late *Movements* for piano and orchestra is a condensed composition reflecting the influence of Webern. Stravinsky has had the Mozartian gift to convert to his own idiom whatever music around him attracts the whole of his attention.

It may as well be confessed here that no twentieth-century composer of the first rank has been able to compose a piano concerto that stands in equal authority with the best of his other music. Debussy and Scriabin failed entirely. Prokofieff, Bartók,

Stravinsky, and Schoenberg came near succeeding, but each wrote a violin concerto of equal or more commanding stature. Only the Second and Third Piano Concertos and the *Paganini Variations* for piano and orchestra by Rachmaninoff have equaled the popularity and prestige of the violin concertos by Sibelius, Berg, Prokofieff, and Bartók. The fact may be melancholy; I do not attempt to explain it.

The combination of piano with full orchestra appears not to succeed in a twentieth-century idiom. Bartók tried twice to invent a new sound-relationship between piano and orchestra; his most playable piano concerto, the Third, lies more nearly within the neoclassical tradition. His Sonata for two pianos and percussion is the most successful—and one may doubt, agreeing with the composer's title, whether it is a concerto at all.

Alexander Scriabin alone among Russian composers invested the prevailing Italianate harmony with chromaticism, learned not from the Germanic tradition but from the keyboard art of Chopin and Liszt.

During the three centuries of modern music, homophony and monody had projected the independence of the keys, and counterpoint an awareness of the surrounding realm of dissonance. In fear of dissonance the limitations of harmony were drawn more tightly, the logic of the rules meanwhile inviting greater extremes of dissonance. The full acceptance of equal temperament for the tuning of all instruments had made all keys alike. The single chromatic scale, however refined and restrained by the authority of tonal theory, allowed the possibility of unrestrained tonal combinations. Within this conflict of possibility and rule Liszt and Wagner less and less restrained themselves, being careful however to keep the dissonance prevailingly sweet, a retrogression from the art of Beethoven.

Conventional modern harmony had been built of the thirds of the triad, which in meantone were concordant; why not invent new harmonies, for example of superposed fourths, which in equal temperament are more nearly concordant than thirds? Dissonant combinations a whole step above or below the octave had domesticated the seventh and ninth. Scriabin, a mystical enthusiast, believed himself inspired to create a chord of superposed fourths, which treated the resulting ninth as consonant. His many preludes and short sonatas, which he played very softly in the

same manner as Chopin and Debussy, evolved away from consonance, through sweet dissonances, into a rhapsodic, esoterically
interpreted ultraharmony. More powerfully performed, his music
becomes noisy and indeterminate, for lack of the fixed harmonic
reference his chord could not supply. His last works predicate
that elimination of key-reference which is called *atonality*.

Though it had many lesser imitators, the independent Lisztian
style brought forth two other composers of importance, Ferruccio
Busoni and Béla Bartók.

The pianist-composer Ferruccio Busoni began by imitating
Brahms, inadequately; then, repudiating the earthiness of Brahms,
which is the very body of his musical wisdom, Busoni went on to
master Chopin, Beethoven, Mozart of the piano concertos, and
finally Liszt, whom he most resembled. The superiority of Busoni's intelligence, his great knowledge, the fastidious judgement
that would not yield to other men's opinions, destroyed him as a
composer. When he put on the magician's cloak as Bach-Busoni,
he adapted a part of Bach's keyboard compositions to his own
taste. At the height of his powers, the cynosure of pianists, not
the most popular but as the best men thought, the best, traveling
constantly to perform, weary of repertoire though never freed of
it, he completed in turn three versions of the unfinished four-part
fugue, containing Bach's signature in notes, which ends the *Art
of Fugue*.

First he completed the unfinished fugue of Bach, prefacing it
with a chorale prelude in his own style as Bach-Busoni. Then,
drawing upon the entire misappropriation of his knowledge, he
rewrote this *Fantasia Contrappuntistica,* in a passion of self-
indulgence, as a phantasmagoria of styles and devices, to the
limit of his technical capacity; and being still discontent, reset it
for two pianos. This was no longer the aristocratic complacency
of Liszt amusing himself by writing for display a fantasy on the
well-known melodies of an opera; here the highest and most discriminating judgement had grown crazed and tasteless. Afterwards, as though awakening, Busoni composed his lovely small
sonatinas for piano, his *Arlecchino* (some of the melodies are to
be found in his *Sonatina ad usum infantis,* written for a child to
play at the harpsichord), and his opera *Doktor Faust.*

Busoni, composing out of the past, prophesied, as if it were an
escape from despair, the new anticlassical music which since his

death has come into existence. Edgar Varèse finds authority for his nontonal and electronic compositions in Busoni's book *Towards the Esthetic of a New Music.*

Béla Bartók alone of the twentieth-century composer-pianists was able to reach the highest level of proficiency as a pianist without sacrificing or impairing his primary gift as a composer. He ranks among the supreme composers for the piano because, like François Couperin, he knew exactly how to do what was possible within the limitations of his period and medium. Beginning with Wagner and Brahms but increasingly influenced by Debussy and by a more useful comprehension of Liszt than that of Busoni (with whom he collaborated in an unfinished edition of Liszt's compositions), Bartók soon put aside the conventional pianistic idiom and, much affected by his studies in folk music, developed a new art of small intervals and clashing tones, threaded through by keyless melody.

Unlike Busoni, Bartók did not mold his understanding of past music to his own preoccupations. He could hear, underlying the decorative fancies of Liszt's B minor Sonata, passages which spoke his language. Editing for publication volumes of Bach and Beethoven, and more particularly Domenico Scarlatti and François Couperin, he found in them further idiomatic resources.

For a century collectors of folk tunes had been conventionalizing and covering up the melodic consistency of folk music by forcing it to wear harmony. Bartók learned from Scarlatti how the sound of folk instruments could be conveyed in abstract forms, without program or scenery. He borrowed from Couperin the atmospheric suggestiveness of articulated small-note ornaments, making of them, with silence, movements which he called "night music," for example in his piano suite *Out of Doors.* He took apart folk melodies and recombined them, in extreme concentration, to compose new melodies.

At a time when composers sought eloquence in large forms with plenty of stuffing, Bartók was writing his *14 Bagatelles* in acrid intervals that forbade a superfluous note. He tried to enlarge the sonority of the piano by building massive chords, incorporating the dissonant acciaccaturas which Bach and Scarlatti had used more reticently. He borrowed from the American composer Henry Cowell the use of tone-clusters, clumps of neighboring tones which go beyond harmony into noise. Cowell played

13

them with fists and elbows; Bartók kept them under the fingers. The method culminated in his Piano Sonata. This is, to my knowledge, the first borrowing from American experimentalism by a European composer: Bartók acknowledged the permission with a letter of thanks. Though Bartók may not have known it, the American composer Charles Ives had already used tone-clusters of several sorts even more drastically in his two piano sonatas.

Bartók's chief and most singular achievement was to create the first mature keyboard literature for the student since the compositions of J. S. Bach. The charm and taut delicacy of his folk-tune settings *For Children* were designed not only to please and educate but to train the ear away from the fat harmony, the assured key-references, the flabby rhythms, the accepted tonal combinations which were thought to be the whole of music. Where Debussy stirred a recognition of Oriental sound-patterns by his imitation of the Indonesian *gamelan,* Bartók tried to convey, through the piano, the clashing higher overtones of the harpsichord and the Hungarian *cembalom,* the folk fiddle and the pipe. He set his clashing sounds to powerful rhythms, additive rhythms outside the normal experience of European counting, enforcing a fresh comprehension of the piano and its potentialities, stressing the percussive nature of the instrument.

Bartók's concern for every detail of pianistic composition and performance, in his own idiom, is epitomized in the 153 progressive piano pieces of his *Mikrokosmos,* the most precious gift made by any twentieth-century composer to the true Amateur who reads at the piano. The first pieces of *Mikrokosmos* lie under the five fingers in the most elementary position of keyboard playing, as free of harmony as plainsong and as satisfying. The most difficult provide no display of obvious virtuosity.

Though Bartók compromised tonality by his preference for close intervals and pre-diatonic melodies, explored atonality, and adapted the tone-row to his own purposes, he never abandoned tonality for total chromaticism. Within his compressed idiom he left no problems unsolved.

Germanic twentieth-century composers turned almost entirely to the orchestra and chamber music. A direct inheritance of style runs from Brahms to the crabbed, uninspiring counterpoint of Max Reger and the heavy keyboard formalism of Paul Hindemith. Brahms's idiomatic "tiny-work" became the inheritance of Arnold Schoenberg.

Schoenberg's Three Piano Pieces, opus 11, explore through the idiom of Brahms and, less evidently than Bartók, the contrary inheritance from Liszt. Liszt had eliminated the ground-tone of improvisation, the thoroughbass; in the third piece of his opus 11 Schoenberg does away with the theme and its key-reference, to create the first freely composed example of his twelve-tone chromatic pantonality. (Though no more *atonal* than the mature music of Debussy or Scriabin, Schoenberg's music was the first to be called, in derogation, *atonal*.)

In the Six Little Piano Pieces, opus 19, Schoenberg reduced the chance relationships of pantonality to a profoundly considered group of elementary intervallic relationships and distinctive rhythmic binders, each self-subsistent, grouping them together economically, like the ball-and-stick structural analyses of new chemical compounds. Occupying only six minutes playing time, these pieces are the imaginative nucleus of a new creative chemistry. Through them one enters the unique, tiny cosmos of Anton Webern.

With these Six Pieces, Schoenberg decisively emancipated the dissonance, substituting for key-related form what he believed to be the no less traditionally authenticated procedure of continuous variation. His resolution of the possibilities of these new types of keyless intervallic relationships occurs in the Piano Suites, opus 23 and opus 25, tentatively exploring the formality of the new *twelve-tone method*, in which each of the twelve notes is related only to the others. With these, one should list for study at the keyboard Anton Webern's piano Variations, the almost diagrammatic esthetic summation of his art. Except the two small pieces of his opus 33 and his powerful but archaic Organ Variations, Schoenberg composed no more for the solo keyboard.

With the emancipation of the dissonance, the procedure of continuous variation, and the syntactic grammar of the 12-tone method, Schoenberg established a system of orderly reference, supplanting the former key-system, bringing to an end the period of modern music, the three centuries during which, with a few such exceptions as the work of Berlioz, the art of music had been related to the keyboard.

Before the turn of the century, Arnold Dolmetsch and a little later Wanda Landowska revived the building and playing of the older keyboard instruments. Dolmetsch crafted his instruments in the older style and built them himself; Landowska designed what is in essence a new, larger twentieth-century harpsichord with sixteen-foot register and pedal stops, a magnificent instrument, built for her by Pleyel in Paris, with which she devised what is in effect a twentieth-century style of harpsichord performance. In recent years there has been an increasing but cautious tendency among harpsichord players to revive the earlier instrument and to follow Dolmetsch in learning its correct performing conventions.

At the start of the twentieth century the long-lived organ was a century dead; the piano and reconstituted harpsichord had been left to shift for themselves as soloistic means; opera was in extremities and the symphony orchestra, once an integral part of opera, survived like the opera house by civic pride and sufferance; chamber music had left the patron's home to exist on the small charity of the public audience.

Audience and performer had been dissevered by the footlight glare of money and a universal incompetence to do for oneself what could be done dazzlingly well by hired artists. The audience, idealizing its performers, had slight experience of them as persons; the performer felt himself deprived of creative leisure by his never-satisfied antagonist, the public. Its critics' mouths fawned and yapped. The performer could not deny the mass favor of the public; the public, however exasperatedly critical of itself as mass audience, could not escape the mob consequences of its anxiety to be pleased. We do not yet see clearly that the titans of pianistic virtuosity were—and are, although nowadays the precocious mantle wears more lightly—entertainers and buffoons performing before a public which set small value on their aspirations and almost none on their original compositions. I call to mind the cry of one of the greatest of them, Artur Schnabel: "Have I learned everything I know about music to go on performing in public, like a child!" Schnabel performed only work of the masters: a little Bach, much Mozart, the whole of Beethoven and Schubert, and some Brahms; his performances on records became for a generation of listeners the audible embodiment of the previously little-known masterpieces of the classic piano literature. Through recording and broadcast a wider knowledge of music than had been the privilege of the elite audience in a few cities became the common property of indistinguishable millions. Their enthusiasm and the increase of their opportunities would soon reduce the sublimest art to an appreciative indifference.

Until the twentieth century the great musical artisans had not felt themselves accused because of a time-lag in the acceptance of their music. Until towards the mid-nineteenth century the performance of contemporary music outweighed the revival of the classics. In the twentieth century the drag of the long past of modern music seemed to hold back the public and its performers from recognition of the contemporary; the composer, exactly to the degree of his unique gift, was accused of being an enemy of the past. Eventually, some became so. Yet the seemingly most perverse twentieth-century composers did what they had to out of no disregard of tradition; they knew that tradition—even to reject it—more familiarly than those who criticized them. They set forth in their compositions new answers to old questions, reawakened possibilities which had been put aside by a trend of no longer consequent events, restated forgotten habits in new ways which concealed but did not at first deny their origins.

At the age of forty Erik Satie commenced studying classical polyphony at the Schola Cantorum. Webern and Schoenberg lamented every step by which their conviction forced them to go beyond their knowledge of tradition. During the first half of the century not much was done new that was not historically founded, but the awareness of musical origins was now reaching beyond native folk music to the traditional scales and melodies of Asia, the Orient, and—through jazz—Africa.

The first half of the twentieth century saw a flowering of creative individuality, unequaled in number of composers and the high level of individual capacity, in variety of modes, rapidity of change, and uncertainty of eventual direction, since the sixteenth century. The uninformed habit of deprecating composers of the present in comparison with the chief masters of the past exasperated the living composer to deliberate defiance. New compositions challenged the complacency, the comfort, the patience, the perceptiveness of the audience, throwing back at it its own incomprehension by forcing it to receive incomprehensible events as if they were musical compositions.

No one composer has so thoroughly reconceived the course of

music in his lifetime as Arnold Schoenberg. No living composer has been so widely accepted over so long a period and by so many people as Igor Stravinsky. No composer of such complete obscurity while he was living has more dramatically influenced the composers of an immediately succeeding generation than Anton Webern. No composer, alone and disregarded, has created a music of national individuality more vigorously independent of its extranational origins than Charles Ives.

It is not surprising that America, which did not commence to admit the authority of the greater twentieth-century composers until after 1950, should have failed to recognize the foremost of its own composers, Charles Ives. In America, fashionable taste has accepted the work of European composers with less resistance and more rapidly than it accepts the no less valid work of American composers.

Charles Ives, who is often called a "primitive," was a thoroughly educated practical musician. As a boy he gave public recitals at piano and organ. He studied at Yale with the preeminent American scholar-composer, Horatio Parker. He became an experimental composer under the influence of his father, a pragmatic Yankee-experimentalist bandmaster. In his work the two conflicting traditions of twentieth-century American musicianship, an academic traditionalism drawing authority from Europe and an experimental individualism determined to speak the musical language of a new continent and nation, were bound together in restless argument.

Ives composed the greater part of his still incompletely published and very inadequately performed work between 1895 and 1920. His idiom reports the habits and native musical speech of an era almost as remote from present-day American experience as if it were another culture: the hymns of countryside camp meetings and marching bands and dances of community picnics, the excitement and noise of ball games, popular tunes and the pervasive ragtime, the melodies of Stephen Foster, and national anthems—particularly the now seldom heard but not forgotten "Columbia, the Gem of the Ocean." In the greatest of his solo songs, "General William Booth Enters Heaven," the poem by Vachel Lindsay, Ives sets the refrain, "Are you washed in the blood of the Lamb?" to the melody of the revivalist hymn *Fountain:* "There is a fountain filled with blood . . ." The devotional-dramatic irony of this great marching song for the emancipation of the underprivileged mingles the vividly realized scene with its message by an art so commanding that only the utmost skill of singer and pianist can achieve it.

Ives instructed his copyist to be sure to include the "right wrong notes." American performers of Ives have been eager to make corrections and play the wrong "right" notes, so that much of the strength and rightness of the idiom are lost. Only a very few of the performances on records do justice to the music.

Ives gave to the keyboard two large piano sonatas. His marginal comments on his manuscripts are as humorous as Satie's but more pertinent. The First Sonata consists of five movements, bound together like a fantasy, made up of town and country scenes, including the hitting of a home run, divided by brief interludes marked by hints of a type of sentimental melody. It was written more immediately for the piano than the Second Sonata.

Of the Second Sonata, titled *Concord, Mass., 1840–60,* Ives wrote in a footnote to an accompanying book, *Essays Before A Sonata,* now at long last fortunately, and doubly, reprinted: ". . . the first movement (*Emerson*) of the music which is the cause of all these words, was first thought of in terms of a large orchestra or a piano concerto, the second (*Hawthorne*) in terms of a piano or a dozen pianos, the third (*Alcotts*) of an organ (or piano with voice and violin), and the last (*Thoreau*) in terms of strings, colored possibly with a flute or horn." The second of the two subjects around which, with continuous variation, the entire sonata is composed, includes the opening of Beethoven's Fifth Symphony, reflecting Ives's awareness of the American cultural debt to Europe.

Both sonatas are as difficult to perform, as large, and as rewarding in renewed hearings as Beethoven's *Hammerklavier Sonata,* opus 106, although the form, character, and idiom are absolutely different. When performers and audiences are able to convince themselves of the truth of this statement, the two sonatas will take their proper place among the chief masterpieces of the keyboard literature and, very likely, as the two principal large piano compositions of the first half of the twentieth century. They demand of a sophisticated listener the waiving of nearly all technical preconceptions.

The two sonatas were composed, in total isolation, during the years between 1902 and 1912 and in the spare hours after business, when Ives was heaping up quantities of more or less finished compositions, songs, sketches, and studies, and recombining these into orchestral *sets* (suites) and symphonies. During these years Ives was also creating a new type of successful insurance business and writing manuals of instruction for the salesmen that revived the relationship of trust between the insurance business and the public.

The composer Lou Harrison, who edited for publication several major works by Ives when the composer had become too ill to do such work for himself, wrote in an excellent short analysis: "In his use of song, dance and hymn tunes it must be emphasized that Ives used *popular,* not folk music . . . ; not as with Bartók, ethnic. . . . Mr. Ives's inclusion of popular music was a perfectly logical one, for he was himself cultivating a new music by every means, and every so often he made a piece entirely out of new means. Of the many new means first extensively employed by Ives I think the most important is his heterophonic polyphony. Without this (a freeing of melodic lines from any formal pre-arrangement as to the kinds of chords their several junctures should make) the daring venture of what he called a 'prose' style could not have existed. There were precedents. Mahler and Strauss often let the 'vertical warfare' take care of itself; but a more direct opposite comes closer. Reger's peculiar polyphony was composed, I think, with some such basic idea in mind without his ever grasping what was grasped at once by Ives—that the free progress of the melodies was the essential. Ives proceeded to the making of a polyphony in which phrase and section cumulate from motive-germinated melodies alone."

The technical aspect of the condition of music in the twentieth century as well as its effect on the world-wide creation of new national musics comes to focus in this paragraph by the Hungarian composer Zoltán Kodály: "Let us not forget that the greater part of the world . . . has only homophonic music to our very day. Eastern monophony does not tolerate the yoke of polyphony which developed from European melos. After a certain time polyphony modifies the style of melody; the vertical component influences the horizontal component and the melody cannot fly so freely. In order to accommodate the melody to the harmony, at first its rhythm becomes simplified and sometimes poorer. But the line of sounds also becomes more limited in movement. Instead of self-sufficient melodies new ones arise which demand harmony. Contemporary western European melody almost bears its harmonies in itself, whereas the harmonization of self-sufficient eastern melody, which, by its own nature, would not be necessary, always confronts the [arranger] with new and specific problems. Nevertheless the process of making eastern music polyphonic is going on, slowly but surely, and follows the traces of European civilization. With the collaboration of foreign musicians, the forms of European musical life are first established and for a time European and traditional musical activities flow side by side in two separate channels. Later the leadership of musical education on a European pattern is taken over by natives trained abroad and finally the currents merge into a new, national school of composers and a kind of synthesis is born between the two factors. This can be found in Japan and is what happened in Hungary and in every country where polyphony was not known from the beginning: as in Russia, in the Scandinavian countries, in the Balkans, and more recently in Turkey. This same phenomenon occurred in North America. . . . The peoples of the earth are approaching each other in the field of music. Uniformity need not follow from this. If some kind of a musical world language could be created, this could be only a means of expression: the real subject-matter must be taken by the people from their own soil." (*Folk Music and Art Music in Hungary*)

Throughout the world the condition described by Kodály is now well advanced; its consequence, accompanying the disintegration of European harmony, has been the creation of new types of polyphony and of sound-means which deny horizontal-temporal voice-leading.

In one of his conversations with Robert Craft, Igor Stravinsky, for forty years the leading twentieth-century exponent of tonality (with its consequent, polytonality) against atonality (with its consequent of complete chromatic dissonance), admitted the end of the period that I have called modern music:

"Harmony, a doctrine dealing with chords and chord relations, has had a brilliant but short history. . . . Today harmonic novelty is at an end. As a means of musical instruction, harmony offers no further resources in which to inquire and from which to seek profit. The contemporary ear and brain require a completely different approach to music. It is one of nature's ways that we feel often closer to distant generations than to the generation immediately preceding us. Therefore, the present generation's interests are directed to music before the 'harmonic age.' Rhythm, rhythmic polyphony, melodic or intervallic construction are the elements of musical building to be explored today."

More than two decades earlier, a few composers, particularly in America, had begun breaking away from the limiting conception of the twelve-tone scale, from the determinate intervals of tuning by equal temperament, from the very necessity of tuning and of fixed notes, and indeed from the idea that sounds notatable by any manner of indicia need be tones.

When young Henry Cowell in the 1920s began sounding tone-clusters at the piano with fist and elbow and leaning over inside the instrument to pluck and swish the strings, he was initiating a new practice which in the *Winter Music* by John Cage and the performances of David Tudor (creatively the most important pianist, world-wide, of the 1950s) would convert the former king of the harmonic instruments into a mere sound-producing means, a resonating box.

The revolution in methods of organizing sound, in listening, in projecting sound for esthetic purposes, has already struck so deep into our surviving conceptions of music that we can no longer predict what will be the next step towards the final disintegration of all that we have known and recognized for music and its replacement by an entirely new understanding of tonal relationships and of sound in its relations with other sound as *field* or as melody.

The future will never be what we imagine but what we have become ready to accept.

The alternative courses of music into the future may be by a return to the natural acoustical relationships of tones, in a scale of just intonation, as it was before the period of modern music; by a rediscovery of the variable possibilities of tuning; by intervals varied in mathematical relationship according to the instructions of the composer; by more intervals within the octave; by artificially prefabricated intervals such as those used by John

Cage in his music for "prepared piano"; by a complete recon-
sideration of our use of instruments; by tonally indeterminate percussion; by noise; and by the invention of electronically created
artificial tones, sounds, or noises. Each of these new types of
music is already in existence.

The Art
and Pleasure
of Being
an Amateur

16

WHAT IS AN
AMATEUR?

No definition will satisfy. Being an *Amateur* is a state of mind, an attitude. Call it recreative leisure.

My favorite art teacher, Sister Magdalene Mary IHM, puts it this way to her evening class of adult painters: "The professional has solved his problems before he starts painting. An amateur discovers his problems while he is painting. We are amateurs."

She says also: "A professional insists on the rules, because he is afraid of what an amateur may do without them."

The professional thinks of himself as one who knows how to get things done, with a certain public suavity that may be called tact, at the right time, in the right style, according to accurate and usually predetermined standards. That is why a genuinely creative artist, or a creative thinker, is often, and rightfully, reproached for being unprofessional. He is perplexed by unanticipated problems his work brings to recognition.

An amateur never knows how he will get anything done, or worked out, or when, or if according to any standards. The professional has to get a job done. An amateur, while he is being an amateur, doesn't have a job to do, and he need not ever finish. A professional is a busy man; an amateur should be leisured.

Leisure can be an escape from busyness, a withdrawal, an emptying, or another kind of concentration.

H. L. Mencken said in a recorded talk: "It's foolish for an

amateur to get too good, because he wastes time on it he could use for something else."

I would say: It's foolish for an amateur to measure what he is doing by any purpose outside what he is doing. The line he draws, the music he makes are his experience—nobody else's. What he does pleases him better than what he accomplishes.

An amateur is a lover, and like most lovers he is sometimes exalted, sometimes dejected, always passing through some sort of love-trouble he will never quite get out of, from which he hopes for a very intimate reward.

There is this sympathy between any genuine amateur and a true artist, that neither can tell—or sell—what drives him, or put a price on the misery of being driven, or evaluate the discipline of being every so often lost without purpose, or the hope, or the very intimate reward. There is this difference, that the true artist usually manages to preserve some report garnered out of his experience, an artifact or note, or the esthetic object which we call the work of art. Insofar as producing an esthetic object satisfies his purpose, he is a professional. Because of all he has put into the object and learned while making it, he will stand by the object and expect others to share by means of it something of what he himself has experienced.

This is the ritualistic aspect of art, a ceremony or form that by being done over again or seen again, or by being remembered, relives an actual experience. It becomes a common experience only after it has been an individual experience. It survives as a discrete replica of experience, a form or model, either an abstraction or a substitute, a transcendence or a euphemism, bringing in the dangerous relationship of *beauty,* so that one can say of an *Et incarnatus est* or a *Crucifixus,* or of Socrates drinking the hemlock, it is beautiful.

A professional artist works to a predetermined pattern of skill, making objects that he believes are beautiful because they resemble other beautiful objects. A true artist sets his skill in competition with predetermined patterns to produce something which will be, however devoid of obvious beauty or originality, quite individual. What the true artist produces will deny the pattern even while suggesting it and suggest the pattern even while denying it. Therefore it is his own and likely to be at first unwanted, refused or rejected because it is thought to refuse or reject the pattern.

In the work of the professional artist we recognize the accredited pattern of some beauty we presume we know. Before the work of a true artist we must go outside our normal habit, to seek an individual beauty in that work by that artist. Recognition of individuality in the work of an artist does not usually occur at once: we see first the negative of it. I began by disliking nearly every one of my favorite composers.

The *time-lag* in recognizing the nonreferrable individuality of a composer can be a significant means of distinguishing between a true artist and a merely fashionable artist. A true artist seldom grows by nonimitation or merely negative originality (being unlike anybody else); he swallows and digests past and present in gulps of knowledge, too big for most of us to get away with. The time-lag that denies him quick recognition is not his fault but the result of our inability to travel as fast as he does from experience to consequence—from our present to his present.

A true Amateur tries to realize within himself in some degree the omnivorous capacity of a true artist. He looks to the past; he frees himself as well as he is able from the tradition or convention of his time; he anticipates the future and responds for posterity to the living artist.

Amateur has other connotations, such as *connoisseur* or *dilettante*. These refer to the exercise of taste, fashion, or arbitrary opinion. Though formerly each had a meaning similar to the present usage of the word *amateur,* they describe in our present thinking one who exercises his judgement on the finished product. So an *Amateur* makes music for himself at the keyboard; a *Dilettante* distinguishes among keyboard performances; a *Connoisseur* likes to believe that he knows which are the best performances. Let us keep these words separate, not in hope of purifying the language, which like art is always changing, but to understand what we are talking about.

I should explain that a *Snob* is one who presumes upon the freedom of a true Amateur without knowing what that is. Because he lives lazily on the old plantation, he thinks of himself as an aristocrat.

We are Dilettantes when we listen to music; when buying tickets or records we try to become Connoisseurs; when we make

14

music for ourselves, we are Amateurs. When we live on opinions without working for them, we are Snobs.

In the presence of art, which is a part of wisdom, we are all mixed of these four elements. The words are not absolute values, nor are there any absolute values in art. An absolute value would have to be a work of God.

17

THE WASTAGE OF

PROFESSIONALISM

Whatever is to be done well the professional aims to do as well, if not better, according to precise, acknowledged standards of accomplishment. The measure of his worth lies outside himself. If he fails, he is still a professional.

Perhaps a typing mistake on my typewriter can guide us to a particular meaning: the professionally skilled artist who has never given up or has retained his amateur independence. Let's call such a person by the lovely, Japanese-sounding word *Amateru*. It is a new word; it has no meaning but that we give it.

And I hope that at once a presence flashes into mind, a music teacher or performer who was *Amateru*. Perhaps he was immured in a small community or in a professional routine, perhaps he was ill-tempered or addicted to wrong habits; nevertheless his presence causes a slight, memorable radiance, conspicuous and motionless, or swinging in a local wind, like an arc lamp over a crossroad.

I saw recently a catalogue put out by one of the big national concert agencies: pages of bright-faced young pianists, the very tiptop of the crop, chosen for looks, presentability, ease of manner with a hostess or when cornered, tired, at an after-concert party around midnight. Equable above all else, capable of reproducing the same routined performance at who knows how many one-night stands, where the artist must seem technically invincible while remaining glamourous. Every year brings another crop.

Of the hundreds of thousands of children who have studied piano, these are the competitive survivors who have made their way to the top. These have and reflect the glamour of accomplishment. They are prisoners of the currently accepted repertoire, happily larger than it used to be, prisoners even of the currently accepted style within which they must play it. They are prisoners of success and will be, before long, nearly all of them, its victims.

If, poised before flight, one of these admired persons should sit near you at dinner in professional company, you will hear from him or her little talk about sonatas, concertos, the new music, interesting points in playing. Not that shoptalk is avoided; it is all shoptalk: tours, hotels, conductors and orchestras, managers and their failings, traveling conditions, the bugs which drop from the ceiling on a South American hotel bed. On occasion, in the right company, they will speak also of music, a sort of reminiscence.

When they do speak of music, it is often to recall some great musician who was, in the special word we have invented, *Amateru:* Artur Schnabel, who talked by the hour unceasingly about music, literature, philosophy, the world of knowledge and ideas; Josef Hofmann, whose mind was like a natural vehicle of music, from which he turned aside to work successfully at his hobby of mechanical invention (he invented an air brake widely used on railroad freight cars); Leopold Godowsky, the little man who missed nothing and turned it all to wit, whose tiny hand required him to become a master of technique; Ferruccio Busoni, whose mind was like an encyclopedia of music perpetually rewriting itself in new considerations. During his last illness, visited by friends who were musicians, Busoni would spring from bed to demonstrate at the piano a thematic reference, the point of an argument.

There is another, though you will seldom hear him spoken of among the virtuosos: Arnold Dolmetsch. We owe to this amateur of a dozen instruments, more than to any other, the rediscovery of the composers, the proper building of instruments, and the performing habits of music before the age of the piano, particularly the music of the sixteenth, seventeenth, and eighteenth centuries. He engaged in his musical passion both wives and his several children, each of whom learned to play several instruments; they could play together a consort of viols or of lutes. After his death, the Haslemere Festival he had founded with his family in an English country village, the instrument-building workshops, the habits of performance, all became professional.

The present-day pianist, if sufficiently unknown, interested, gifted, young, may risk playing in public one difficult new composition without pedigree. The majority are content to accept the limitations for the sake of the success; they do not indeed recognize any limitations, having been trained from an early age to concern themselves with nothing but the technique of the instrument and a repertoire of music not less than fifty years behind the times—composed by famous persons who are safely dead. (A dead composer can compose no more scandalous "new music"; that is what makes him safe.) It is in this environment that suffering begins for the elect.

There was the evening I spent listening to an eminent younger pianist, already established at the level where one plays concertos with the best orchestras. Invited to read trios with two others scarcely less eminent than himself, he erupted at the end of every movement in voluble denunciations of his host's piano and was only by flattery persuaded to continue to the end of the third trio. In the fullness of his ego he desired a piano with a proclamative tone, even for chamber music; and I was interested to observe that, in struggling with a piano that would speak but not shout, he reverted to the finer discriminative rhythm and phrasing of his early reputation. He did not appear to be aware that he was playing better or to value the skills which enabled him to do so. I do not expect to hear him play so well again, and to the present I have not. He has covered up his fine early style in vulgar assertiveness.

The wastage of professionalism fills the Sunday pages of the New York newspapers with more publicly announced weekly music-making than the halls of Europe a hundred years ago offered in a season. The spring-legged critic bounces from hall to hall, snipping concerts and recitals, taking in his dozens of *Appassionatas,* his annual quota of the favorite symphonies, recording the evolution of musical taste as one might note the growth of tree rings. He is grateful to hear new music but, having no positive opinion concerning what he has heard, usually derides it. On the periphery the new music groups and the old music groups garner praise and objections, their programs designed as often to crowd in novelties as for taste. There is too much of everything, too much desire of reputation masking as disinterested achievement. The audience is as professional as the players, as seldom capable of a naïve delight.

Into this morass of frustrated talent and diseased ambition the young performers hurl themselves by dream and effort, thousands failing for each one who succeeds, the returning failures surrendering to what they and their mentors consider the honorable verdict of society by hiding away and eventually giving up their single talent. If the verdict is not favorable, what else is one to do? They withdraw from music, accepting failure as the sole alternative.

The wastage of professionalism is not only the too much that is done at one time in one place, the eagerly prepared and built-up recitals performed at great expense, for the sake of printed notice, to an audience huddled in a corner of the floor-space; it is also the infinitely more that is not done elsewhere, the narrower limitations, prospects, and lost opportunities of the provinces.

18

WHAT HAPPENS
TO ALL THE CHILDREN
WHO STUDY PIANO?

The children begin by taking music lessons. Starting with an
innocent pleasure in making musical sound, they are sent to a
piano teacher, who tries to help them get the music-making into
head or fingers so they can bring it out as pieces. To do this requires practice. A good teacher knows that many children profit
by studying music even if they don't practise. Parents whose child
doesn't practise soon convince themselves that the child should
give up studying music. Regular practice is the rationalizing
formula by which parents justify to themselves the cost of music
lessons. It is adult logic, and sensible children, having to disagree
with their parents about many more important propositions, are
content to go along with this one. The child doesn't see any
future in it either. So the music ceases. It has become work, and
for the child that ends it.

We write off the whims of children, because children's whims
are not expected to grow up. Parents who have themselves no
need of music cannot take seriously a need of music in their
children. Some children, like myself, defeat the most expert and
loving teaching, yet continue dinging away at the piano year after
year without supervision.

A child may discover his innate musical interest, or skill, in
jazz, or listening to records, or taking up an instrument in the

school orchestra. He does the best he can with the opportunity at hand. As he grows older he may go to concerts.

Out of school he finds no time to keep up his instrument or place to use it, so he abandons it and usually abandons the musical life as well. Or he may, when able, continue buying records and going to concerts. That is as much as he knows how to do and as much as society encourages him to do about his innate capacity for music.

Such activity does keep alive in our society some musical interest in the socially useful condition of entertainment. It emphasizes the distinction between the amateur who lends his ears and only occasionally his talent and the professional who works at music all the time because he makes his living by it. Between the two sags an empty gully of washed-away true Amateurism: the songs of the people that we perpetuate museum-fashion as folk music; the artful vocal madrigals and chansons and instrumental consorts of the fifteenth, sixteenth, and seventeenth centuries, when everybody played and sang as naturally as we drive in traffic; the hymns and church music that the congregation sang in parts; the house-and-home music of the eighteenth and nineteenth centuries. Instead of this abundant and communal music, we are left with tunes, forever changing, a "popular music" so called, whistled or sung for a few weeks and forgotten. This popular music springs up and vanishes, weeds in the gully.

We have among us another musical condition, still unreckoned with, that is tragic. It is the condition in which those young pianists find themselves who do not give up music after their early teaching but go ahead studying and practising, concentrating and intensifying their skill, until somewhere between the ages of fifteen and as late as twenty-five or thirty they are forced to admit that this training, to which they have devoted undivided attention, will not support their claim to artistic recognition, though it might furnish them a livelihood.

Nothing in our system of musical education has prepared these young pianists to be frustrated. For ten or fifteen years they have been encouraged to devote several hours a day of intense disciplinary effort to studying and practising the performance of a concert music, which needs and expects an audience. While they were young, an immediate future of preparation, recital, audience, reward, advancement, perhaps scholarship, unrolled constantly before them. Then, at the height of their skill, trained, ambitious, these accomplished students are turned loose on the community to make their way, deprived of audience, reward, advancement.

The parents, who have invested money and enthusiasm, are no better prepared to meet a situation which might have been anticipated but which, because of the love and hope and ambition in them, they did not anticipate. In the self-justifying fantasy of the American dream they have expected a reward from their investment. They have no philosophy to help a disappointed young artist adjust to a new life without promises.

Because his musical education has been directed to working up concert pieces for performance, the young pianist has been taught little more than generalities about the literature of music. His repertoire is meager. He has not been encouraged or educated to read music as he would read books. He is left with a collection of recital pieces to polish, the same pieces he has heard played by other pianists—often discouragingly better played. His skill degenerates to a manual habit of no absorbing interest, the small repertoire he knows and believes to be all the music worth playing.

His musicianship deteriorates to a shoptalk of preferences and opinions, often strongly conservative, reactionary against music he doesn't want to know, refreshed by no new insight. This narrowness, this indifference, this actual lack of acquaintance with the larger possibilities of a private musical life, he passes on, if he is a teacher, to his pupils, while stirring again in them the same fruitless ambition.

19

THE AMATEUR AS
POSTERITY

Art is ritualistic in that it repeats itself, but our experience of art is not ritualistic; it grows, changes, and can be returned to in search of a renewed experience. What any rite binds, it condemns to spiritual death; what it renews, it revives to spiritual life.

The great force of art today is acting through a desire for spiritual revival, expressed first of all as liberation from the rule. In art as in spiritual renewal there is no forward; there can be only progress in the individual, his maturing. The distinction falls between the art object, as simulacrum of beauty, and the renewing experience.

No music can wear well under the pressure of practising it, but come to again and again, each time after an interval, it renews freshness.

My little niece, when she first visited in our house, would sit at the piano or the spinet harpsichord, instruments she did not know, and delight herself and delight us by laying her small hands on the keyboard to release moving sound. Moving—we think of the word as an emotional metaphor. The pleasure in listening to my little niece make music was to hear how under her fingers the unpremeditated, uncommitted sound could move. She played at the piano as a child fingerpaints. Then we praised her too often; she wakened to her tiny power and lost it. The sound became hard, clumsy, trying to be impressive: in a word, noise. She pounded the keys, and there was no music; it had ceased to

move. Trying to show off, she was no longer giving pleasure or
finding pleasure. Within a few days she had traveled the
virtuoso path from pleasure shared to staleness.

The arts throng in our kindergarten. Jaded teachers cannot
keep up with the flair of these awakened children. The children
do not yet appreciate; their art blooms in companionship. At
home, afterwards, they have their music lessons; they must practise alone, and in trying to obtain control they risk losing art.

The children know, better than we, that society is antagonistic
to these pursuits. When a little older, they will be sharply re-
minded that, if you can't make a career out of art, you had better
drop it. What is charming in the child, praiseworthy in the adolescent, is in the adult thought waste of time, eccentric. A com-
mon-sensible child, responding to the atmosphere around him,
refuses to practise in the first place. Parental discipline seldom
conquers: do the parents themselves want these things? Is music
celebrated in the family life?

Let a school allow time for playing instruments or singing, let
a family delight in making music, let a touch of leadership, not
argument, light on the child mind, let art in any form be accepted
as a measure of companionship, and the child will respond to it,
freely, without needing discipline—and the same is true among
the felons in our penitentiaries.

Yet in our society, which professes the highest regard for the
arts and their performance, for the presumably enlarged life,
adult concern for art is relegated to teachers, to society women,
to retired or affluent businessmen who can afford the indulgence,
and to students who are expected to repair the imbalance as soon
as they enter business.

"I can well imagine," writes the imaginary Hadrian of Margaret
Yourcenar, "forms of servitude worse than our own, because more
insidious, whether they transform men into stupid, complacent
machines, or whether to the exclusion of leisure and pleasures
essential to man they develop a passion for work as violent as the
passion for war among barbarous races."

"Our era is thus the first which poses civilization as a problem
—which asks itself, what is civilization?" André Malraux told a
Time interviewer. "That is a great adventure of the spirit."

The spirit has had many adventures, ventures in innumerable
directions, to innumerable goals and without goals—these last are

the more daring. Works of art are preserved artifacts, or trophies, of adventure. Adventurers do not travel for pay, though some may be well rewarded. The work of art is an aspiration realized, an achievement of daring: daring before it is achieved, daring and courageous in the achievement.

Adventures are solitary in the doing, but they begin and end in companionship—I am tempted to alter the word and write instead *compassion*. Where success is the incentive, compassion is scarcely possible, companionship becomes alienated. Competition for power or for prizes brings out the wrong incitement. We compete from ignorance, from lack of compassion, in despite of companionship.

"Poetry," R. P. Blackmur tells us, "is one of the things we do to our ignorance. . . . We have the interesting relationship that as we intensify individuation the society of individuals tends to disappear . . ." He is speaking in favor of a new type of intelligence, the *master layman,* who "is committed, not to the creation of experience but to the response to experience no matter what the experience is of, and no matter how far short of direct knowledge of the experience his sensibility might come. . . ."

Most of us who come to art are precious failures. We believe that we have tried and failed. We know what we like, or believe we do; if we teach it, we teach what we have ourselves been taught. We have the taste, usually an acquired taste, but no real appetite for the thing itself. We share, we appreciate; we do not turn to art to renew ourselves. Art comes to us easily, but it isn't natural to us.

One skill of the artist is to know how to be used. The true despair of an artist is not failure of ambition but failure so to adjust himself to the known and the unknown that he may be used—that he knows himself fully put to use. When he knows that, other reward is incidental to him. His skilled hand answers any argument. While the critic abuses him and the creditor denies him credit, posterity hangs over his shoulder waiting to applaud and purchase; but he works as if in God's presence.

Any form of art deserves the attention that it wins, but attention must be directed. We live in the first era of common, vulgar, nonaristocratic, nonaccredited *appreciation*. For us, art is no longer presented in public symbols of mystery and power. The symbols are private, and individual, and secret. We share, all potentially equal, the authority, formerly reserved to noble esthetes and their courtiers, to enjoy or to reject. But we are not sure that we know how to enjoy or what it is that we reject.

Most of us approach art, to begin with, ignorantly, following current habit. We don't try very hard, and after a while, growing self-conscious, we stop trying, pretending to ourselves that knowing about art is for specialists. So art is evaluated as if it were a public spectacle, and when we have anything to do with art we judge it not by what we bring to it but according to the entertainment we expect it to bring us. The big music operators see to it that we are seldom allowed on a program any item that might alert us that we are not being entertained. That makes the whole affair a bore, really, a respectable bore, from which we turn to speak about the personality of the performer, the quality of the playing or the sound of the orchestra, or other entertaining substitutes.

Many of us are aware that something more needs to be done about art or music than just taking it in. Art is beautiful, we think, and if we can find out what it is that makes art beautiful, then we shall be able to recognize the difference between what is genuinely beautiful and what isn't. You can't put a work together by dissecting all its parts. The taste of experts is just as fallible as the taste of any ordinary person. Appreciation of art grows less by accumulating information about it than by accustoming oneself to give it full attention—putting it to use.

For a number of years I have been exposing listeners to unexpected musical experiences. Almost without exception they respond to the unusual experience with either a downright "I don't like it" or a qualifying "It's not so good as"—something they know better. When an unfamiliar composer displays a sure sign of his unfamiliar "genius," the effect shocks, as if he had committed a public vulgarity or a moral error. Those trained listeners who might be thought to have the capacity to appreciate what is being done are quickest to condemn it.

In approaching any work of art that lies outside my habitual experience, I try starting where the other fellow usually leaves off. I keep going back to the work that has defeated me until I feel able to comprehend why it is what it is—instead of being what habit tells me it ought to be, which it is not. That is to say, I put complete attention first and only afterwards—and always provisionally—apply judgement. If the new work is large and of unusual scope, or small but of unusual concentration, I may have no more than a single opportunity to hear it. If I put judgement in place of attention, I may hear it incompletely.

Observe that this comprehension is esthetic, not intellectual. Many a bright person believes he can explain the *why* of a work of art he esthetically detests. Of course the *why*, the intellectual explanation, has been prejudiced by his dislike. To dislike a work of art is not to pass a final judgement on it; it may be as often a failure of adaptation. But mere adaptability, without severe resistance, signifies failure of attention. To love a work of art we must first recognize it as it is—not idealizing the vague symbol of perfection. If God has made man in His image, He has given us not a mirror to look into but the faces of men.

A work of art is not beautiful of itself but by the composition, the resolved oppositions, the balancing of counterthrusts, the intertwining of impossibles. In spite of this, the final effect, when the work of art is music, is not beauty until the ear has learned to follow it.

Some of us nowadays can hear a large share of the world's music, even the more complex, almost as simply as if it were a melody. This is not because the music has become any simpler than it ever was but because we have accustomed our listening to a quite extraordinary discriminative process. We recognize that the great composer's simplicity is not the ordinary listener's simplicity. We are continuing to discover that even more complex acoustical adjustments can be brought within the composer's grasp.

This simplicity is more than what many today define in outline as *form*. It is a guide and a consequent, the report of someone who has been elsewhere and come back. Form may be incorporated in a guidebook and become a rule of the road, but it is not law. Form establishes no moral responsibility.

My favorite Amateur, Roger North, writing about the year 1710, describes this communicable simplicity of music, which he terms *Ayre*, as "a sort of musick that seems to flow from Nature, one sound following another as if they were of a family, so as nothing occurs that occasions any one to say Why, or What means this? Every thing proper, and nothing fantasticall or in the least defective, but as the Thames, . . . still full but never over-flowing."

But in the same passage he continues: "I would willingly find a master that would give us a peice of musick intirely new; that is, without our comon formes of cadences and passages, which are to be found the same in all musicall compositions whatever. Of all the products of art in the world, musick pretends most to novelty and hath least. If they say it is confined by Nature, the bounds of which they cannot exceed, I ask why is there such a different caracter of musick in severall countrys, if there were not a possibility of variety, greater than appears in the musick of any one country. Why may not a man diversifie at home, as the neighbours are diversifyed from us?"

More than two centuries later Arnold Schoenberg wrote: "If we imagine that the perceptive faculties of audiences will advance nearly as far in the future as in these past years, then we must have faith that we shall achieve a true knowledge of the ideas presented today and an understanding of their beauty. The difficulty is to recognize and to feel in the dissonant polyphonic sounds the capacity to be joined successively; to see in them elements of form . . . and to feel also their relative measure of weight and significance just as in the older harmonies. Theoretical knowledge is not the most essential need. . . . Probably habit is all that is required; for it is able to prevent the recurrence of shock and the resulting lapse of presence of mind. He who is frightened is seldom in a position to follow exactly what is happening. Should such a one be accepted as a witness, or rather one who does not lose presence of mind?"

We think of posterity as making the important decisions, forgetting that we are posterity. We are those who have no reason to be frightened, who should not lose presence of mind. We have to learn to do by individual discriminative adjustment what the expert tries to do out of the book. That is not to say that we can slide along making judgements without effort or knowledge—just the opposite. We are accustoming ourselves to be aware of what is not yet in the book.

Experts try to make their rules compulsory and shove them down the throats of the succeeding generations, like a mother robin feeding her chicks regurgitated angleworms. The new creative generation, out of the uproar of its labors, cries back at the misdirecting critics: "Esthetic gossips! Spiritual scandalmongers! What can you know of the blood and dogma, the height and the humility of our forefathers! Come and live with us in our glory, as we live with them in theirs. Then in the muck, in the hazard, and most of all in the common failure, the ceaseless failing of creative effort, you may understand how art is moral and what creation means."

But the complacent critics, the sidewalk engineers, the satisfied whistlers who blow the same tunes over and over, stroll away hands in pockets. "Who"—they shrug—"is paying for the job?" Or someone asks: "What's it good for?" No answer to that question.

A good critic can't do much to help, except as he's been through that sort of country and knows the ground. There are no short cuts, though many are offered; these go around the foot of the mountain but they miss the view.

We amateurs can deserve as we can share art. By the individual artist, or amateur, the question is more pertinently stated: Is what I am doing worth while?

An Amateur
in the
Community

20

RELEASE

"But it is so unhappy that gentlemen, seeing and observing the performances of masters, are very desirous to doe the same; and finding the difficulty and the paines that is requisite to acquire it, are discouraged in the whole matter, and lay it aside . . ." (Roger North).

We have heard and read so much about faith that we are inclined to lump it with other theological concepts, using the word as it may please us and leaving any definition to the experts. Faith is reliance on being able to do in any case with what one has. In good fortune, such faith may be complacent, unable to meet disaster. In bad, it may be only a bare existential affirmation. On the naked limb of faith the believer may try to graft what potency of bud he wishes. While we often speak of faith, we seldom test it. Few of us have moved mountains, yet mountains are removed, more often by a person so concentrated on his object that the shifting of millennial inertia is complementary to his purpose. He may not see what he has done.

Dr. Suzuki quotes Ummon, a great "staff-wielder" of the tenth century: "Is there anything that will obstruct your way in any sense? Does your hearing do this? Does your sight do this? Where is the world of differentiation which you imagine to be obstructing your freedom? Where is the bondage you wish to escape from?

"If you tarry even for a moment you have already lost the trail."

Three times during my boyhood I went to a piano or an organ teacher and, defeating the teacher, defeated myself. Then, failing to make music after having learned to read it, I began enjoying the piano. For more years than I care to count, my fingers have been stumbling over the notes of Bach and Byrd and Mozart, Field and Bartók, Scarlatti and Telemann. I was playing Beethoven's *Diabelli Variations* before ever I had heard them performed. When I sit alone at the piano or harpsichord I can read, not gracefully but with fair ease, such music as the Couperin *Orders,* including all the indicated ornaments. I can even translate back, in many instances, the bungling written-out notation of some modern pedant into the originally intended embellishments. Yet if anyone comes near when I am playing, my fingers and mind go stiff. What skill I have developed in solitude leaves me at the first try in performance.

A while ago I talked over this situation with a friend and corresponded about it with a player of the older music whom I admire. The friend explained to me that such is the way of the world: I may never hope to be free of my impediment. The player of older music, who retains somewhat in defiance her amateur spirit, replied that whatever is most exquisitely arrived at in solitude may be lost or contorted in performance. This, each explained to me, is why performers must painstakingly practise, until the unpredictable has been worked out and thoroughly overcome.

I don't agree: the unpredictable is proof of the adventure in a great performance.

For all my lack of freedom, my incompetent dexterity, I resolved to free myself to read among friends some if not all of what I can play happily by myself, not to display it, but so that when the occasion arose I should not appear helpless. My method, for which I found guidance in such old practical modes as the techniques of Zen Buddhism and my successful experience with the Bates method of eye-training, would be to eliminate myself by forgetting my presence, to read directly from eyes to fingers by removing effort: not to try to play what I see before me but to play it. (Such lack of self-conscious inhibition is probably the way of child prodigies.)

I am able to report of my method that it will work. It is possible to play, as I have learned that it is possible to see, not by straining but by doing so.

The chief handicaps are misplaced emotion, the emotion which

is not feeling but self-feeling, not awareness but self-consciousness (of which I was born with generous measure); and trying
to do without first conceiving what is to be done—this makes for
stumbling.

Being knowledgeable about the interference caused by unnecessary emotion does not help me to be rid of it. As easy to
put off one's personality. A person well aware of the damaging
influence of his emotionality may at any one time be incapable
of correcting it. Anyone who has learned to use his eyes properly,
without glasses, knows that his vision will decrease with weariness or emotional disturbance. Emotional tension comes on like
weariness from the breaking of concentration, the checks of
tedium and irritation. Fully concentrated, one can work almost
indefinitely, unaware of exhaustion. At such times one is scarcely
sensible of emotion outside the object, or of distraction.

Emotion, like weeping at a sentimental movie, may be the result of intensified self-consciousness, the sort of feeling so many
people expect of art because it can reach them in no other manner.

A musical instrument need not be solely a medium of public
exhibition. A friend of mine carried his violin as companion
through the trenches of the First World War. A harmonica player,
barring the professional exhibitionist, plays as happily alone as
in a group. Of all instruments the keyboard is the best adapted to
complex musical experience. To enter fully into this experience
one needs no audience.

The external or listening experience can also to a degree become internal, until the listener forgets himself in listening, a
complete adaptation of the auditory-rhythmic capacity of the
body to the recording, articulating mind. Such listening does not
translate music into feeling, emotion, or analysis; in the largest
sense it takes the music in. The listener does not listen, notebook
in hand, as it were, but afterwards, returning to what he has
heard, restores to deliberate consciousness as much as he has
received. The ability, needless to say, grows with experience. My
past listening listens with me.

I am not so far from ignorance that I have forgotten my early
experience with extended music, when I received from it almost
nothing but the meaningless, interminable progression of sound.
My sympathy goes out to the willing, patient listener who has

not passed this stage of unawareness. He can only hang on by his ears, hoping to break through to attention. My hearing is not now more analytical, but I hear more completely and through dimensions of difference which shape variety of meaning.

I do not now more than at that time detach the first subject from the second in a sonata movement, unless a doctrinaire pattern forces this fact to my attention, nor welcome the return to the home key like a traveler in sight of his native threshold. Such recognitions break in, but when they do, it is less often a sign of triumph in the form than a mark of inadequacy in the presentation. In fugue one should not always mark the re-entry of the theme. If Beethoven had wished me to hear infallibly the famous false entrance of the horns in the first movement of the *Eroica Symphony*—which you read of in the books—he would have taken pains to ensure it; the little joke, like many pleasures of great style, is received unconsciously. Listening for it every time, I should miss more than I would gain.

The mind rejects what it does not comprehend; comprehension is the grasping of the whole. To hear music merely as patterned formula or to receive it only as emotion is not to hear it. Hence the faults charged by inadequate listeners against new music; hence the faults committed against new music by inadequate performance.

Inadequate listening waits on the shock when the communicative intention appears momentarily explicit. Much response to performance reacts crudely to no more than the way it has been brought off, the "big bang" which Richard Strauss recommended to the young Stravinsky as a sure means of making a hit with the crowd. Today many listeners who are too sophisticated to respond to the bang seek the same response in orchestral dexterity or instrumental tone, or in "know-how," pleasant enough in themselves but of slight musical significance. How many solemn listeners who know nothing of the piano or its literature will compliment a pianist for his "touch"! And there are those who marvel at the ability to play a large number of notes rapidly, cleanly, and correctly or to carry about in memory, as in a portmanteau, a big repertoire of standard concert pieces.

When you are too much concerned with formal details as things to be listened to, your mind may have been too blocked to hear the work itself. This is a common experience of critical listening: the expected obtrudes.

One needs to be able to listen to a great quantity of music in performance without engaging oneself in it, yet recognize at once that moment when the routine is transfigured into the exceptional. At such times everything becomes new; the organism reacts to the moment with a needle sharpness. But it is the past experience which listens, and if the past experience has been inadequate or routined, the present will be as inadequate and unable to go beyond knowledge of routine.

The listener who knows the bang he wants will wait for that bang.

Concentrated listening should stimulate expectation, which the work of art must satisfy at every moment. A work of art should balance in space, a conceptual metaphor like Brancusi's "Bird." But the fault of failure may not be in the work.

Art for art's sake is conspicuously practised by those who direct the argument to the crowd. The innate artist is unaware of any audience. He enters into difficulties with no thought of solving them outside his work.

Anyone enjoys watching the entertainer with a good routine. He has been doing the same act over and over; his timing and technique are second nature; when he goes up he has nowhere to go but down. It's always the esthetes of the next generation who discover the technical capacity and invent the legend of the genius-clown. He begins crudely enough. The entertainer who would go beyond his routine must go by the way of the artist, through no less danger, by giving up self-consciousness; until he may find his private life exploited as the converse of his release. Naïve, he may seem fool or villain to the crowd that wishes to adore his skill and will not let him alone. The entertainer is seldom a complete person; he licks the public which laps him.

Release is dangerous, and most of us who have at some time let ourselves go know that for any moment when we have given pleasure there may have been another when our action seemed peculiar or we were called "Ass!" for inadvertence. That is what the ordinary person fears who sits down to make music.

Opening the letters of Holmes to Pollock: "As long as one continues to write, the question is always of tomorrow and not of yesterday, and tomorrow may show what a fool one is."

The fear is common and not to be ashamed of; the shame is to succumb to it. To succumb is to be self-conscious, to feel that one's failure matters, and therefore to fail.

An alternative is to adopt the brazen armor of the performer. This can be done without talent; it destroys genuine talent as a vine destroys a tree. That temptation is thrust today on any artist who, however temporarily, succeeds. The armored talent wears his name as a knight his coat of arms, the face behind a vizard. In the glittering panoply of display he charges through concerto or aria, thinking only of his honor. And he relaxes in the adulation of courtiers and fair ladies. He is clumsy afoot, helpless on his back, and incapable in a strange country, if there is not a proper ground for his horse. Imitating inspiration, he paints a cross on his armor. The natural musician goes afoot by strange ways as a pilgrim.

Now for theory and practice: the human body may be regarded as a mechanism or as a self-functioning unit. If as a mechanism, it must be directed by intelligence or will, hiding somewhere around the premises, to perform mechanically as it is trained. You may object that a mechanism is not trained. The difference is that the mind and body are indissolubly linked. All of us have observed instances, beginning in ourselves, of mechanically well-trained bodies which break down because of some impediment in the linkage. This explains why a qualified instrumentalist may be incapable of showing to advantage in a solo performance. The mind, or intelligence, becoming aware of its situation before an audience, shuts itself apart and refuses to go along with the well-trained body in exhibiting its routine.

If the body is regarded as a self-functioning unit, a deliberate adjustment may be tried to release the will and allow the body-mind combination to work together, the eye seeing as it were directly to the hand, the hand carrying out what the eye sees without willful intervention.

One qualification is necessary: the music should be seen with full awareness.

When a painter using ink and brush in the Japanese tradition sets about to paint a landscape, he does not try to visualize or reproduce the landscape as he sees it, nor does his line follow the normal contour of the land. What he is to produce will be a single concentrated act of mind and hand in awareness of the landscape. Each stroke is final; there can be no overpainting, no sketching or filling in. The painting is a group of actions, each decisive, linked like the muscles of a forearm by a single act which is thought. Thus is preserved the tension, or balance—for in such conditions these are the same—so often lost, or distorted in Western abstract painting towards a violence of expressionism.

I read a fascinating little book about the Zen method of shooting with the bow and arrow. The bow, with a tension of ninety pounds, is parted by the arms extended straight above the head, not drawn from the shoulder as in Western archery. Not muscle but concentrated thought and breathing, detached from will, part the bow. Learning to part the bow, one thinks only of the act, not of the target; the released arrow finds its goal, not by aiming, but by the oneness of the entire action. This is archery as art, act of mind without effort, in purpose noncompetitive. Hitting the mark is not the object, as we should think it. The shooting may be a contest, but the competitors do not compete.

That is where most of us fail: we want the thing to happen to us, not out of us. We think less of doing than of being able to succeed. In the Bates eye-training the first flash of perfect vision without glasses, though it may last scarcely a second, is as miraculous as it is unexpected. The flash of vision proves that a perhaps lifelong defect of vision originates somewhere else than in the eyes themselves. You cannot argue the point, practically or metaphysically, with anyone who has had the faith to try it and found it happen.

Actually, it doesn't matter, so long as one has the idea of it.

This is of course the true meaning of the word "inspiration," the drawing in of breath, followed by release. It is one intention of art, now grievously lost sight of in our age of educated repetition. Two opposites prevail: the resolute confrontation of an outward audience, which awards success; and the inward awareness which in its own moment, like a breath, may be freshened and released.

Place a piece of music before you which you know well. Do not try to guide the fingers or the mind; see and hear the notes you wish to play and release the hand to play them. The measure of your success will be the measure of your release. You cannot have the release by wishing the success. Errors indicate either false visualization, very easy when one is strained or anxious, or failure of detachment in concentration, that is, in release.

When you begin to get the idea, you may forget the preliminary visualization and all the rest of it. Because when you sit down to play you know what you are going to play, as you wish it; that you are playing for yourself; that to do so will require a preliminary warm-up; and when the warm-up starts you will already be anticipating the pleasure lying ahead.

At this point you may wish to reinstate a methodology of practice, thirds, sixths, and octaves, all the Czerny business, as remorselessly as if you had never sought release.

Let us instead recognize and reassert our amateur status. The hand is quick as the eye and will move as rapidly and accurately, if we are reasonable in our expectations. Not the finger but the effort is at fault.

The hand will interpret the music as we comprehend it, and the more exactly as the comprehension is our own. We shall not expect to play a piece as we have heard a master perform it. This is a common cause of failing, very common in would-be artists. They measure a success by lack of failing, whereas success is giving as much as one can give.

Released, we must search as assiduously for good expression as if we practised a single passage all day long. But the search has been transferred from will to comprehension. We try to play not like the master but like ourselves, to the best of our ability. A wrong note is of no more intrinsic importance than a misprint on a page. The art, as much as we have of it, is our own. The listener, if there is one, must wait upon us.

We shall never play better than we are able, but we shall not, as many facile talents do, fake the virtuoso. We shall not borrow a pattern to be followed like a dogma. We shall have to seek and seeking find, in our degree, an understanding of music more flexible than pattern, the same comprehension that both Josef Hofmann and Artur Schnabel implied when, being asked in their maturity how they practised, each answered: "In my head."

That is why I maintain a wide repertoire of reading at the keyboard, and especially in the older music, where I must seek out the interpretation for myself. The older keyboard music was intended to be read in just this fashion, to be interpreted afresh by the player at each time of reading.

As for fingering, a touchy problem that goes back to the earliest writings about keyboard music, let it be guided by anticipation but begin in the hand. The hand, being a natural instrument, will seek out the fingering that suits it best. Insofar as we hold securely in awareness the musical design we wish to make, our fingers will contrive to let the music sound that way, possibly not to the extent that we desire, but sufficiently. Think the manner of playing with the sounding of the phrase. The better we know the music, the better, with concentration, we shall play it. Precisely as we are able to release ourselves to make music in the full enjoyment of it, we shall find ourselves released to play it.

We are not performing, we are reading; we are enjoying the experience of sounding music. The *summum bonum* of faith is faith; not more faith, or better faith, or better faith than that of someone else, but as much as we have, which is sufficient.

In each mind there is a gift, which used can be enough to live with; enough, released, detached in concentration, to appear genius; enough, accepted, to counterpoise the wastage and the emptiness of grief; enough that, by it, sorrow may become fruitful through release.

Patience—not will but starting now can do the job for you.

"If you tarry even a moment, you have already lost the trail."

21

ACCOMPANYING,
CHAMBER MUSIC,
AND FOUR HANDS

"The solitary hath two intents: first, practise, in order to acquire a dexterity or perfection in the use of certein favorite instruments, and nothing more conducing; but on the other side, respecting time, and application to consort, as much disabling. For the most exquisite solitary practiser coming into consort is enervous, and at a loss how to goe on; for he is not used to comand his pace, and to act with complyance. And besides his time is corrupted, for no one, in the exercise of difficultys, or when his private satisfaction in what he doth is unequall, can keep an equall measure of time long together; but at hard places he will retard, and getting the better, goe too fast, and so also when he is better pleased. And when he comes to consort, these failings, unthought of alone, will shew themselves grosly, and spoyle all. Therefore solitary practise is good to make a hand, but it corrupts consort; and in general no practise is profitable to all purposes, but onely in consort." (Roger North on *Solitary Musick*)

Each true Amateur should seek to let his musical interest or skill serve the community, without egotistic self-display.

I am a solitary musician, subject to all the faults described by Roger North. My service to the community has come through making programs and getting them performed or broadcasting them, and in writing and lecturing about music.

Another service, of which the community may be more often in need, is accompanying at the piano or organ.

A good accompanist must be able to count. This counts me out. I can count, but under any stress I don't count accurately. Given practice and experience I might overcome these disabilities; those few who have tried to play joint music with me have never encouraged me to go on.

An amateur accompanist may be especially useful in a small or middling-size community, where the few professional pianists are fully occupied, with little time to lend their services freely to singers, instrumentalists, or choral groups who cannot get along without a competent pair of hands to keep things moving at the keyboard. A moderately well skilled pianist or organist can help bring along a singer or solo instrumentalist, a chorus or a choir, by unobtrusive means which provide the inward self-satisfaction of good workmanship.

A good accompanist must (a) keep time, and (b) enable the soloist to be free of it. To keep time, the accompanist must make sure that the principal notes of the piece are sounded always at exactly the right place. Between these principal accents the accompanist will distribute the remaining notes so that they either hurry things forward ever so little, if the soloist is lagging, or hold them up ever so slightly, if the soloist is running ahead. This is not too easily managed, but expert accompanists do it all the time as a matter of course.

The accompanist should know the acompaniment at least as well as the soloist knows the solo, and since the greater part of accompanied music is more difficult in the accompaniment than in the solo part, a good accompanist will have to be a good musician as well. He should be a more competent sight-reader than any soloist is expected to be.

If in spite of such help the soloist does not slow down, the accompanist may have to swallow a couple of notes and reach the next principal note when the soloist arrives. If the soloist will not speed up, the accompanist may have to throw away a principal accent and then bear down hard on succeeding subsidiary accents, in the hope that the soloist will more or less unconsciously get the point.

Ordinarily the accompanist sets the pace of the music at the start and adjusts it throughout. To do this as the music requires will need tact, sometimes flattery. An accompanist should never argue with the soloist; argument destroys rapport and threatens the soloist's necessary confidence, of which there may be no surplus. A good accompanist learns many other ways of getting things done as they should be, without argument.

The accompanist should be prepared to help the soloist make up his mind about anything to do with performance, including dress or deportment; he should even be prepared to choose the music to be performed—this again needs tact. To show the soloist to best advantage he will study to display the soloist's accomplishments, such as they may be. A well-trained, well-behaved, musicianly, and properly self-assertive soloist is a credit to his accompanist. The accompanist should avoid crushing the vanity of the soloist, however often he corrects him.

An accompanist should expect to receive no more credit for a well-managed soloist than a second violinist receives for controlling the rhythm and balance of a string quartet. Accompanists and second violinists are among the most valuable and the least praised of musicians. A violinist may have good professional reasons for not playing a second part, but not good musicianly reasons.

Soloists are not expected to listen to accompanists, but a good accompanist can often make one do so. Accompanists must always listen to the soloist, even if in pain. A soloist not too set in his ways can usually be brought into line by an experienced accompanist; not even the most experienced accompanist can do anything to correct or help a soloist who has become set in bad habits.

A violinist friend of mine used to play as concertmistress for a wealthy conductor who maintained an orchestra so that he could beat a stick over it in public while trying to follow the music in his score. It was interesting to watch how she would keep the orchestra together, in spite of the conductor, by unobtrusive signals to the other leaders of the various sections of the orchestra, so that a clean performance would result and the conductor could follow the music with his stick.

One evening the orchestra had as soloist a famous elderly violinist no less untimely than the conductor. My friend and her associates had to keep the orchestra balanced together in such a way that neither the soloist, who knew nothing but his solo, nor the conductor would be too separate. Such a skill is accompanying raised to a high art.

This same violinist is the only one I have ever heard who, in playing a Mozart violin sonata, could defer to the pianist. She did not, that is, expect the pianist to perform the major part of the sonata as if it were no more than an accompaniment to the violin; instead, she kept her solo part where it belonged, within the larger scope of the pianist.

These are the skills a true Amateur should learn to detect and admire more than the display dexterity of soloists.

▶ Readers of this book may have been given to suspect that I have little or no use for professional musicians. Far from it! I have known, admired, honored, and worked with professional musicians by the hundred. Without competent professional musicians, no music, not even tribal or ethnic music, can exist. To recognize certain common bad habits of the professional musician, in his various phases as composer, performer, thinker, repository of convention, and less-than-competent historian (the professional musician *appreciates* musical history more naïvely than many a callow amateur and unless carefully brought around to it shares the most reactionary suspicions of anything new in his line), is not to disallow his extraordinary gifts in making music come alive. No one in the audience can shout a louder *Bravo!* than I do when this happens. I have worked for the benefit of musicians during my adult life and have never lost my trusting affection for them. When we are not criticizing them, which is our privilege, we amateurs are to be found exchanging superlatives in admiration of them. But however much or often we may lose our hearts to them, we must never lose our heads.

In all instrumental sonatas the keyboard part contains a larger portion of the music than the solo. A good accompanist will insist on having the music heard as a whole, but must do this without disturbing the ego or upsetting the aplomb of the soloist, who is seldom aware of the significance of this fact. To do this, the accompanist should not play more loudly but better, at once more accurately and more freely, so that the listener's hearing is diverted, while his conscious attention is not diverted, from the more noticeable goings-on of the soloist. Such an accompanist can often make a routine soloist seem to be a good one. For this reason an expert accompanist is in constant demand.

A solo pianist unused to accompanying will at the start embroil himself with the soloist by playing his part so that it is equally well heard: this is known as "covering the soloist." Intimidated, he will then reduce his tone to so slavish a level that the music loses all character; and the failure will be charged against the soloist, who will not understand why.

The rules for playing chamber music at the piano are not essentially different from those for accompanying. The pianist hardens his character against snubs from the other instrumentalists, and, if he is strong-minded, turns the group into something that is not quite a miniature piano concerto among equals. If he cannot do this, he must function expertly, or as expertly as possible, as accompanist to the group, treasuring his solos as much as any second violinist.

No chamber musician except the pianist really enjoys having a piano take part in chamber music, because the piano is the one instrument which is always in tune. *Intonation,* on a string instrument, signifies playing the exact pitches of the notes; but it signifies also playing each tone slightly above or below its exact pitch for the sake of the combining harmony with other instruments, especially in chamber music, and for the shapeliness of the melodic line. (But refer to the contrary opinion of Rudolf Kolisch, p. 93.) *Correct* intonation is therefore one of the self-canceling contradictions dear to the hearts of professional musicians, whose faith in their ability to discern the exact right of them never ceases. It is as ingrained and infallible as their belief that a conductor either has or has not "a Brahms style." Composers, who apart from such exceptions as Berlioz and Schoenberg are usually happiest at the keyboard, though aware of the imbalance between fixed and flexible intonation, have seen to it that there shall be duos, trios, quartets, quintets, and still larger combinations with piano, to include themselves.

Song-accompanying differs from instrumental accompanying in the fact that from the beginning of accompanied song and choral writing the vocal part, in the nature of the human instrument, has had first place. From the polyphonically accompanied songs by Luis Milan and John Dowland to the German *Lieder* and the songs of Debussy and Charles Ives, the keyboard part, however interesting in itself, has yielded primacy to the voice. To play songs at the piano is an art more specialized than instrumental accompanying; it must be learned in the company of singers.

A small voice, well managed, may enhance the accompaniment by singing within instead of in front of it. Anyone who believes that the art of singing begins in the enlargement of the voice is not well informed. Esthetic like athletic skill depends more upon art than upon the cultivation of muscles. A very large voice may be advantageous for Wagner but not for Purcell. Some of the most beautiful voices, of which Handel or Mozart would have taken advantage, are nowadays lost because of the vast spaces of concert halls and opera houses.

Choral accompanying, whether with a secular group or in church, requires of the accompanist a firm hand, decisive rhythmic control, and ability to emphasize the beat without beating it. I am told, not having tried it myself, that rhythmic control of group singing can best be managed by use of rhythmic accentuation, distributing the unaccented tones or subordinate accents in such a way that they either hurry forward or retard the pace between major accents.

These skills can be only hinted at. Practice of them, experiment with them, carefully observing their consequences, can very much enhance the pleasure of group singing, for the singers as well as the accompanist.

A good accompanist will be, or should be, among the more intelligent of musicians, less limited in scope than he appears in his subordinate place. If he is not or is unable to become so, the accompanist will degenerate to a time-beater.

▶ As for appreciation of the accompanist by the soloist—I saw recently a full-page advertisement, with adulation, of an album of the complete violin sonatas of Beethoven in performance by a famous violin soloist; the names of the recording company officials who officiated were also displayed, but not the name of the accompanist. One ventures to believe that in the superhuman presence of this violinist the piano

16

plays itself. Indeed, violinists generally fail to observe that Beethoven inscribed these sonatas "for keyboard and violin."

The prevalence of time-beating upon the recital stage explains the proficiency—resulting from a deficiency of musical attention—of the two-piano team. Composers have been chary of writing for two pianos, though to do so is convenient, because they know how difficult it is for two pianists to accompany or keep time with one another and not dwell too heavily on the beat. Because of the sparse literature, two-piano teams soon overlearn their routine and drum it out as if paying no attention. Good two-piano playing is possible, because I have heard it, but uncommon.

Mozart and Schubert wrote some of their most attractive music for four hands at a single keyboard; this more intimate art the two-piano teams seldom attempt. The present-day two-piano team insists that the instruments should be identical—which was probably uncommon in earlier times—and the styles of playing indistinguishable: two keyboards, two soundboards, two sets of strings beaten by four hands in a civilized inflexibility that would appall a savage at a tom-tom. The attempt to create orchestras of pianos has, fortunately, not succeeded.

Because I am an unregenerate solo sight-reader married to a pianist who disposes with skill of the Beethoven *Diabelli Variations* and the Ives *Concord Sonata*, I have never been able to enjoy the essentially domestic art of playing four-hands at a single keyboard. I have been invited to do so often enough, but the disparity unmans me. Recently my wife cut from *The New York Times* a column by the critic Harold C. Schonberg about the pleasures of playing duet at a single piano. Because he has so evidently enjoyed to the full a pleasure my inhibitions have denied me, I have obtained his permission to reproduce what he has written.

"For the large part, duet playing has been confined to amateurs. And, for the amateur, there is nothing like it.

"Duet playing is the most innocent and the most personalized way of making music. It follows a formalized pattern, like that of two cronies meeting weekly over their chess board, being intimate, leisurely and faintly Victorian. Almost, but not quite, it suggests ruffles and old lace, big chandeliers and massive up-rights.

"Had not Charles Lamb despised music he would have written another Old China essay about its joys. Nowhere can one dupli-cate the unique mixture of participation and general well being that surrounds four busy hands playing Mozart.

"Only old friends really get the most out of piano duets, and then only when no audience is present. Strangers generally come out poorly. They eye each other with the bristling suspicion of dogs meeting by chance. Complications ensue. But old friends are informal, like the music they play. Old duettists caress lov-ingly their tattered editions of Bach fugues, bound in heavy leather, carefully fingered, stained and creased at the lower right by many a hasty thumb. They make mistakes; they are not vir-tuosos; perfect performances are not for them—and little do they care. They realize their shortcomings but defer to none in their mellow love for music. Humble in their approach, they inherit the kingdom.

"Well it is that duettists perform in private. Although their hearts are pure, the music sometimes suffers. So do bodies. Feet engage in subterranean war about the pedals. Fingers tangle (blood is sometimes drawn by a jabbing fingernail) and piano benches, buckling under double weight, seldom have the capacity to sustain comfortably two earnest rears. One partner in the course of events generally drops behind, protesting that the other is forging ahead. A muttered one and two and three plays a verbal harmonization. There are knit brows and occasional halts, quiet oaths, hurt glances and much counting of measures.

"But always the last fortissimo chord is struck in unison and two beaming faces assure each other that after all it wasn't *too* bad. Then on to a fresh piece, both players vowing that each is reading at sight and each knowing that the other is, if not exactly lying, not exactly truthful either.

"One does not have to be an especially good pianist to play duets, which vary from elementary arrangements to real finger twisters. There has been a literature for piano duet ever since the Elizabethan composer Thomas Tomkins interested himself in the form. Mozart, Schubert, Schumann, Dvořák, Brahms, Mosz-kowski, Ravel, Poulenc, Hindemith—these are some of the com-posers who have contributed original music to the four-hand repertory. Except for those pieces composed expressly for the medium, textual adherence is not the most important thing, since most of the literature is in the form of arrangements. Many of us grew up learning the Haydn symphonies, Mozart chamber music and Beethoven overtures through duet arrangements. Consequently, what if a measure is slid over, or a passage is sloppy? Things can always be readjusted, and in the meantime the pair has the pleasure of recreating music they heard in the concert hall.

"Virtually the entire classic and romantic repertory has been arranged in duet form, plus a good percentage of the moderns. In the days before radio and phonograph, the duet was one of the primary ways of introducing new works to the music lover, and few scores would be published without an accompanying four-hand edition. . . ."

I thank Harold Schonberg, who from behind the frowning countenance of a major contemporary music critic has contributed this testimonial to the spirit of a true Amateur.

22

PROGRAMMING

An amateur will be sometimes a program-maker, either by engaging in local concert and recital activities or by no more than playing from a collection of records. A well-made program is a composition giving reward beyond the individual content of the music; everything reacts with or against everything else.

A well-made program grows from living literature, is selected as carefully as a rose gardener cuts blooms, for the sake of the bush as well as the bouquet. Your hothouse commercial grower forces the blooms until all are alike, beautiful and characterless. A sufficient program can have one bloom, a preparation and an afterthought. The first is received with pleasure in anticipation, the last with satisfaction after what has passed. A program can drive forward; it can linger from the beginning. Or it can be all masterpieces and too much.

A good program shows on its shining face of pleasure why it has been put together and the special enjoyment to be looked for in hearing it. A good program has shape, design, contrast; like a well-made composition, it has texture and it moves.

A well-made program does not promise that it will be well played, but the presumption is in its favor. It can be less well performed than it deserves, yet hold the audience to attention by the interplay of its design. Such a program will sometimes bring its audience to so great concentration that, if it is being played live, the musicians will be stirred to surpass themselves. When you have made a program do that, you are a craftsman of the guild; when you can predict it, you are a master.

Programs which are not well made defeat the best that is in

them and call undue attention to their weakest members. That is the common fate of those new music programs so often dumped before an audience like coal down a chute. Nobody wants to hear a program that offers itself without references. The ear needs something it can begin with and something it can return to. But there is a special effect, worth trying for, that begins in strangeness and leads on through strangeness. Such a program, successfully achieved, delights the craftsman and rewards the master.

The best program may not seem the best when it is being heard; the listener, remembering, returns to it as to a divide in awareness.

Good performance may be the wrong consideration. Can you imagine how the Ninth Symphony must have sounded that night when Beethoven, post deaf, conducted it for the first time in Vienna and had to be turned around to see the audience cheering and weeping!

A program should be made for the audience but not directed to it. Some put together for a program whatever they believe will draw an audience. This is a little different in theory and vastly different in practice from choosing what an audience may wish to hear.

The program-maker who sets himself above the audience cannot help but condescend. His condescension is cheap, and so is his programming. Being so cut off, he is incapable of the common sensibility which is the source of any good programming. He tells the audience, This is what you should hear, though he may like it no better; or, This is good enough for you—a sure sign that his own taste is no better. To know a large quantity of music is not necessarily to have good taste. Learned opinion may be as often wrong as right. Historically it is more often wrong; it cultivates the current fashion as assiduously as it presumes judgement concerning masterpieces of the past, that past when a similar intelligence would have been denying the same masterpieces on similar false assumptions.

An audience is what we make it. It reflects not so much our judgement of music as our taste for it. A conscientious program-maker listens to his audience and is rewarded to the degree that he hears his audience listening. If he knows his business he can anticipate, with some error and occasional amazement, how his audience will respond. His programming persuades the audience to seek the music. He will know that the masterpiece thrives only in a proper setting. To furnish that setting, out of the widest ranges of music, is his proper business.

The well-intentioned program-maker cannot afford to forget the audience or curse it for its inadequacy. To bring the audience to the music—within reach of it—is his business. The skill here, as in all art, is to make something fresh, to begin with showmanship not at the box office, to balance the unexpected against the known. What is well known will be heard in a freshness of remembrance when it is returned to out of something less well known. We observe this in any gathering of paintings, where the well-remembered springs before our vision like a living presence, an acquaintance among strangers.

Before music as before his audience the shrewd program-maker will be humble. He will temper his sophistication, knowing that in any audience someone may be hearing a familiar classic for the first time. The public, always changing, will not temper its experience to his maturity.

Ideally, each type of programming has been designed for a certain place and method of performance. A concert or recital may be presented in a church, in a hall with high or low ceilings, in a room with or without acoustics, or in the open air. Any one of these may be the best available place for the occasion. Each of these conditions will alter the validity of the programming. There is no best performance; there is only, given the conditions, the best possible performance.

Some record-collectors believe that the only tolerable performance is one made up of selected, preserved masterpieces, in transcendent readings, reproduced on their equipment. If this were true, the newer records, made without interruption and more accurately reproduced, would surpass any made by the older, agonizing procedure of fragmented playing and stops. We know this is not so.

If the program-maker aims at uplifting his audience, he will be well advised not to aim at it too directly. The word "uplift" is dangerous, implying moral rather than esthetic decisions or the sentimental affirmation which, besides entertainment, is the most that perhaps a majority of listeners expects to borrow from good music. The belief that a worthy subject can exploit any means is as fallacious as the belief that pure form can substitute for content.

Morality and ethical affirmation or tragedy are characteristics of much great art, being a common ground of understanding but not essential to it. Comedy is the scarcest and the best release. Art rests upon the indigenous ethos of its culture, against which it eternally protests. When it no longer protests, it becomes either traditional or ritualistic, esthetic convention or moral habit, stabilizing but incompetent to modify experience. Enlarging dimensions of experience are the utmost reward of participation in art, not to be arrived at by short cuts nor denied by extraneous moral or ethical considerations. In spite of cynicism, most of us do recognize the pre-eminence of the moral-ethical response and the art that not only calls it forth but qualifies it.

An audience pays to be amused, but it wishes to be released out of its condition as an audience. An audience comes together like a mob, vaguely intending the execution of some project; the program-maker makes the occasion urgent. Each listener feels that he alone is listening; this individual reaction is relieved of self-consciousness by the group reaction: *I alone feel this, but I do not feel it alone.* The group response imparts new dimensions to the individual response.

A program is the measure of the taste that makes it. Bad programming, though not always avoidable, should not, except in knowledge of the particular circumstances, be forgiven. Making a bad program, you have lost the chance to make a good one.

A program-maker needs both guile and craft, if he is to maintain standards of programming which will arouse an audience to seek what he is offering instead of continuing to attend by habit. A certain number of lesser pieces can be thrown away each season for the sake of the others—masking, as it were, to direct the attention. To throw away a piece in this manner is not always to lose it; the reaction may work both ways.

When you insert unusual effect or unfamiliar composing into a program, place it in such a way that the listener is not fully aware of the unlikeness as something he must automatically resist. An audience can rise to the most unusual or demanding music in an enthusiasm that grows with its increasing sensation of release. Such events trigger the mutations by which yesterday's oddity becomes tomorrow's symbol of genius. Genius is a type of revelation, both in the person who realizes it within himself as content and in the public world that will eventually receive it.

For every miracle of unexpected realization there will be error, failure, boredom, acute discomfort. Yet once the nonprofessional, naïve public has been encouraged to seek the unexpected good, by occasionally and delightedly finding it, they will leap often beyond the acute professional discernment. Their adventure of discovery—or rejection—contributes a new personality, an unpredictable excitement, to the routine of concert attendance. Incompetent admirations will be sloughed off.

Guile and craft do not connote virtue; from fair beginnings they can degenerate into a self-admiring smartness. It is well to have some impersonal standards and the conscientiousness to admit when one falls short of them.

Why is a program made? What is its purpose? What is to be accomplished by it? How shall it be arranged to reveal the utmost there is in it? What is that utmost? What are the physical and acoustical limitations imposed by the setting, and how are these to be used to advantage or their disadvantages overcome? These questions should be answered separately for every program. To give cynical answers and believe them is to be self-condemned.

Examples of good programming! I can offer examples; I have my secret spells, my alchemical formulae. But spells and formulae, however precisely rendered, will not summon up good programming. Any example, and formula, like a musical theme, is only as good as the taste and skill which uses it. No program-maker, however self-satisfied, is good enough to be as good as he might be. No audience is so weary that it cannot be stirred, startled, irritated, inspired to the renewal of attention that makes musical performance glorious.

23

THE CRITICAL
FUNCTION

The function of the critic is to make evident that works of art exist. It is a publicizing, propagandistic, journalistic, but enjoying function. Lacking enjoyment, it is lifeless.

If the critic is expert enough, he may raise the making evident to such a level of expressiveness that his words are themselves work of art. In this service explanation and poetry both have a share. By its enthusiastic concentration, its attention to the evocative detail, the criticism should of itself demonstrate art. Criticism may become an art but cannot replace art.

The living literature of music does not consist of so many scores taken from a shelf. The living literature is the music we make, cherish, bring fresh alive. Living art is a garden that changes fruit and season with new generations. Much withers. Some dies. A great part will go dormant.

One thinks of posterity as not being born yet or no more than in the cradle. The fact is, we are ourselves posterity. As critics of performance, we are, as we customarily think ourselves to be, posterity of an age gone by. As critics of music composed in our time, we have to learn how to become posterity.

Critical listening, rightly used, corrects what is too often misrepresented by the term *communication*. We should not expect the composer to communicate with us in our language but in his; technically, conceptually, emotionally, we must tune our receptors to his channel.

The critical listener trains his attention to receive what is in the music, to shape for his own understanding what may be thought of as its meaning, and to transmit this improved comprehension both to others and back into the music. Critical listening is a constant exchange, until we have used up, to the limit of our capacity, all that the work of art is able to bring us. By active criticism we enable ourselves to comprehend *beauty*, nowadays an unfashionable word.

Beauty consists in the relationships among events that occur in the presence of the human mind: through its sensibilities, which are passive; by its active ability to think. The relationships may be deliberate or accidental, or by wear or growth, positive, negative, determinate or indeterminate, measurable or incommensurable, fortuitous by suggestion, symbolic or without meaning, or contradictory, or mixed.

Except through the attention of a human being, there is no beauty, though the elements of beauty may be present. Beauty is therefore also the result of a spiritual attentiveness. We study, we train, we discipline ourselves to concentrate the attention beauty requires of us.

No matter how good a performance or how great the composition, the listener must recognize and compose with *his* mind all that he is able to make of the opportunities that are given him. A few years ago only the exceptional listener could hear any work by Béla Bartók and make a composition of it. Today that is a common privilege.

When an unknown composer places his wares before you, by means of a performance, it is you, not he, who must compose the composition. The performers may help or they may hinder you in doing so; as you grow more skilled you will be able in some degree to discriminate the work itself from the differences in performance.

Keep in mind, however, that there is no such thing, in sound, as the absolute work itself apart from any performance. There is only the remembered composition that each individual, in his own re-creative response, has tentatively composed and is able to call up by recollection. The score is only a design to be realized in performance. The critic, at least in part, criticizes his own re-creative capacity—himself.

What does the composer do? Or what has he done? Quite simply, he composes his composition and recomposes it, until, in his opinion, it is successfully composed. Whatever rules, or forms, or habits, or conventions he may borrow to compose it are no more than a convenience. He so orders events that some of us, eventually, or perhaps too easily, will be able by hearing it to recompose his composition. The composition, as it becomes final, has its own built-in resistance, which the composer dare not violate or alter and the listener must learn to recognize. Then the composition is not his only but ours; and then recomposing that same composition again and again becomes a habit. This habit, often enough asserted, enters into what is called tradition.

For a great many listeners the reassurance of their habitual expectation, with perhaps a nuance of difference to be noted in the individual performance, grows to be a comfort to them which replaces the challenge of art. Or the stylistic individuality of a great performer may command, by the attraction or the assurance of its deviation, the critical responses of a great majority of listeners in its generation. Wanda Landowska imposed the anachronistic sixteen-foot stop upon the modern harpsichord by the eloquent and assured deviation of her usage.

When we listen critically, we need to be constantly challenging the habit of expectation in ourselves, so that we can return with renewed attention to what is actually happening: the composition occurring in sound and the manner of performance.

We think of our habit of recomposing the same composition over and over again as if that were the art of music. It is not. The art of music is in seeking the composition. The composer sought it first, with greater trouble and more delight than we can know. The performer has sought it again, to bring a realization of it to performance. When he has prepared the performance so well, through many repetitions, that he stops seeking the composition when he plays it, the art dies.

Sharing in and searching attentively through this double experience of composer and performer, the listener also seeks the composition.

Public criticism is concerned with the responses and discoveries of the critic. If the critical listener has listened well, his responses and discoveries may become useful evaluations for others with whom he shares his experience. Between spontaneity and care for an evocative language he will seek an expressive means, through which to convey to others the work of his liberating critical attentiveness.

The first duty of any critic is to learn how to praise; it should be his pleasure, for by that means he conveys delight to others. The second duty is to describe, accurately and concisely, what he has observed. Description should be the body of his art and message. The third duty is to explain; this is supplemental and cannot succeed if he is unable to praise for the right reasons and describe what has happened. The least, but on occasion the most salutary, of his duties is to condemn. He may be his own victim.

Bad criticism is usually no more than an opinion; the work isn't what the critic thought it might or should or ought to be. Blind criticism blinds the vision of others who might enjoy what the artist is doing, if they were encouraged or left free to enjoy it. Bad criticism puffs itself with catchwords about everything else except what the creative artist has actually done in each instance. Bad criticism is lazy; it appeals to the ignorance and false prejudices of those who respond to it.

If the critical amateur will begin his response to a work of art by speaking of it as well as he is able in his own language, he has gone already a long way towards saying what he means. If he borrows words from others, he may lose what he himself believes. In criticism too much information can be treacherous; it tells the wrong things, offers the wrong facts. The more information a critic has, the more careful he should be in applying his information to the particular event. Learn to describe accurately, so that you may learn to perceive. Sharpen the general explanation to the individual content.

Yet the range of elaboration, the reach of comparison and contrast, the authority of the critic in putting to use all he knows and has experienced, his ability to generalize upon sufficient content, and not least his skill in speaking or writing, distinguish the work of a true critic from that of the critical reporter, the appreciator, the explainer. Criticism can be work of art.

When you believe that a work fails or is badly composed, say so. Say why. Don't escape into a generalization. Be wrong as grandly as you please, but do not be indifferent. Try not to rationalize indifference; better to be silent. If you have traveled farther than the composer, remember that he hasn't come there yet. Out of your greater knowledge speak his language, but not to condescend. The informed traveler knows and enjoys where he has been; a snob boasts of it. Wherever the artist is may seem an absolute in the development of art, for him. Or it may be that while you are presuming upon a trip to Europe, he is already at the antipodes. If the artist has gone farther than you, don't expect him to wait for you to catch up. The artist owes you nothing. Chase after him with all the critical energy you have. It's pitiful to stop and stay where you are, grumbling and cursing the artist who has left you behind.

Beware of critical "idealism," which is putting yourself, idealized, in place of the artist. Many a critic believes he stands upon a foursquare image: it is the track of himself chasing himself around the block where he lives.

If you compare, be relevant. "It's not so good as" speaks for a lazy response. "Better than" is a short cut. Enthusiasm will often take a short cut. Be careful that condemnation doesn't. Be merciful; but when you shoot to kill, take exact aim.

Save your best energy for praising, and praise at the top of your skill. Distinguish with distinction. Choose words carefully, but when words spill out, let them. Spontaneity can outreach reason. If a work of art touches you, speak for it from your heart. If tears come, shed them. Keep clearly in mind, however, that your emotionality is not a criterion of the work of art.

Fight for what you believe. Don't be afraid. The more effectively you release your feelings, the more you will share them. A critic will be no better than a gossip if he can't blow up a spark of the creative fire. Share with others your own vision of the creative miracle, and remember that it never ceases. The adequacy of your responses will prove to others that works of art exist.

The critic is responsible, himself personally, for the esthetic life of the community. Among the audience he is a leader, by attention, by responsive presence. To impose his will upon art in the community is vain. He must work with and through others, lead, persuade, stand upon his integrity but not so rigidly as a statue. "Pull down thy vanity." Be wise; know when to yield, and never cease to try again.

The esthetic spirit is a part of the religious spirit, to be cultivated, not to be allowed to degenerate into hedonism, pleasure-seeking, diversion, or an amused indifference. When there is no spiritual core, no culture that speaks to a man in his own language, he becomes like a primitive tribesman who has been deprived of his tribal gods: his civilization ceases. To convey this awareness to others, you will have to realize it for yourself. At the least, a community needs to keep up its esthetic morale, as it keeps up its public services. The esthetic spirit can be hidden and rapidly lost behind a screen of cultural pretensions. Don't be satisfied that the ritual presence of art in the community signifies esthetic health. How many in the community, at all social and financial levels, are actually using it? How widespread is the conscious need of art, the esthetic literacy?

The control of public art is foul with power politics, evasion, cruelty, dishonesty, deception. Simple forthrightness may compel you to emulate a St. George willy-nilly, though you feel a self-conscious Don Quixote. But just at this very moment of high virtue, recall to yourself that painting of Adolf Hitler as virtue on a white horse, his bare head sticking out above plate armor, bearing on a lance the banner of St. George. Restrain your immodesty with humor. Thoughtless sincerity can be heartless. Your well-aimed barb may be poisoned and, unknown to you, destroy a living spirit.

Forgive failure, as in your own failing you will need forgiveness. Rereading what I have written here, I remember my own guilt.

24

AN AMATEUR IN THE
COMMUNITY

To round out his experience—or sometimes to begin it—an Amateur should seek his place in the communal music.

He has a passive place when he turns on the radio to hear music or equips himself with a player and records; he will be concerned about what music is being broadcast or what records to buy or the availability of certain works. He will start to discriminate and concern himself with the literature and performers, the affects and details of performance. His response will be less passive the more he concerns himself with what he hears. He may write and send to the radio station a request to play certain music, or a letter of complaint; more often he will think of doing so but not do it. He may feel the need to share his records with others, to discuss his opinions, his impressions. He acts in this way as impresario or critic. His passive attitude is coming to be active.

When he attends public recitals or concerts, he will concern himself with the quality of the event and, over a span of time, with the general quality of such events in the community. If sufficiently concerned, he may wish to effect change or improvement. How is he to go about doing this?

Alone, he is almost helpless. He will have to join others who feel as he does. Together they may decide to act in some way for the improvement or enlargement of the communal music.

When I was a child I was given operatic records and built a stage on which to set scenes for the music. Not having a reproductive mind, I did not attempt to reproduce the correct scenes for these operas. My art was serious fun instead of scholarship. I could not understand why looking at these scenes while listening to the music did not give pleasure to others as it did to me.

At college, a friend commenced my wider musical education by playing from his library of records. Several years later he came to live with us; we continued this education through long evenings of concentrated listening, inviting others to share the experience with us. We learned all periods of music at the same time, finding none wrong or strange.

I married a trained concert pianist. The few opportunities of playing in public scarcely compensated for the labor to keep her repertoire alive. Instead of giving up music, she started reading it, widening her knowledge of the literature without the strain of having to retain it, uselessly, in memory.

In 1939 we founded together the Evenings on the Roof chamber concerts in Los Angeles and kept them running for fifteen years; after twenty-five years these concerts are still in existence, called now Monday Evening Concerts. The programs we gave during the first years were built around her reading repertoire. Her habit of reading from the score became the Roof practice.

During the fifteen years, Evenings on the Roof presented more separately programmed recitals and concerts than any other chamber-music group I know of. I don't say this to boast but because it was the consequence of two policies, each stated in one sentence, which we would not change.

At the bottom of the printed program of our first concert was the statement: "The programs are for the pleasure of the performers and will be played regardless of audience." The statement engendered a corollary: No member can be denied programming for any reason. This unwritten rule served for a discipline, enforced by myself against myself and against any pressure of dislike from other musicians or from the audience. Once a musician had become a member, he could play what he pleased or as badly as he might. It was a trust that encouraged risk, a confidence that encouraged deviation. A musician became a member by taking part in three concerts during two seasons, in any capacity: accompanist, obbligato player, member of a group, or soloist. All were equal in duty and in opportunity; there were no exclusive soloists. As our membership increased to and beyond

17

a hundred musicians, we had to provide more concerts to fulfill our promise.

The Roof was a co-operative organization, without underwriting or salaries, and the musicians were paid. To challenge the professionals, I kept a few amateurs performing, with equal status. They were volunteers, who also helped get out the work. In the early years many of the regular musicians helped, too. Co-operative morale involves group sacrifice, and the best sacrifice is of oneself. I co-ordinated the programs in my spare time, while fully employed elsewhere. In the last years we had a paid executive secretary, an increasing deficit with no decrease in audience, and underwriting enough to break even at the end of each season. At the height of our activities we were sending series of concerts to the University of Arizona, to Arizona State College (as it was then), and to a chamber music society in Santa Barbara, California, and single concerts elsewhere.

We gave repeatedly whole programs of music by Béla Bartók, Charles Ives, Arnold Schoenberg, and Igor Stravinsky (the two latter lived in Los Angeles), as well as numerous other single-composer programs. We played extensively the music of resident composers; several were among our regular performers. We reserved a concert each season for less-known local composers.

When Otto Klemperer resigned as conductor of the Los Angeles Philharmonic because of illness, he came night after night to sit in our audience. For over ten years Igor Stravinsky sat in the front row every concert night he was in town, with Aldous Huxley often beside him. Stravinsky granted us first performances of several of his smaller works.

The young conductor Robert Craft came to Los Angeles to assist Stravinsky. After Schoenberg's death, Craft prepared several works by Schoenberg as part of the four retrospective programs of his music we presented. Stravinsky attended the rehearsals and soon afterwards began adapting the tone-row to his own use. The following year Craft directed nine works by Anton Webern at one concert. Afterwards he went ahead to produce his recorded album of the complete works by Webern, the most influential single musical event of the decade. Every musician who took part in recording that album lived within greater Los Angeles. All—or practically all—were Roof members. At that time Stravinsky dedicated his *Three Songs by William Shakespeare* to Evenings on the Roof.

In our programming we maintained a steady balance of two-thirds classical and one-third contemporary music. We went through the cycle of the Beethoven sonatas, piano, violin, and cello, three times. We played the Schubert sonatas. We introduced Couperin and Byrd. We performed the entire Bach *Clavierübung*, the 48 Preludes and Fugues, the *Art of Fugue* three times in two arrangements (for two pianos and for mixed instruments), both by Los Angeles musicians. My wife played all the compositions for solo piano by Mozart. Joseph Szigeti played in one evening the three Bach solo violin sonatas.

Given the opportunity, the local musicians formed groups to provide chamber music for us; others set up competing series. The three members of our first associated chamber-music group, a string trio, became after two years the first-chair men of the Philharmonic. Our musicians responded to challenge like musical athletes, performing works which would not otherwise have come to their attention.

We set up an ancillary group, the New Friends of Old Music, to give scope for Wesley Kuhnle's studies in keyboard practice and the historic tunings and Sol Babitz's work with the old-style violin and pre-Tourte bows. We invited the splendid musicians of our Japanese community to play for us their classic music.

During the last five years we instituted a committee elected by the musicians to assist in directing the concerts, hoping they would take charge permanently. I gave up control; after a few weeks they asked me to take it back. I had put a term of ten years on my direction of the concerts. I looked for a successor and after fifteen years turned over to him everything but the name, my one property in the organization. I use the name now for my FM radio broadcasts of music, for which I am not paid.

Somebody may be thinking: But you are not really an Amateur. If an Amateur works successfully as an amateur, he is supposed to be a professional, though that is exactly what he is not. I write about music as an amateur; I lecture as an amateur for amateurs. I am an Amateur because I have done for love, and sometimes for money, what a professional would not feel willing to do except for guaranteed payment. I learned the literature of music by training myself to hear it and the literature of the keyboard by training myself to read it. After many years working for and within music, my activities now so engross my time that I have resigned my other employment.

A great American amateur of music, Henry S. Drinker, defined the work of an Amateur in these words: ". . . intelligent and musically educated amateurs may be the most effective critics in molding the development of public taste and in preventing the foisting of cheap musical products on the public." I believe an Amateur can do more than that.

To be a real Amateur you have to know your responsibilities and fight for them without cease. You have to dig tirelessly to break through the great American institutional negative that has come between the American audience and the living artist.

I go a little farther in the direction indicated by the title of a lecture I have given at several universities, *How To Become Posterity.* I am serving as posterity to composers half my age.

To become posterity to living composers you have to learn who they are; you have to hunt down performances; you must train yourself to hear the occasionally performed work with extreme attention, so that you are able to make connections and comparisons over long gaps of time. You must try to outgrow the absoluteness of many youthful convictions, while striving to remain youthful and flexible in new responses. Your maturity consists in the breadth, depth, scope, and versatility of your experience, in the assurance to decide, and in the flexibility which admits the authority of other alternatives as it admits wrong decisions.

Too many cities are leaving the cultivation of the arts in their community to a small group of socially inclined persons with a taste for power, who know nothing about the arts or showmanship, who control and discipline the local art institutions to their uncreative tastes, who feel no urge to bring the arts to any other social level than theirs (of course, anybody can come who will buy tickets!), who may be expert at raising money or dunning the tax funds to meet their deficit but have never considered widening the public base of their endeavors to exist without a deficit.

Any single isolated group working for the arts in a community is likely in the end to have a growing deficit, if it must depend for survival entirely on its own efforts. Just as a community improves its parks and recreational centers, adds a zoo, puts in a botanical garden or an arboretum, so it should improve its local orchestras and song groups, make sure that recital halls are open and operating at a reasonable rate to provide for its recitalists. No group working for the arts in the community, no artist alone and unfavored determinedly making art as he sees it, should be overlooked or neglected.

Where is the money to come from? From where it is to be used: the community. How are we to raise money when we can't pay for our schools? No community refuses to pay for anything it takes pride in; and we know, though often we forget it, that the community is wealthier as a result. Industry comes to the community where its employees will be happy to live.

True pride is not vanity; it's a combination of enthusiasm and personal excitement in seeing the job done more than adequately, outgoing, expansive joy in knowing that the community is doing the job right. If a citizen can die for his country, he can live for it, too; this may not be easy, and you'll be surprised how many well-intentioned citizens will oppose you. It isn't the end that counts but the doing, being at the heart of it. For all that, we should never expect one citizen to do singlehandedly the work that a community can do.

Nowadays more than ever there is need that the communal leisure be well directed. If you have a symphony orchestra, does it provide its members full-time jobs, or must they scrounge the other half of the year to make a living? Have they formed string, wind, and brass groups, and percussion and chamber-music ensembles? Is there an outlet for this smaller music? If you have a conductor, music director, business manager, do they speak the language of the community—if with an accent? Is their job merely to arrange entertainment for those who can afford and know they want it, or does each recognize his personal responsibility to all who live in the city and its environs?

How do we persuade the television-watching, drive-in-movie-inhabiting local citizen to take pride in the arts? The ordinary retired person won't start coming to hear music just because he has leisure and years to do what he wishes for the first time in his life. His leisure terrifies and haunts him; he doesn't know what to do with his years; how is he to know what he wishes? Are we then to bring down the level of the arts to the level of the unaccustomed people? Just the opposite.

If programming is directed to the pleasure of the audience,

that pleasure will become gradually narrower, until even the so-called "best" audience grows weary to satiation of just being pleased. The arts offer a perennial challenge; the audience wants not to be pleased but to be stirred, until each subscriber buys his tickets with a tingle of anticipation. To make him feel so is showmanship, the artist's business. When you plane down the level of showmanship to a polite cultural routine, you destroy art as surely as you destroy artists. Showmanship can be vulgar, and will be, if given no better incentive. The true spirit is to raise showmanship to the highest level. A good show costs no more than a poor one; while you are gradually raising your audience to the level of good showmanship you are also filling empty seats.

At the same time that you are getting the esthetic plant in order, you should also be looking out for the native artist. No other society but our own depends for music on imported artists.

If you want to find the artist who is worth supporting, look for the rugged nonconformist who puts in most of his time working at his art, who isn't on the gravy train; an artist radical to life, whose individuality disturbs you; one to whom the future may turn with reverence but who is now ostracized by the makers of safe programs. We speak in admiration of the great cultural communities, where genius has grown: shouldn't yours be one of them? Look for the real man in the product, not in his self-advertisement.

Our first purpose in the arts should be to make the native artist's path from self-discovery to maturity not plain, straight, or simple, not luxuriant, but possible. Here is shelter; here is a small guaranteed income: go to work. Though your sins be as Strindberg's, we shall not abandon you. Be as rich or famous as you can by your own efforts, but let your work be your life; we shall ensure that you and your family have comfort enough and do not starve. Not Parks of Culture and Rest in the Soviet style with consequent restrictions, nor jackpot grants of funny-money, a year at a time, which deflect the artist from his purpose. Only the real artist will be happy to thrive on this regimen.

Our concentration camp for the nonconforming artist has been silence, a polite exclusion, no grants, no performance, no distribution, therefore no reputation and no income, modified by the saving intervention of a minority who provide occasional jobs,

occasional grants or gifts, occasional performances, but can't overcome the largest problem, distribution.

Just as soon as the American community, coast to coast, starts
taking pride in its artists, the artists of the community, the one
in the community, the odd man down the road, just so soon will
the arts come to full and fruitful life all across this continent.
When the local community plays in pride the work of the local
composer, not asking the pleasure of the audience but inviting it
to pride, the local boy may not be a great man, but he is on his
way; if he has it in him, he will be recognized. When the local
orchestra invites the competent local conductor or composer to
direct a concert this season or next, it may soon find itself pride-
fully refusing to hire another conductor out of Europe.

Too many young artists are being expensively sent overseas to
obtain a European postmark: to learn form and style and cultural ingratiation that leaves their work formless and derivatively
styleless and culturally worthless. What is the American artist
doing in Europe on his Fulbright? Is he selling American music,
styles, composers, to the natives? Let him stay at home, paid with
less money, to learn his native idiom working full time at his
art in his home town, where it's needed. Let the entire community be aware and proud of him. Let them work out together
their mutual responsibility.

The traditional artist trains by working at his art in the local
community, until he is sufficiently routined to go elsewhere. The
American artist goes to school; as a reward for competence he is
sent abroad. When he returns, nothing more is expected of his
maturity. The university opens its monastic gates to him.

A community art center should be a place of communal meeting. It need be no more comfortable than a cathedral, but it need
not be an imitation cathedral. Such community centers, like park
and recreation areas, should invigorate a healthy circulation of
amateurs and artists, provide for the work of art and for the
audience. They should not be showcases for performance, or
schools.

By simplifying and combining facilities, a community program
for the arts can reduce deficits; by growing in service it can
eliminate them. The constant flowing of people through well-
designed, well-managed community centers—not performance
palaces—will create new thousands of "intellectuals" for the arts,

until the bad name, like so many bad names thrown at art, ceases to function. Use will be the best advertisement, as we see already in libraries and museums. The artist will feel encouraged to live and work in the place that is native to him. Technical accomplishment cannot make up the lack of native roots, of native pride.

Our first duty to art in our own country, throughout this continent, is to serve the native artist, the creator, the performer. Serving him, we serve ourselves. Helping this to happen, the true Amateur will find his place and his active part in the communal music.

Appendixes

APPENDIX 1

TEMPERAMENT AND TUNING

European music from quite early times until the present has been composed around a system of twelve fixed pitches in the octave. The chromatic intervals between the fixed pitches are known as half-steps. The system of fixed pitches and half-steps which has been in common use during the last 125–150 years is known as equal temperament. In equal temperament the half-steps are supposed to be and in practice usually are mathematically equal, and each of the half-steps is imperfect or, as a very precise ear would recognize, a little out of tune.

Out of tune with what? a musician may ask. To answer that question is the purpose of this discussion.

Theorizing about the tuning of European music is supposed to have begun with the Greek philosopher Pythagoras (sixth century B.C.), a religious mathematician who believed that all relationships in the essence of things could be expressed numerically. To support this belief, Pythagoras examined the properties of geometrical figures and the relationships among the vibrations of stretched strings. Our understanding of these relationships is still based on the arithmetical fractions designating the acoustically correct (low-number) interval-relationships established by Pythagoras, as well as by other early Greek musicians.

To simplify the discussion, let us distinguish the two words *temperament* and *tuning*. Theoretically, *tuning* refers in European music to the system or scale of tones related by simple whole numbers, established by or around the time of Pythagoras. Instrumental and theoretical evidence gives reason to suppose that the instruments of that period were tuned exactly to this system.

Temperament refers to any modification of this tuning system that adapts the tuning to a particular usage, such as the pitch-stabilization of an instrument. To *temper* a tuning is to alter it from *just tuning* (in perfect intervals, the tones related by simple whole numbers) to some practical but imperfect variant. You can *temper* a tuning by widening the octave, for example; more commonly, to *temper* an interval of the scale is to narrow it.

Practically, one has no usage other than the word *tuning* to describe the application of either type of system to the tuning of an instrument. Some dictionaries offer no definition of tuning, as if the word had no individual or substantive meaning.

Using a string giving the pitch of middle C, vibrations of half the string give exactly twice the frequency, or C one octave higher. A third of the string vibrates at the pitch of G, the first new tone of the overtone series, a twelfth (an octave plus a fifth) higher than middle C. One-fifth of the string will give E. These two higher partials (a partial is an overtone, or in effect a part of a string), G and E, brought down into the same octave with middle C, form with it the perfect major triad. The whole business is complicated enough to have kept theorists working at it for 2,600 years.

To give a simple example of the mathematics: a string sounds the note A at 440 vibrations per second; the A an octave below requires twice the length of string and sounds A at 220 vps. If you sound a string two-thirds the length of this low string, you get E at 330 vps. You thus have the three notes $\dfrac{\text{A} - \text{E} - \text{A}}{220 \ \ 330 \ \ 440}$ and can quickly see that the ratio $3/2 = \text{E} - \text{A}$, and $4/3 = \text{A} - \text{E}$, thus proving that the ratios are exact analogues of the real sounding events.

I might add: the elementary terminology of music is so chary of precise definition that it consitutes a "secret art," clumsy and often totally inaccurate, hiding as much as it explains.

For example, the *fifth* in musical terminology does not mean the tone produced by the vibration of the fifth of a stretched string; such a division produces a *third*—more precisely, the interval denoted by the simple mathematical relation 5/4. A *fifth* is an interval embracing five successive notes of a diatonic scale, denoted by the mathematical relation 3/2. A *third* (or 5/4) embraces three successive notes of a diatonic scale. On the keyboard, C–G

is a fifth (3/2), C–E a third (5/4). But the fifth C–G embraces
eight notes of the chromatic scale (including the black keys), or
seven half-steps (intervals), or three whole-steps plus one half-
step. (It will be better to reread this and make sure you understand it before proceeding. You can see it best sitting at the
keyboard.)

The fifth, being the first *different* tone or *overtone* to appear in
the overtone series, would be very likely the first tone within or
outside the octave to be arrived at melodically by ear (in theoretical but not in ethnic development). Pythagoras, as a mathematician, was more interested by the fact that an octave derived from
twelve mathematically perfect fifths (3/2s) would result in a
larger, or as a tuner would say, "wider" octave than the perfect
octave (2/1). This fraction of difference is named after him the
"Pythagorean comma."

In the same way, an octave made up of any accumulation of
perfect ("just" or "low-number") intervals would be other than a
plain octave (2/1).

Early European composers and musicians were not troubled by
harmony, the vertical relationship of tones simultaneously
sounded. They were interested only in the melodic scale, as in
varying circumstances it would be sung.

The method of tuning a scale at the keyboard is a *tuning order*.
To tune a Pythagorean scale of perfect fifths, begin with C,
tune perfect (beatless) fifths forwards (that is, upwards) through
G sharp; then beginning once more with C tune perfect fifths
backwards (downwards) through F, B flat, and E flat.

These two directions from C (or from A in modern tuning) are
the two cycles of fifths fundamental to a number of tuning orders
(including the Chinese and some Indian).

In the Pythagorean scale, when tuned to a keyboard, the
Pythagorean comma may be disposed of by a very narrow fifth
placed where it is least likely to interfere (for example, G sharp–
E flat). With such a tuning, the intervals of the third divide, surprisingly, into two groups of equally imperfect thirds. The keyboard will have all but one.of its fifths perfect, four thirds which
are approximately perfect, and the remaining thirds all wider
than a perfect third by an equal margin.

There is reason to believe that such a Pythagorean scale was
used, in whole or in part, for the greater part of European music

before the fifteenth century. Anyone who is interested in tuning this scale on a keyboard instrument, and it is not hard to do, will be amazed by the acoustical magnificence of the sound. Medieval plainsong and polyphony, harmonized concordantly at the fifth and octave only, would gain greatly by being sung in this correct temperament, the pure sonorities of the deliberately placed concordances glowing like jewels on the dark robe of the surrounding non-concordance.

For practical experimentation on the piano, it is best to damp off two of the strings and tune only the third string; the damping is easily done with the aid of tuning felts. This method simplifies the tuning and gives a "juster" scale (since it eliminates "outphasing" of the other two strings); the damping must be very firm to reduce such unwanted vibration.

The expansion of polyphonic music into many parts during the fifteenth century required a more extensive concordance, including perfect thirds and sixths. For this reason attention turned to a new scale (based on the Ptolemaic *Diatonic Syntonon*), which would provide as many perfect fifths and perfect thirds as could be managed in different approximations for the more commonly sung intervals, and requiring some adjustment of the imperfect intervals in any modulatory passage with accidentals. This is the scale of *just intonation*.

To obtain a scale of just intonation on a keyboard instrument by tuning order, tune perfect fifths from C to G to D to A (upwards) and from C to F to B flat to E flat downwards. Then tune perfect thirds from C to E, G to B, D to F sharp, D flat from A, A flat from C (or A flat from E flat, D flat from A flat).

Though more practical for voices in polyphony than a Pythagorean scale, the seraphically mellow just intonation is not practical beyond a single key for fixed-pitch instruments. For composing, however, the entire field of polyphonic music has reopened, free once more of the harmonic key-system.

The next solution was to *temper* just intonation by retaining the principal perfect thirds while narrowing the fifths, so that an instrument with fixed pitches could be played, by avoiding a few unacceptably discordant intervals, in more than one key. This is *meantone*, the first scale in European music to be devised primarily for the keyboard at the cost of acoustically correct vocal intonation. The usefulness of such a scale is to be judged by the effect, which to unaccustomed ears will seem at first "out of tune" in comparison with our own equal temperament.

I should explain that *equal temperament*, the tuning we use today, has been known from very early times as a possible alternative to the other scales, which were preferred; but though it had its advocates the objections to it outweighed its merits. Equal temperament is not, as some believe, a modern improvement.

Until approximately 1600, the beginning date of the era of modern (vertical harmonic) music, the voice was the principal means of musical expression, and for voices the just, or perfect, acoustical intervals are the most natural and easiest to sing. Even today, as Lou Harrison has discovered in practice, the change from the artificially tempered intervals of equal temperament to the acoustically pure intervals of just intonation can be managed by singers and players of adjustable-pitch instruments in a few minutes with little trouble. The greater trouble is to change back.

For this reason a musical art governed by the voice would strongly resist in practical use any type of tempered scale, however much individual musicians might agree theoretically to the need for an equal temperament. The adjustments of pitch necessary to avoid occasional discordant intervals, even the presence of a few discordant intervals, would seem to them more desirable and would certainly be easier to sing than a temperament which is all acoustically out of tune. Until the sixteenth century, the tuning of fixed-pitch instruments must have seemed a minor consideration.

By 1600 the instrumentalists had struck out on their own. The era of keyboard harmony had begun. The solo keyboard was demanding a wider range of harmonic possibility than could be achieved within the purely melodic scales of Pythagorean and just intonation.

The first tempered scales were certainly a modified Pythagorean. Leaving the perfect fifths C–G, G–D, A–E, E–B (as tuned for Pythagorean), the tempered fifths might have been B–F sharp, F sharp–C sharp, C sharp–G sharp, F down to B flat, B flat down to E flat. C down to F may have been tempered or left perfect. The enharmonic intervals, E flat–D sharp, A flat–G sharp, B flat–A sharp, G flat–F sharp, may have been adjusted according to the harmonies desired. Other adjusted variants of the tempered

Pythagorean tuning would have been tried. For the listener the general effect of such a tuning would still be that of perfect fifths.

We should keep in mind that from the sixteenth into the nineteenth century tuning was more variable and flexible than it is now, and the capacity of skilled musicians to detect and provide for subtle adjustments greater than at present. A comparable skill in adjusting intonation is expected of string players in chamber music today.

The tempered Pythagorean tuning is very effective for the playing of the earliest keyboard music and for the English keyboard music as late as Purcell. It solves the problems of the modulations in the famous *Hexachord* (see pp. 122–23) by John Bull so effectively that, on the example of this piece alone, the use of tempered Pythagorean for the English Elizabethan music seems very probable—although for a considerable part of the literature a straight Pythagorean would suffice. This would indicate that the Elizabethan keyboard music was conceived around the interval of the fifth, whereas keyboard music using a tempered just intonation (meantone) is figured more often around the interval of the third. This is not dogma but a guide to further explanation.

If it may be asked why no documentation of this tuning for the Elizabethan keyboard music has survived, I would point out that there is also no documentation for the playing of the two commonest types of Elizabethan ornament, the single and the double line through the note stem. Apparently the composers took so much for granted the common elements of tuning and embellishment that they felt and foresaw no need to document them —as, today, no one has effectively documented jazz rhythmic notation. We who take our classical harmony for granted make the same assumption, scarcely realizing that in our lifetime the very foundations of harmony are again changing—if indeed, in music of the future, any harmony as we have known it will remain.

Meantone tuning is extensively documented in a variety of tuning orders. Where tempered Pythagorean has acoustically perfect fifths, meantone has perfect major thirds and narrowed fifths. (The old rule of thumb was to "narrow the fifths as much as the ear can bear.") The third is divided into two equal whole steps: this is the source of the name *meantone*. This tuning varies more markedly than Pythagorean in the character of the individual keys, no two of which are alike in intervallic coloring. Composers attached to these disparate characters of the eight principal meantone keys emotional significances (*affects*) related to the figurative doctrine of the *affections*.

Not least of the advantages of meantone is the ease with which it can be tuned by tuning order. Here is a diagram for the tuning of basic sharp meantone.

E — B — F♯ — C♯ — G♯

C — G — D — A — E

C — F — B♭ — E♭ = (A♭)

Tune equal narrow fifths forward as far as E, until major third C-E is beatless; continue tuning similar fifths forward from E. Then tune similar fifths backward from C. All fifths narrower than in equal temperament. All thirds joined by arrows in the diagram should be beatless (thus checking the accuracy of the fifths). Enharmonic intervals may be tuned sharp or flat, as the key requires. Thus A♭ (if tuned instead of G♯) should give a beatless third with C above.

This tuning will serve for all keys through three sharps or two flats. For the flat keys, raise G sharp to A flat, making a perfect major third with the C above. This change alters the principal "wolf" tone (that tone which contributes to the most discordant interval).

A little practice in adjusting the interval C–E will enable one to come out with a third that is absolutely beatless (acoustically correct). Each cycle can be *proved* by checking the related major thirds, as indicated in the diagrams by arrows, until each is beatless. Thus meantone can be tuned by fifths and checked by thirds for accuracy at each interval. No other tuning can be so accurately verified by an ear with little training, though one will have to learn how to hear beats and to recognize when an interval is beatless.

Apart from the distinctive coloration of each key, the relationship between concordance and dissonance in meantone gives a wonderful sense of the expansion and contraction of the

18

melodic line, which cannot be matched at all in equal temperament.

It is likely that the vogue of *double* instruments (with separate keyboards, strings, and soundboards) originated in the need to provide for variant tunings. The second instrument was often inserted like a drawer in the larger instrument.

Composers of the later meantone period did not hesitate to dramatize certain dissonant aspects of false relationship to enhance the pathos of a single voice or intensify a passage, for example the fall of Goliath in Kuhnau's *David and Goliath*. Knowing how to use these dramatic or pathetic affects of meantone can greatly enhance the interest of seventeenth- and eighteenth-century keyboard music. A few minutes listening to a seventeenth- or early eighteenth-century composition in C minor played in meantone will convey to the listener what the musical intelligence at that time understood by pathos. The hint of false relation within the key can be no less moving than the more recent outright use of dissonance.

But the most important use was to build in by modulation changes of registration more variable and subtle than those that can be produced by pedal changes on a modern instrument.

Many tuning compromises within meantone were tried in hope of finding a *well-tempered* tuning that would preserve in some degree the distinctions among keys, while permitting in all keys full harmony in both hands. The best-known and probably the most successful of these well-tempered tunings was that achieved by J. S. Bach. Well-tempered tuning is not equal temperament but a modified meantone tuned by ear and taste. When well ordered it is perhaps the most expedient, satisfying, and practical tuning for the keyboard that European musicianship has produced.

Well-tempered should be tuned forward (first cycle) and backward (second cycle) from C. The Pythagorean comma is gradually absorbed by progressively and very slightly narrowing the fifths, starting with a correct fifth (3/2) in each cycle. It is capable of considerable variation.

In equal temperament the vertical relationship predominates, and melody becomes an adjunct of the chord. The importance of the key has dwindled to a notational convenience.

The weight of argument that I have laid on the importance of the other tunings does not mean that I fail to appreciate thoroughly the beauty, usefulness, and expressiveness of equal temperament for music written to be played with its advantages, including the enharmonic relationships. In meantone one must tune either a G sharp or an A flat; in equal temperament one note suffices approximately for both, providing dramatic modulatory short cuts.

My effort has been to break through the exclusive attachment to equal temperament by musicians who have no awareness of any other tuning or the consequences of tuning throughout the history of European music, and who have not accustomed themselves to hearing as natural idiom music in another tuning. Listening to Arabic, Indian, and Chinese music will help in accustoming the ear to unusual scales and microtonal relationships.

The experiments of Wesley Kuhnle in realizing the historic European tunings by working out their tuning orders taught me the full meaning of this subject. He has preserved his studies in a *History of Tuning*, with a multitude of examples, recorded on tape, which should be in every musical reference library and should be put to use in courses on harmony, acoustics, and practical theory and music history. It is the best audible guide to the performing practice of the first four of the five centuries of keyboard music. Each of the tuning orders in this Appendix was worked out by Wesley Kuhnle for his *History of Tuning*.

The best reference texts are *Genesis of a Music* by Harry Partch and *Tuning and Temperament* by J. Murray Barbour, though the latter has too easily and falsely "solved" a number of problems for François Couperin and J. S. Bach by assigning them to equal temperament. I have referred also to the school paper, *The Influence of Tuning on 20th Century Music*, prepared by my eldest son, Peter Barheidt Yates.

This Appendix as I first wrote it was glossed on every page with amendments by Lou Harrison. But since I have not included every one of them, any defects in the argument must be charged against myself.

APPENDIX 2

RHYTHM AND EMBELLISHMENT

The time or regularity of music is articulated by recurring emphases, or beats, divided in units of two or three notes or multiples of these. A *measure* is the group of notes set off by bar-lines.

Melody, consisting of melodic periods or groupings, can exist without measure or beat—like a prose sentence. In some primitive music the melody and the accompanying recurrent rhythm proceed independently, without cross-relationship.

The melodic period may have its own system of articulating emphases, or stresses, which proceed in greater or less independence of the beat. Such measure need not have bar-lines; when it is printed with bar-lines, like Elizabethan keyboard music in modern editions, one should disregard them.

Many composers, from early times until today, do not always write out their notation to the exact subdivision of time but occasionally leave the adjustment to the player.

Simple melodies or tunes usually have their principal accent on the beat. Shifting of the melodic emphasis from the normally accented note to an unaccented note, with the beat remaining relatively strict, is called *syncopation*. Shortening the accented note and lengthening the unstressed note, without altering the beat, produces the so-called "Scotch snap," as in bagpipe music, very common in the seventeenth and eighteenth centuries. Marches and dances often shorten the unaccented notes to emphasize the beat.

A traditional method of distinction (especially during the seventeenth and eighteenth centuries) is to call the *stressed* note "good" and the *unstressed* note "bad"—without moral connotation. One can speak also of "strong" and "weak" notes, but this has the effect of seeming to require a dynamic accent (sounding the note more forcefully or loudly), whereas the emphasis may be only by length without change of dynamic or loudness, or by displacing the bad, or weak, notes in such a manner as to throw greater emphasis on the good, or strong, notes. This last is the general principle of *rhythmic alteration.*

The cross-play of stresses and accents between the beat and the melody, with consequent displacement of notes to sound elsewhere than as notated, may be divided in two categories: *rhythmic alteration* and *rubato. Rubato,* which signifies robbing one note of its time and giving that time to another note or to a silence, is the generic term, but the significance of rubato has been so vitiated by contradictory usages that the distinction can be made clearer by using *rhythmic alteration* for a complementary term.

Let us confine the term *rubato* to signify any changing of the beat and *rhythmic alteration* to the displacing of notes or stresses in the melodic figure or period.

The most common rhythmic alteration emphasizes the first note of the rhythmic unit (of two or three notes), so that the good note is held slightly longer and the bad note proportionately shorter.

During the seventeenth century, it was generally believed that Italian composers notated their keyboard music very nearly as they meant it to be played, but that French composers expected their music to be played quite differently from the manner in which it was notated. In fact, Italian music used both the common rhythmic unit, with a delay of the bad note after a slight extension of the good note, and its alternate, a shortening of the good note followed by a lengthening of the bad note. French music commonly required holding the good note much longer than the succeeding bad note, in a proportion of 3 to 2, 2 to 1, or even 3 to 1. These customary variants were not indicated by the written notation.

In the older English music, through the end of the seventeenth century and in the works of Blow and Purcell, the uneven fall of the bad notes was the commonplace, with varying degrees of flexibility between short-long and long-short, as well as a quick snap from a bad note to a succeeding good note.

A further distinction should be made between the relatively

even flowing of the melodic line in an Italian *coranto* and the strong cross-rhythms, articulated by decisively displaced notes, of a French *courante*.

During the eighteenth century the French habit of uneven playing prevailed throughout much of Europe, reaching an extreme during the lifetime of the Bach sons and Haydn and continuing into the works of Beethoven and Chopin.

In music of this broad period (from the sixteenth well into the nineteenth century) the dot after a note indicates an extension of the time of the dotted note by as much as the length of the dot and very often more, usually followed by an aspirate or silence and a late entry of the note after the dot.

A dotted note is often played as if double-dotted, to compensate for the uneven playing of undotted notes, and is followed by a silence, the note after the dot being very late and short (though not more lightly sounded). This last is particularly true of the movements called French overtures, of passacaglias, chaconnes, and sarabands. The present-day habit of subordinating the rhythm of a saraband to a dramatic rendering of its melody is quite incorrect; the rhythm should be marked.

Throughout sixteenth-, seventeenth,- and eighteenth-century keyboard music, the prevalence of the temporal unit consisting of a longer good note followed by a shorter bad note or notes is demonstrated by the several types of embellishment used to indicate the contrary (e.g. the two-note slur, until around 1750) and by the care of some composers to indicate whenever the notes are, instead, to be played evenly.

For the spirit or atmosphere, let us listen to Roger North: "And it was my fortune to be in that company which introduc't the Itallian composed enterteinements of musick which they call *Sonnata's*, and in old time more imitated by our masters in what they called Fancys. The Court, about this time [after the Restoration of Charles II], enterteined onely the theatricall musick and French air in song, but that somewhat softened and variegated; so also was the instrumentall, more vague, and with a mixture of caprice or Scottish way, than was used by the French; but the Italian had no sort of relish. . . . The old English Fancys were in imitation of an elder Italian sort of *sonnata*, but fell from the sprightlyness and variety they had even in those times, into a perpetuall grave course of fuge; and if the fuge quickened into a litle deviation, or an air of tripla was prick't in, it was extraordinary. . . . but I ever was pleas'd with it, and esteemed the best of them . . . as agreeable as I desire."

Strict counting of the triplet, as is done now, came in slowly, for an occasional rhythmic variant. The older style was called *tripla*. "It may be doubdted whether in truth the tripla measures of time in reallity differ at all from duple," North comments, "or whether the seeming difference be not the result of emphasis more than of proportion, for all the pulses are supposed to be equal. . . . And in a word, a tripla is an emphatick breaking the ground tones into 3, as the comon time is into two, and wherein there are great libertys taken, whilst the ground bass moves *equali passu* [with equal step], and there is no rupture or dislocation of the musicall current . . ."

So the first note of the triplet is frequently held, to enhance the melodic articulation of the line, and the two following notes played more rapidly, either legato or skipped, depending on whether the first note is dotted. This basic rhythm is subject to constant melodic variation. In a three against two (or two with the first note dotted) the second and third notes of the triplet will fall in close relation with the second note of the two—thus making melodic and easily moving such an otherwise buzzing and metronomic movement as the *Courante* of J. S. Bach's B flat harpsichord Partita. The late entry of the second note of the duple, after the dotted note, will cause it to fall more closely with the three of the triple instead of the two, so that the rhythm skips.

Regular repetitive rhythm (meter) can be emphasized either by stress (length) or by accent (loudness). When the emphasis is by loudness, it is possible to play in strict time without distinction by length.

This last is the method which has long been used when performing on the piano music composed originally for the harpsichord or the organ: the piano permitting accent by volume, while the harpsichord and organ require stressing the length of the good notes without consequent displacement of the bad notes. Present-day harpsichordists too often try to imitate the incorrect pianistic accent by volume, with metronomic strictness, distorting every aspect of the music for this wrong purpose.

Rhythmic accentuation by good and bad notes prevailed

throughout European music, until the rise of dynamic accent by volume in music of the later eighteenth century composed for clavichord and subsequently for piano. With dynamic accent, the distinction between good and bad notes lost conventional usage and merged with the new practice of rubato. (The word *rubato* was not new but was given different meaning; Chopin appears to have been the first to write a rubato indication in a score.)

Composers of the sixteenth and seventeenth centuries agreed that the playing of keyboard music should not be subject to strict time but should permit expressive fluctuations among slower and faster parts, with very slow introductions and interludes, and expressively silent pauses. Here is the origin of the practice which I distinctively call *rubato:* a changing of the beat to let time flow expressively and to conform it to changes in the melodic rhythm.

One should also distinguish as rubato the type of freedom required for playing an embellished slow movement of the type favored during the period from C. P. E. Bach to Chopin, of which it is said that the left hand "does not know what the right hand is doing." The right hand plays the moving line with a very great freedom of conventional altered rhythm, against a seemingly exact flow of accompanying notes in the left hand—like a very high-class boogie-woogie. An almost imperceptible extension or reach of the accompanying note may dramatize the outcome of a flight of independence.

There is also the so-called "elastic" rubato, where the beat is very gradually widened and again compressed, or the reverse, having dramatic effect somewhat like an extended harmonic modulation; the beat should return to the same measure from which it departed.

"Elastic" rubato of another sort is exemplified by Chopin's habit of playing the three beats of a mazurka in a rhythm of four beats.

The whole complex reaches climax in the keyboard music by Chopin, where rhythmic alteration over a strict beat will be followed by a rubato or delay of the beat, for example, to accommodate an elaborate written embellishment, which is played as if on a single beat, though it requires more time. Such a short rubato is succeeded by a resuming of strict time.

Rubato degenerated into a mindless, wavering emotionalism

and is today held in grave suspicion—by keyboard players who prefer instead an equally mindless metronomic inexpressiveness.

The most fascinating gamesmanship of musical performance is in the playing of liberated melodic rhythm against strict time, balancing to the very margins without ever falling out of judgement.

Before proceeding to list the general principles which govern the embellishment, here more particularly the gracing, of sixteenth-, seventeenth-, and eighteenth-century music, I should repeat that these principles are not exact rules. Like a good shorthand they leave much to the intelligence of the reader. Any attempt to indicate these principles by notated examples, as is commonly done, may be good for one composer but not another and supplants the broad method of application by a single, isolated instance, denying the first principle of all embellishment: that the same figure alters its style and rhythm according to its location in the passage and in relation to the rhythmic character of the movement.

No possible method of notation could begin to list the subtly variable applications of any single ornament as it should be played in different circumstances, or in repeating the same movement, or in different positions within the movement. If exact notation had been preferable, the composers would have been well able to supply it; in doubtful instances they often preferred to do so. Thus an ornamental indication may be repeated in a more difficult position, to show that it should be played, whereas in a more obvious position the ornament is taken for granted and no indication shown.

When the convention changed, the method of notation changed with it. Only in the context of this long-established convention can one understand the criticism of J. S. Bach by Johann Adolph Scheibe: "Every ornament, every little grace, and everything that one thinks of as belonging to the method of playing, he expresses completely in notes . . ." Though the increase of notated embellishment in Bach's later compositions seemed to Scheibe so absolute, it was really not so, as we learn by comparison with the more detailed notation of C. P. E. Bach or Haydn. Even in Haydn's music, the conventions of altered rhythm and embellishment still govern the performance to such a degree that few of our pianists are able to give a convincing account of them in playing.

Some composers preferred their own signs of gracing and embellishment, complicating the labors of the modern reader. Here again, knowledge of the general principles will overcome many difficulties. By comparing what one composer indicates with what another leaves to the convention we can widen our knowledge of acceptable variants.

Another problem for the modern reader is to retranslate an editor's written-out notation of the gracing signs into the more intelligible original. Don't ignore the editor, but don't believe him: he may use one version, where a skilled reader would employ a dozen variants.

I have no doubt that this manner of setting out the principles of embellishment will be subject to criticism, because the method does not conform with standard practice and may be thought unmanageable by players who will not try it. The "proved" and easy method of imitating a few notated explanations is too generally preferred to the more subtle, exact, and careful learning of the art.

The *acciaccatura* is a tone outside the harmony, a diatonic step above or below the harmonic tone, occasionally at a greater distance, which is struck with the harmonic tone, more rarely just before it, and immediately released, the purpose being to accentuate the tone or add brilliance to the chord. It was ordinarily added by the player to taste, like pepper, and not indicated. J. S. Bach and Domenico Scarlatti added them in quantity. It may be shown by diagonal lines between the notes of a chord, indicating where the acciaccaturas should be played; or the extra-harmonic notes may be written out as part of the chord, in which case they should be sounded and at once released, even though the notes appear to be all of equal value. The acciaccatura was often written as a small note before the note with which it should be played—and for that reason is easily confused with an appoggiatura similarly notated.

Acciaccaturas of more than one note and at wide intervals occur, and are played in the same fashion but a trifle more melodically, so as not to sound like a chord.

The little note with a line through the stem, called a *grace note*, is often substituted by indifferent editors for every manner of correct elaboration. Where it is correctly placed, it raises the delicate question of the relation between the acciaccatura and the appoggiatura. For example, the ornamented opening note of Beethoven's *Diabelli Variations* may be played as either an acciaccatura or a short appoggiatura, though the former is more likely. Such an accent, *pace* Schnabel, should not be smoothed into a triplet. In sonatas by Domenico Scarlatti the majority of such indications should be read as acciaccaturas.

The *appoggiatura,* whether short, even, or long, is always played on the beat and is always the main accent. It is dwelt on but not sounded appreciably louder than the succeeding tone which it ornaments.

The common appoggiatura divides the time of the note it ornaments approximately in half. The volume and quality of each tone should be alike. Properly articulated, this is the most balanced and graceful of ornaments, allowing a great variety of inflection. A coarse unbalance or an inarticulate sliding from one tone to the other spoils the effect.

If the ornamented note is followed by a dot, the appoggiatura is held through the time of the ornamented note, which retains approximately the time of the dot. The silence imposed by the dot is stolen from the succeeding tone.

A long appoggiatura occurs in the manner of a suspension, for melodic as well as harmonic reasons. The length and sounding of the appoggiatura and its relation with the note it ornaments permit much elegant variation.

A *passing appoggiatura* may be played at the end of the time of the preceding note and before the time of the succeeding note, making a sort of tonal aspirate. It is clearly indicated by a small note tied by a slur to the preceding note; there may be several in succession. In French style, where the passing note is usually played late, a passage written with appoggiaturas indicates that these notes should fall as nearly as possible in exact time. (A good, and simple, example is measure 14 of the 6th Couplet of Couperin's *Les Folies françaises* [*La Persévérance*], where the appoggiaturas in the right hand require that the six notes be played to strict count while the four notes of the parallel passage in the left hand are altered, the F sharp and D entering late.)

Another sort of passing appoggiatura occurs when the intervening note is dropped in before the beat in the middle of a rising or occasionally a descending third. C. P. E. Bach dismisses this grace as facile or undesirable, thereby showing that it was rather widely used. A graceful example may be found, written by another hand, in the manuscript (published in a facsimile edition) of J. S. Bach's first *Invention*. Whether this records Bach's own manner of playing or was written in for another reason, the grace is here graceful and not undesirable.

The *slide* consists of two or more small notes written before the main tone and played in the single beat and time of the main tone. The slide indicated by a sign is usually an ascending diatonic scale figure of two tones rising to the main tone; the slide from above is less common. More extended slides occur in the manner of fast scales with a single beat; these are often written out. From these develop the scalewise cadenza or arpeggiated figure, written out or added by the performer as an enlarged embellishment in a slow movement or at a fermata.

The *two-note slur* is an ornament of importance only less than the appoggiatura, which rhythmically it complements. The normal appoggiatura divides the time of the note it ornaments and may be very slightly dwelt on without accent. The two-note slur very slightly shortens the first note to place a gentle legato emphasis on the second tone. The second tone is never cut short or played staccato like a slur in nineteenth-century music, and the break between tones is lightly aspirated only when the same note is repeated after the slur (when you should change fingers).

In slower movements the slur marks an emphatic legato, a going ahead to place the weight of the melody on the second tone. In lighter, faster movements it may emphasize a counterrhythm. The delicately counterrhythmic effect of two-note slurs opposed to even appoggiaturas is often wittily used by Couperin and Haydn.

With the advent of clavichord and piano, relying on accent by volume (around 1750), the two-note slur reversed emphasis, the first note now being held longer and the second note played shorter with a slight dynamic accent, detached from the succeeding note.

The slur over an arpeggio indicates that all the tones should be held under the fingers until the end of the arpeggio, within the distance covered by the hand or until a note is repeated, at the discretion of the player. In harpsichord, clavichord, and early piano music, without pedal, the holding and retaining of notes under the fingers was the method used to obtain mixtures of resonances like those now obtained by use of the piano damper pedal. An arpeggio should be played in relatively strict time, as a counterpoint to the general leaning of the passing notes.

The slur over any group of notes indicates that the notes under the slur should be played with relatively even value, in contrast to the prevailing altered rhythm, and without aspiration between tones. The first note may be held somewhat longer than the remainder, which are otherwise played evenly. Groups of tones so marked may be overlapped or blended by holding them with the fingers. Such an effect gives richness and sonority to an Alberti bass. Even on a modern piano the effect so obtained will be more delicate and accurate than bringing in the entire heavy sonority of the instrument by using the damper pedal.

The *shake* or *trill* is a reiterated appoggiatura, beginning on the beat, often with a turn at the end for rhythmic emphasis, the balance of the sound divided between the tones, and the whole played slightly faster than the time of the passage—but never to an exact count. Couperin and C. P. E. Bach use a distinct sign for the shake and turn (the sign for a turn written over the sign for a shake). The same grace and articulation between tones should be used for the shake as for an even appoggiatura. The number of beats, their speed, which may include an accelerando or very occasionally a slowing, and the inclusion or omission of the turn, should be constantly varying with the passage or phrase.

When a shake is tied to the preceding note, the preceding tone serves for the auxiliary (appoggiatura) of the shake; the shake is sounded starting with the main tone, after a delay equivalent to the length of the implied appoggiatura which is not sounded. This is one of the less understood rhythmic variants, essential for Couperin. When the shake is not tied, and the indicated or implied auxiliary is the same as the preceding tone, it is better to repeat this tone as the starting tone of the shake.

A three- or five-note shake from the main tone, without appoggiatura or a final turn, occurs in Italian and Spanish keyboard music, less often in German, French, or English. The many admonitions by seventeenth- and eighteenth-century composers that the shake should begin with the upper note, instead of from the main tone, show that the opposite may have been common practice—as it has been for the last century.

To omit the appoggiatura and play a so-called "inverted mordent" from the main tone alters both the melody and the rhythm. Observe how carefully Chopin writes out this inverted mordent when he wishes it to be played instead of a shake—indicating the ordinary shake by the usual sign. Chopin played the inverted mordent on the beat, though the habit of playing it before the beat began during his lifetime.

The designs, emphases, and rhythmic forms of the shake and its relations with the appoggiatura furnish material for endless study and experiment. It is essential to begin by learning to play a quick, smooth shake, ending either in a brief holding of the last note of the shake, with or without aspiration, or with a turn which leads directly to the succeeding note. Or there may be an aspiration at the end of the shake, followed by the turn to the succeeding note, but not a turn followed by an aspiration.

The turn should be never slower than the shake and often slightly faster. Modern performers consistently violate this rule. C. P. E. Bach lists it first among "other errors as ugly as they are frequent: The appending of a limp suffix to a trill . . .; failure to give trills their full length, which (excepting the short trill) must always agree with the value of the note over which the symbol appears; plunging directly into a trill without playing a preceding appoggiatura or properly joining both ornaments; performing such an impertinent trill loudly in a subdued, plaintive context; trilling excessively . . ." The last is the one fault we seldom suffer today.

The *vibrato, tremolo,* or *trillo* is an Italian coloratura embellishment, borrowed by composers of other countries: the single tone is sustained sometimes with and sometimes without exact rhythmic articulation, either by rapid repetition or by rapid alternation with a tone above or below. It may be elaborated into a cadenza or embellished cadence; it may begin on the main tone instead of with an appoggiatura; and it may have no final turn. It may begin with a turn, include a turn, and end with a turn.

The *turn* is most common as the termination of a shake. It begins usually with an appoggiatura from above. In many instances the first three notes are played more rapidly. When a turn follows a dotted note, the sign is written over the dot, and the figure begins with or after the time of the dot. When a turn is written over a note followed by a dot, the turn is played in the time of the note and followed by a silence. Turns may often be used to elaborate the melody without being indicated. The turn is a useful improvisatory embellishment. It may replace a shake in quick movements.

The *mordent* begins on the main tone, in combination with the tone a diatonic step below it. It is sometimes written with an appoggiatura, normally from a lower tone, though it can be from above. The appoggiatura from below can be often played where it is not indicated, giving the mordent the rhythm of an inverted shake. When a mordent is tied to a preceding tone, this tied note serves as the auxiliary of the mordent, which is sounded after a delay equivalent to the length of the implied auxiliary which is not sounded (very usual in Couperin, and see the first measure of the *Goldberg Variations* by J. S. Bach). A mordent should ordinarily be played rapidly.

The mordent, like the acciaccatura, may be thrown in rather freely for emphasis or accent where no indication has been given. In rapid passages the lower tone may be sounded and immediately released, without releasing the tone above. Interpolated mordents and turns may be very useful in articulating the melody of a composition which contains few or no indicated embellishments.

I should add that throughout harpsichord music a dot over the note means *hold*—not a staccato. A dagger sign or short vertical over the note indicates a shortening of the note-value.

Arpeggiation: in seventeenth- and eighteenth-century keyboard music any vertical combination of more than two notes should be broken, rolled, arpeggiated, or intensified by the interposition of acciaccaturas. The rhythmic, accentual, or melodic use of arpeggiation, fast or slow, ascending, descending, or both, or spread freely across the measure, or expanded to a cadence, provides the background of color and enriches the harmony. In harpsichord playing and accompanying it prevents the thump of several jacks plucking and falling back at the same time.

Couperin restricts the amount of arpeggiation (*battery*), but only by comparison with the extended arpeggiation of the contemporary Italian style. (Several good examples of elaborated arpeggiation in the older style may be found in the first piano entries at the beginning of the Brahms B flat Piano Concerto. Brahms knew and practised in his fashion many principles of the earlier embellishment, notably the long appoggiatura or suspension.)

Compositions having few or no notated embellishments are meant to be filled out by the player. Simple melodies should be freely elaborated, but the knowledge and taste to do this can come only after extensive playing of fully embellished compositions. With such experience, the lack of needed embellishments will become evident, and the elaboration will sing itself into place according to the skill and taste of the performer. Don't be afraid to overornament experimentally; by the time you are able to do this, you should be acquiring also the taste to remove the excessive ornaments after you have tried them.

Fine embellishment is distinguished by the rhythmic freshness and individuality of its gracing, and the originality of its occasional exceptions to the normal pattern. Good ornament intensifies the listening experience; it is never trivial. Taste in the placement and delineation of ornaments, with subtle extensions of time and beat to allow for playing them, is the very spirit of rhythmic emphasis but should never deteriorate into an arhythmic rubato mannerism. Playing an embellished composition should never fall into a repetitive routine.

When the fundamental principles given here have been practised, with attention to the examples given by each composer when you play his music, you may learn many more details and variants from such exemplary authors as C. P. E. Bach and Arnold Dolmetsch.

The method of applying a glossary of examples to a few isolated compositions will result only in such confusion as one hears constantly in public performance. Under such conditions, an ear habituated to the still predominant nineteenth-century strict tempo, broadly elastic rubato, accent by volume, harmonized melody, and other habits and mannerisms of the wrong century, will translate these into a functional substitute for sixteenth-, seventeenth-, and eighteenth-century idiom and call the result good taste. During the time I have been writing this book I have observed among performers some improvement in the reading and rendition of altered rhythms and embellishments, giving hope of a generally improved keyboard practice.

". . . And every night as he went to bed, the harpsichord standing in the gallery at the door, he and I must have a litle of diversion that way. I should not mention such levitys as these may be accounted, but because I thinck they are, being vertuous and ingenious, for his honor; because they shew he was honest even in his recesses, and had no vicious, luxurious or debaucht ways, in the injoying himself."

—ROGER NORTH, *The Lord Keeper North*

BIBLIOGRAPHY

This bibliography has been designed to suggest the inclusive range of a practical keyboard library. It is short, yet large enough that no Amateur is likely ever to own the whole of it. I have not gone beyond the needs of an Amateur who reads keyboard music for his pleasure; therefore I have not listed concertos or chamber music; but a brief list of piano duets has been provided. I have not tried to make the bibliography complete, nor can I be certain that every edition I have listed is the best. An Amateur should keep in touch with his own music dealer, watching for new editions and collections of keyboard music and making his own comparisons. Through the dealer and by writing to music publishers or their American distributors, one can maintain a file of current music catalogues. Such activity encourages the local music dealer to enlarge his stock of music not ordinarily called for and in this way benefits the community.

On the whole, it is more economical over a longer period to buy the complete works of a major composer one volume at a time than to patch together a library of single pieces and selections. One can then make a practice of reading clear through each new volume as one obtains it. For composers not available in complete editions, or whose *Complete Works* is expensive, one can start with an album of selected works or an anthology. It is wise, especially with anthologies, to check the editing and inclusiveness of several alternative albums. Identify in particular the few anthologies which cover the most ground and offer the best representation of composers whose works you don't know well enough to start buying them complete; this is a better plan for music composed before 1700 than for the nineteenth century.

Consult your playing ability but avoid stocking up with Easy editions. If you keep working at it, you can make your way into the more substantial music. And Easy editions, consisting only of smaller works or larger works made easy, oftentimes present more editorial problems than standard editions. The slightest eighteenth-century pieces for keyboard require for enjoyment a real feeling for the idiomatic swing of the period, whereas you can chew away at larger compositions and get nourishment from them using any stylistic means. If this weren't so, most of our virtuosos would go out of business.

The best reference manual I have found is *Music for the Piano, A*

Handbook of Concert and Teaching Material from 1580 to 1952, assembled
by James Friskin and Irwin Freundlich (New York, Holt, Rinehart &
Winston, Inc., 1954). The listing is thorough, with separate sections for
early keyboard music, European, American, and South American music.
The comments supply, in brief space, well-chosen and discriminating information about composers, styles, and editions. Many excellent publications
have appeared on the market since 1952, especially works of the early
masters and new practical editions of the classics based on original sources;
I have included some of the best of them in the bibliography.

Piano teachers may disagree, but in my opinion the best score for the
amateur reader is the urtext with the least visible editing (fingerings, interpretative markings put in smaller type or in parentheses, explicatory
alterations or omissions gravely described as helpful, masses of footnotes).
A good reader should seek his own fingerings and should change them often,
as Busoni advised; he should positively defy any interpretative markings
except the composer's; alterations or omissions indicate more prejudice than
scholarship; footnotes clutter the page. A good introduction and notes
set apart from the music text can be helpful; these should be pertinent and
not discursive, after Couperin's example. The Henle Beethoven urtext, for
example, includes a paragraph which says only that the editor does not
know how Beethoven played a shake or trill. A Bülow, or Busoni, or Bartók,
or Schnabel edition of Bach or Beethoven may be educational; these were
all pianists of the first rank, and in some degree composers, who had earned
their opinions, but their opinions are not those of Bach or Beethoven. Use
them for reference. Don't necessarily prefer the edition with the larger
notes; the distribution of white space among the notes is more important in
providing a readable score.

For all composers included in their catalogue I recommend without
exception the *Lea Pocket Scores.* These are photographic reproductions of
the finest old urtext editions, many not otherwise obtainable. (Some of
these have been superseded by new editions which are editorially superior,
especially those of J. S. Bach and Mozart.) For J. S. Bach, the *Lea* score
is the *Gesellschaft,* including the complete works for organ (and in the
Supplementary Volumes a large number of compositions not by Bach);
the Mendelssohn also includes the organ works; the Handel is the Chrysander
edition, and the volume of the instrumental sonatas gives only the original
figured bass, a good score for an accompanist to work from in developing
his own skill in playing continuo; the Schubert includes the early sonatas
usually omitted from standard editions. Since the originals of these scores
were all expensive, well-engraved editions, the best on the market for a
half-century or more, the miniature score is quite clear, except in copies
which have been badly printed. Be sure to look through any copy before
you buy it. Some are more readable than others, depending on the proportions of the original edition. Any person with normal eyesight should be
able to read from these scores at the keyboard, as I do. The price is less
than that of other standard editions. A set of *Lea* scores will make a good
start for any keyboard library; for the major composers these provide a
second copy to carry with you to recitals or for reference.

ANTHOLOGIES

There is a great variety of old music anthologies; the best contain
individual works not easily to be found elsewhere. In selecting these one

will learn much about the literature, as one tries to patch together a fairly complete survey of the lesser or less obtainable composers.

Early Keyboard Music, 2 vols. (Oesterle-Aldrich), Schirmer, 1904. Volume 1 has been for many years the most rewarding single-volume anthology of earlier keyboard music, especially for the seventeenth century. The editing and indication of embellishments vary. The selections from the English virginalists will serve for an introduction but should be replaced or corrected by reference to more authentic scores. Volume 2 is not of equal importance, much of the space being given over to François Couperin and Rameau, for whose music other editions are preferable.

Keyboard Music of the Baroque and Rococo, 3 vols. (Georgii), Volk, 1960. A broader spread than the Schirmer, freshly edited from original sources.

Early Keyboard Works, 5 vols. (Buchmayer), Breitkopf & Härtel, 1927. North German pre-Bach composers, principally for organ, transcribed for piano, with the urtext in an appendix to each volume.

Music of Early Times, 2 vols. (Apel), Schott, 1934. The best small collection of very early keyboard music, with some lute compositions including a *Tombeau* by Denys Gaultier. Several of the pieces are in reduced versions.

Spielbuch für die Kleinorgel oder andere Tasteninstrumente: Old masters from the 16th to 18th centuries, 2 vols. (Auler), Peters, 1951. Early compositions for small manual or cabinet organ, more suitable for your harmonium than for piano.

Silva Iberica, Easy Keyboard Music of the XVI, XVII, and XVIII Centuries from Italy, Portugal and Spain (Kastner), Schott, 1954.

Cravistas Portuguezes, 2 vols. (Kastner), Schott, n.d. Older Portuguese music, Volume 2 principally works by Carlos de Seixas.

English Virginalists, 5 vols. (Dawes), Schott, 1951.

The following are also anthologies, contemporary with the period, of the English virginalists.

The Dublin Virginal Manuscript (Ward), Wellesley College, Wellesley, Mass., 1954. This inexpensive treasure will test your musical skills. It includes, for comparison, a selection of Italian lute pieces on the same tunes.

The Mulliner Book (Stevens), *Musica Britannica*, Stainer & Bell, 1951. The selection in *English Virginalists*, Volume 2, should suffice.

Fitzwilliam Virginal Book, 2 vols. (Fuller-Maitland & Squire), Broude, reproducing the original edition 1894–99. A beautiful, and expensive, edition to own and work at for a lifetime. Now also available in an inexpensive paperback reprint edition by Dover.

Parthenia, or The Maydenhead of the first musicke that ever was printed for the Virginalls (Stone), Broude; the original first published in 1611.

Twenty-five Pieces for Keyed Instruments from Benjamin Cosyn's Virginal Book (Fuller-Maitland & Squire), Chester, 1923.

COMPOSERS

In the following pages the listings consist of composer's name, title of the work, editor's name in parentheses, and publisher. Most European publishers have an exclusive distributor in the United States (see List of Publishers and Their American Distributors, pp. 283–85).

In compiling the list of composers and editions, I have tried to indicate only those editions which are in general the best. Where the *publisher's name only* is shown, this indicates that all or the greater part of the composer's keyboard works are available from that publisher. Where a *composer's name only* is shown, I recommend some acquaintance with his keyboard music; where I have listed one or more works by a composer, I do not necessarily limit my recommendation to those works. The failure to indicate any particular works by a composer should not be taken as downgrading or undervaluing his contribution. Every composition by Messiaen, for example, is of importance, so I have not singled out any one of them for particular reference. I have listed in the same way several earlier composers, more notable like Johann Schobert for their influence, whose work only occasionally turns up in an anthology.

ALKAN, CHARLES-HENRI VALENTIN (1813–1888): *Oeuvres Choisies* (Delaborde & Philippe), Costallat, Paris, now out of print.

D'ANGLEBERT, JEAN-HENRY (c.1628–1691): *Pieces for Clavecin* (Roesgen-Champion), Publications of the French Musicological Society, 1934; in U.S.A. obtainable through Broude, in uncut sheets, which you will need to have cut and bound.

BABBITT, MILTON (1916–   ).

BACH, CARL PHILIPP EMANUEL (1714–1788): *Six Sonatas, Eighteen pieces to illustrate The Essay on the True Art of Playing Keyboard Instruments,* 2 vols. (Doflein), Schott. These are Bach's exemplary pieces, of first importance for the foundation of the post-1750 improvisatory and sonata styles.

   The Prussian Sonatas, 2 vols. (Steglich), and *The Württemberg Sonatas,* 2 vols. (Steglich), Nagel.

   Six Volumes of Sonatas, Free Fantasies and Rondos (Krebs & Hoffmann-Erbrecht), Breitkopf & Härtel. These are the very important late works of the Hamburg period.

BACH, JOHANN CHRISTIAN (1735–1782): *Ten Sonatas,* 2 vols. (Landshoff), Peters.

BACH, JOHANN SEBASTIAN (1685–1750): For the complete keyboard works consult the old *Bach-Gesellschaft* edition (see *Lea Pocket Scores*) or the old Peters edition. The Bischoff edition, reprinted by Kalmus, is editorially obsolete, but I am not the only one who, because of the lie of it on the page, have found it the most enjoyable to read. The new complete Bach edition in progress should eventually supersede all other editions. In the meantime, some of the recent Peters editions and the Henle editions seem to provide the best texts.

BACH, WILHELM FRIEDEMANN (1710–1784): *Sonatas,* 3 vols. (Blume), Nagel.

BARBER, SAMUEL (1910–   ): *Sonata in E flat minor,* opus 26, Schirmer.

BARTÓK, BÉLA (1881–1945): Boosey & Hawkes.

   Selected Works for the Piano, Schirmer. A fairly complete collection of the earlier half of Bartók's keyboard writings.

BEETHOVEN, LUDWIG V. (1770–1827): Kalmus, Henle.

BERG, ALBAN (1885–1935): *Sonata,* opus 1, Universal.

BLOCH, ERNEST (1880–1959): *Sonata,* Carisch.

BLOW, JOHN (1648/9–1708): *Popular Pieces for the Virginal and Harpsichord* (Pauer), Augener.

   The Contemporaries of Purcell, vols. 1 & 2 (Fuller-Maitland), Chester.

The editor wrote out all embellishments in such style that I find it almost impossible to recover the original.

Böhm, Georg (1661–1733): *Collected Keyboard Works*, 2 vols. (Wolgast), Breitkopf & Härtel.

Boulez, Pierre (1925–   ): *First Sonata*, Amphion; *Second Sonata*, Heugel; *Third Sonata*, Universal.

Brahms, Johannes (1833–1897): Peters; Augener; Henle.

Bull, John (c.1562–1628): *Keyboard Music* (Steele & Cameron), *Musica Britannica*, Stainer & Bell.

Busoni, Ferruccio (1866–1924): Breitkopf & Härtel.

Buxtehude, Dietrich (1637–1707): *Clavier Works* (Bangert), Broude. *Organ Works*, 4 vols. (Hedar), Hansen.

Byrd, William (1543–1623): *My Ladye Nevells Booke* (Andrews), Broude. Beautiful, accurate, expensive, indispensable.

   Forty-five Pieces for Keyboard Instruments (Tuttle), Lyrebird. These two collections plus the *Fitzwilliam Book* and the *Cosyn's Virginal Book* give a complete Byrd. I cannot recommend the Fellowes edition of Byrd's keyboard works.

Cabezón, Antonio de (1510–1566): *Music for Keyboard, Harp, and Vihuela*, 2 vols. (Kastner), Schott.

Cage, John (1912–   ): *Sonatas and Interludes for Prepared Piano; Winter Music*, Peters.

Carter, Elliott (1908–   ): *Sonata*, Mercury.

Castro, José María (1892–   ).

Chambonnières, Jacques Champion de (1602–1672): *Complete Keyboard Works* (Brunold & Tessier), Senart.

Chávez, Carlos (1899–   ): *Sonatina*, Arrow; *Sonata*, New Music; *Ten Preludes*, Schirmer.

Cherubini, Luigi (1760–1842): *Six Sonatas* (Alati), Carisch.

Chopin, Frédéric François (1810–1849): *Complete Works* (Paderewski et al.), the Frédéric Chopin Institute, Polish Musical Publications. A handsome, expensive new edition; some say, the best. In U.S.A., Marks. (Mikuli), Schirmer, ". . . perhaps as trustworthy as any," Friskin writes.

Clementi, Muzio (1752–1832): *Twelve Sonatas*, 2 vols., Schirmer. *Rediscovered Masterworks* (Mirovitch), Marks.

Copland, Aaron (1900–   ): *Piano Variations*, Arrow; *Sonata*, Boosey & Hawkes; *Fantasy for Piano*, Boosey & Hawkes.

Couperin, Louis (1626–1661): *Complete Keyboard Works* (Brunold), Lyrebird.

Couperin, François (1668–1733): *Pieces de Clavecin*, 4 vols. (Brahms & Chrysander), Augener.

   L'Art de toucher le Clavecin (Linde), Breitkopf & Härtel. Includes complete text in French and English and 8 preludes.

Cowell, Henry (1897–   ): Many compositions, including unusual piano-sound experiments not too difficult for an Amateur to learn.

Cramer, Johann Baptist (1771–1858).

Czerny, Carl (1791–1857): *Art of Finger Dexterity*, opus 740, Peters.

Dahl, Ingolf (1912–   ): *Sonata Seria*, Presser; *Sonata Pastorale*, unpublished.

Debussy, Claude (1862–1918): Durand.

Diamond, David (1915–   ): *Sonata*, Southern.

Dohnányi, Ernst v. (1897–1960).

Dowland, John (1562–1626): *Lachrymae* (Warlock), Oxford.

DURANTE, FRANCESCO (1684–1755): *Sei Studii e Sei Divertimenti* (Paumgartner), Bärenreiter.

DUSSEK, JOHANN LADISLAUS (1760–1812): *Sonatas*, 2 vols. (Racek, Sýkora), MAB.

    Sonata in F sharp minor, opus 61 (Hermanns), Peters.

DVOŘÁK, ANTONIN (1841–1904): *Slavonic Dances*, 2 vols., Boosey & Hawkes.

ECKARD, JOHANN GOTTFRIED (1735–1809): *Oeuvres Complètes* (Reeser), Heuwekemeijer.

FARNABY, GILES (1560–1640): *Seventeen Pieces* (Dart), Stainer & Bell.

FAURÉ, GABRIEL-URBAIN (1845–1924).

FIELD, JOHN (1782–1937): *Nocturnes* (Liszt), Schirmer.

FOSS, LUKAS (1922–   ).

FRANCK, CÉSAR (1822–1890): Peters.

FRESCOBALDI, GIROLAMO (1583–1643): *Orgel- und Klavierwerke*, 5 vols. (Pidoux), Bärenreiter.

FROBERGER, JOHANN JACOB (1616–1667): *Masters of the Cembalo*, Vol. 1 (Schultz), Peters.

    Selected Pieces (Schubert), Schott.

GABRIELI, ANDREA (1510–1586): *Organ Works*, 5 vols. (Pidoux), Bärenreiter.

GABRIELI, GIOVANNI (1554/7–1612): *Keyboard Works* (Bedbrook), Bärenreiter.

GALUPPI, BALDASSARE (1706–1785): *Dodici Sonate* (Benvenuti), Bongiovanni.

GAULTIER, DENYS (c.1600–1672): volume of transcriptions (Tessier), Publications de la Société française de musicologie, 1932–33.

GERSHWIN, GEORGE (1898–1937): *Preludes for Piano*, Harms.

GIBBONS, ORLANDO (1583–1625): *Complete Keyboard Music* (Glyn), Stainer & Bell. All signs of embellishment assiduously removed, a total mistake to protect the reader from making a mistake.

    Keyboard Music (Hendrie), *Musica Britannica*, Stainer & Bell.

GINASTERA, ALBERTO (1916–   ): *Sonata*, Barry.

GOTTSCHALK, LOUIS MOREAU (1829–1869).

GRIEG, EDVARD HAGERUP (1843–1907): Peters.

GRIFFES, CHARLES TOMLINSON (1884–1920): *Sonata*, Schirmer.

HANDEL, GEORGE FRIDERIC (1685–1759): Schott; Peters.

    Eight Suites (Steglich), in new complete edition, Bärenreiter.

HARRIS, ROY (1898–   ): *Sonata*, opus 1, Arrow.

HARRISON, LOU (1917–   ): *Six Sonatas*, New Music, to be reissued by Presser; *Suite for Piano*, Peters.

HAYDN, FRANZ JOSEPH (1732–1809): 49 *Sonatas*, 4 vols., and 6 *Divertimenti* (Martienssen), Peters. See my comment on page 28.

HINDEMITH, PAUL (1895–1963): Schott.

HOVHANESS, ALAN (1911–   ).

HUMMEL, JOHANN NEPOMUK (1778–1837): *Sonata in F sharp minor*, opus 81, Peters.

IMBRIE, ANDREW (1921–   ): *Sonata*, Valley Music Press.

IVES, CHARLES EDWARD (1874–1954): *First Sonata*, Peer; *Second Sonata*, "Concord, Mass., 1840–1860" (Kirkpatrick), Arrow (many differences from the original edition, privately published by the composer); *Three-Page Sonata; The Anti-Abolitionist Riots; Some Southpaw Pitching;* Mercury.

JANÁČEK, LEOŠ (1854–1928): Artia.

KABALEVSKY, DMITRI (1904–   ): *Children's Pieces*, Leeds.

KODÁLY, ZOLTÁN (1882–   ).
KRENEK, ERNST (1900–   ).
KRIEGER, JOHANN (1651–1735): *Ausgewählte Klavierwerke* (Kreutz), Bärenreiter.
KUHNAU, JOHANN (1660–1722): *Six Biblical Sonatas* (Stone), Broude.
    Selected Keyboard Works (Schubert), Schott.
LeROUX, GASPARD (c.1660–1707): *Pieces for Harpsichord* (Fuller), Peters.
LISZT, FRANZ (1811–1886): Peters; Breitkopf & Härtel; Schirmer.
    Liszt Society Publications, 4 vols., Schott: late, forgotten, and inaccessible works.
MACDOWELL, EDWARD (1861–1908): *Sonata Tragica,* Schirmer; *Sonata Eroica,* Schirmer; *Third and Fourth Sonatas,* Kalmus.
MARTINI, GIAMBATTISTA (PADRE) (1706–1784): *Six Sonatas* (Hoffmann-Erbrecht), Breitkopf & Härtel.
McPHEE, COLIN (1901–1964): for his piano transcriptions of Indonesian *gamelan* music.
MEDTNER, NIKOLAI (1880–1951): Peters.
MENDELSSOHN, FELIX (1809–1847): Peters.
MERULO, CLAUDIO (1533–1604): *Canzoni* (Pidoux), Bärenreiter.
MESSIAEN, OLIVIER (1908–   ): Difficult play with sonorities on motives representing religion, nature, birdsong.
MILHAUD, DARIUS (1892–   ): *Saudades do Brazil,* 2 vols., Eschig.
MORLEY, THOMAS (1557–c.1603):*Keyboard Works,* 2 vols. (Dart), Stainer & Bell.
MOSCHELES, IGNAZ (1794–1870).
MOZART, WOLFGANG AMADEUS (1756–1791): Kalmus (lacks the incomplete sonatas).
    Sonatas and Fantasies for the Piano (Broder), Presser. Includes the incomplete sonatas.
    Pieces (Waller) and *Variations* (Zimmermann), Henle.
MUSSORGSKY, MODEST (1839–1881): *Pictures at an Exhibition,* Peters.
MÜTHEL, JOHANN GOTTFRIED (1728–1788): Two *Ariosi* and Three *Sonatas,* 2 vols. (Hoffmann-Erbrecht), Breitkopf & Härtel.
PACHELBEL, JOHANN (1653–1706): *Selected Organ Works,* 4 vols. (Matthaei), Bärenreiter.
    Hexachordum Apollinis (Moser-Fedtke), Bärenreiter.
PASQUINI, BERNARDO (1637–1710): Seven *Toccatas* (Esposito), Zanibon. In U.S.A. World.
PAZ, JUAN CARLOS (1897–   ).
PERLE, GEORGE (1915–   ): *Sonata.*
PISTON, WALTER (1894–   ).
PLATTI, GIOVANNI BENEDETTO (1690–1763): Twelve *Sonatas,* 2 vols. Hoffmann-Erbrecht), Breitkopf & Härtel.
POULENC, FRANCIS (1899–1963).
PROKOFIEFF, SERGE (1891–1953): Nine *Piano Sonatas,* Leeds.
PURCELL, HENRY (c.1659–1695): *Suites, Lessons and Pieces for the Harpsichord,* 4 vols. (Squire), Chester.
RACHMANINOFF, SERGE (1873–1943): several publishers.
RAMEAU, JEAN-PHILIPPE (1683–1764): *Pieces de Clavecin* (Jacobi), Bärenreiter. (Saint-Saëns), International.
RAVEL, MAURICE (1875–1937): Durand.
REGER, MAX (1873–1916).
REICHA, ANTON (1770–1836): *Fugues* (Sýkora), Orbis.
RIEGGER, WALLINGFORD (1885–1961).

ROUSSEL, ALBERT (1869–1937): *Suite,* opus 14; *Sonatine,* opus 16, Salabert.
RUDHYAR, DANE (1895–   ).
SAINT-SAËNS, CAMILLE (1835–1921).
SATIE, ERIK (1866–1925): Eschig.
   Sports et Divertissement, Publications Lucien Vogel. An expensive re-production in Satie's beautiful script. Witty texts to be read silently while playing. Fun for the innocent.
SCARLATTI, ALESSANDRO (1660–1725): *Harpsichord & Organ Music,* 9 vols. (Shedlock), Bach & Co.
   Seven *Toccatas* for Harpsichord (Nardi), Bärenreiter.
SCARLATTI, DOMENICO (1685–1757): *Complete works for the Harpsichord,* arranged in suites of 5 sonatas, 11 vols. (Longo), Ricordi. Every objection can be brought against this edition and its arrangement, but it is the complete edition.
   Sixty Sonatas 2 vols. (Kirkpatrick), Schirmer. Well edited.
SCHEIDT, SAMUEL (1587–1654): *Song Variations for Clavier* (Auler), Schott.
SCHOBERT, JOHANN (c.1720–1767).
SCHOENBERG, ARNOLD (1874–1951): Universal; except *Suite,* opus 23, Hansen.
SCHUBERT, FRANZ (1797–1828): Kalmus; Henle; Universal.
SCHUMANN, ROBERT ALEXANDER (1810–1856): Kalmus; Henle.
SCRIABIN, ALEXANDRE (1872–1915): Leeds.
SEIXAS, CARLOS DE (1704–1742): Cravistas Portuguezes, Vol. 2. See An-thologies.
SESSIONS, ROGER (1896–   ): *Sonatas,* Schott, Marks.
SIBELIUS, JEAN (1865–1957):Domestic, unpretentious keyboard writing, quite unlike the symphonies.
SKALKOTTAS, NIKOS (1904–1949): Universal.
SOLER, ANTONIO (PADRE) (1729–1783): *Keyboard Sonatas,* 6 vols., edition still incomplete (Rubio), UME.
   Sonatas for Piano, 2 vols., and *Fandango* (Marvin), Mills.
STRAVINSKY, IGOR (1882–   ): *Sonata, Serenade,* Boosey & Hawkes; *Piano-Rag Music,* Chester.
SWEELINCK, JAN PIETERSZOON (1562–1621): Peters.
TALLIS, THOMAS (1505–1585): *The Complete Keyboard Works* (Stevens), Hinrichsen.
TCHAIKOVSKY, PETER ILYICH (1840–1893): Peters.
TELEMANN, GEORG PHILIPP (1681–1767): *Three Dozen Fantasies for Clavecin,* Broude.
THOMSON, VIRGIL (1896–   ): *Portraits* (in 3 albums), Mercury.
TIPPETT, MICHAEL (1905–   ): *Sonata,* Schott.
TOCH, ERNEST (1887–   ): *Five Times Ten Studies for Piano,* Schott.
TOMÁŠEK, VÁCLAV JAN (1774–1850): *Tre Ditirambi,* opus 65 (Pohanka), MAB.
TOMKINS, THOMAS (1572–1656): (Tuttle), *Musica Britannica,* Stainer & Bell.
TÜRK, DANIEL GOTTLOB (1756–1813): Schott, Bärenreiter.
VAUGHAN-WILLIAMS, RALPH (1872–1958).
VOŘÍŠEK, JAN HUGO (1791–1825): *Impromptus,* opus 7 (Helfert) and *Sonata,* opus 20 (Kundera), MAB.
WEBER, BEN (1916–   ).
WEBER, CARL MARIA V. (1786–1826): Peters.

WEBERN, ANTON V. (1883–1945): *Variations,* opus 27, Universal.
WEISS, ADOLPH (1891–   ).
ZIPOLI, DOMENICO (1688–1726): *Complete Keyboard Works* (Tagliavini), Müller.

The following selection of original *Keyboard Duets* was prepared by Wolfgang Sauerlander.

Elizabethan Keyboard Duets (Dawes), Schott.
BACH, JOHANN CHRISTIAN: *Sonatas,* Peters, Nagel.
BEETHOVEN, LUDWIG V.: *Original Compositions,* 2 vols., Peters.
BIZET, GEORGES: *Jeux d'Enfants,* opus 22, International.
BRAHMS, JOHANNES: *21 Hungarian Dances; Variations on a Theme by Schumann,* opus 23; *Waltzes,* opus 39; *Liebeslieder Waltzes,* opus 65 (with 1 to 4 voices ad lib.), Peters, Henle.
CLEMENTI, MUZIO: *Seven Sonatas,* Breitkopf & Härtel.
DEBUSSY, CLAUDE: *Six Epigraphes Antique; Petite Suite;* Durand.
DVOŘÁK, ANTONIN: *Polonaise* in E flat major, and opus numbers 46, 59, 68, 72, in several editions.
FAURÉ, GABRIEL: *Dolly,* opus 56, International.
GRIEG, EDVARD: *Symphonic Pieces,* opus 14; *Waltz-Caprices,* opus 37; *Norwegian Dances,* opus 35; Peters.
HÄSSLER, JOHANN WILHELM: *Sonatas,* Nagel.
HAYDN, JOSEPH: *Il maestro e lo scolare,* Schott.
HINDEMITH, PAUL: *Sonata,* Schott.
HUMMEL, JOHANN NEPOMUK: *Sonatas,* opus 51 and 92, Peters.
MACDOWELL, EDWARD: *Opus 20* and *21,* Schirmer.
MENDELSSOHN, FELIX: *Original Compositions,* Peters.
MOSZKOWSKI, MORITZ: *Opus 12, 55,* and *65,* Peters.
MOZART, WOLFGANG AMADEUS: *Original Compositions,* Henle, Bärenreiter.
POULENC, FRANCIS: *Sonata,* Chester.
RAVEL, MAURICE: *Ma Mère l'Oye,* Durand.
REGER, MAX: *Opus 10* and *22,* Universal; *Opus 58* and *94,* Peters.
SATIE, ERIK: *Various works,* several publishers.
SCHUBERT, FRANZ: *Original Compositions,* 4 vols., Peters, Henle.
SCHUMANN, ROBERT: *Original Compositions,* Peters.
STRAVINSKY, IGOR: *Three Easy Pieces* and *Five Easy Pieces,* Chester.
TCHAIKOVSKY, PETER ILYICH: *Russian Folksongs,* Peters.
TÜRK, DANIEL GOTTLOB: *Pieces,* 2 vols., Schott.
WEBER, CARL MARIA V.: *Original Compositions,* Peters.

LIST OF PUBLISHERS
AND THEIR BRITISH DISTRIBUTORS

Based on the best available information; however, changes in representation do occur. If your dealer cannot help you, you may want to order from the publisher or distributor directly.

Amphion: See United Music Publishers, Ltd.
Arrow: See Boosey & Hawkes, Ltd; Chester, J. & W. Ltd; Universal Edition

Artia:	See Boosey & Hawkes, Ltd;
Associated:	See Schott & Co., Ltd.
Augener:	See Galliard
Bärenreiter:	See Novello & Co.
Barry & Co.:	See Boosey & Hawkes, Ltd.
Boosey & Hawkes:	Boosey & Hawkes, Ltd., 295 Regent Street, London, W.1
Bourne Music:	Bourne Music, Ltd., 34–36 Maddox Street, London, W.1
Breitkopf & Härtel:	See British & Continental Music Agencies, Ltd.
British & Continental Music Agencies:	British & Continental Music Agencies, Ltd., 64 Dean Street, London, W.1
Broude:	See Schott & Co., Ltd.
Carish:	See J. & W. Chester, Ltd. and also Hinrichsen
Chappell:	Chappell & Co., Ltd., 50 New Bond Street, London, W.1
Chester, J. & W.:	Chester, J. & W. Ltd., 11 Great Marlborough Street, London, W.1
Curwen, J. & Sons:	Curwen, J. & Sons, Ltd., 29 Maiden Lane, London, W.C.2
Demets:	See Schott & Co., Ltd.
Durand:	See United Music Publishers, Ltd.
Elkan-Vogel:	See United Music Publishers, Ltd.
Eschig:	See Schott & Co., Ltd.
Fischer (Carl):	See Hinrichsen Edition, Ltd.
Galaxy:	See Galliard
Galliard:	Galliard Music, 148 Charing Cross Road, London, W.C.2
Hansen:	See Chester, J. & W., Ltd.
Harms:	Harms Witmark, Ltd., 25 Denmark Street, London, W.C.2
Henle:	See Novello & Co.
Heugel:	See United Music Publishers, Ltd.
Heuwekemeijer:	See Hinrichsen Edition, Ltd.
Hinrichsen:	Hinrichsen Edition, Ltd., Bach House, 10–12 Baches Street, London, N.1
International Music Co.:	See Swift Musical Service
Kalmus:	Kalmus, Alfred A., Ltd., 2–3 Fareham Street, London, W.1
Lea:	See Kalmus, Alfred A., Ltd.
Leeds:	Leeds Music, Ltd., 25 Denmark Street, London, W.C.2
M.A.B. (Musica Antiqua Bohemica):	See Boosey & Hawkes, Ltd.
Marks:	See Schott & Co., Ltd.
Mercury:	See Schott & Co., Ltd.
Mills:	Mills Music, Ltd., Mills House, 20 Denmark Street, London, W.C.2
Müller:	See Novello & Co.
Musica Brittanica:	See Stainer & Bell, Ltd.
Musicus:	Edition Musicus, 47 Dean Street, London, W.1

Nagel:	See Novello & Co.
New Music:	See Kalmus, Alfred A., Ltd.
Novello:	Novello & Co., Ltd., Borough Green, Sevenoaks, Kent
Orbis:	See Boosey & Hawkes, Ltd.
Oxford:	Oxford University Press (Music Dept.), 44 Conduit Street, London, W.1
Peer:	See Southern Music Publishing Co.
Peters:	See Hinrichsen Edition, Ltd.
Presser:	See Kalmus, Alfred A., Ltd.
Ricordi:	Ricordi, G. & Co., Ltd., 271 Regent Street, London, W.1
Schirmer:	See Chappell & Co., Ltd.
Schott:	Schott & Co., Ltd., 48 Great Marlborough Street, London, W.1
Southern:	Southern Music Publishing Co., Ltd., 8 Denmark Street, London, W.C.2
Stainer & Bell:	Stainer & Bell, Ltd., Lesbourne Road, Reigate, Surrey
Swift:	Swift Musical Service, 7–8 Aldgate High Street, London, E.C.3
U.M.E. (Unión Musical Española):	See United Music Publishers, Ltd.
United:	United Music Publishers, Ltd., 1 Montague Street, London, W.C.1
Universal:	Universal Edition, Ltd., 2–3 Fareham Street, London, W.1
Zanibon:	See Hinrichsen Edition, Ltd.

BOOKS

I have listed here a small selection of books, most of them referred to in the text, two histories of music on tape, one record album, and one record. Because of the rapid turnover of record issues, any list of records is usually obsolete by the time it appears in print. I have not listed any biographies of composers.

APEL, WILLI, *Masters of the Keyboard, A Brief Survey of Pianoforte Music.* Cambridge, Mass., Harvard University Press, 1947. A condensed history of keyboard music, with examples. London: Oxford Univ. Press.

BABITZ, SOL, "A Problem of Rhythm in Baroque Music." *The Musical Quarterly,* Vol. 38, No. 4 (October, 1952).

BACH, C. P. E., *Essay on the True Art of Playing Keyboard Instruments,* trans. and ed. by William J. Mitchell. New York, W. W. Norton & Company, Inc., 1948; London: Hall.

BARBOUR, J. MURRAY, *Tuning and Temperament.* East Lansing, Michigan State College Press, 1951. A thorough study and compilation of the background information about this subject, which denies its own conclusions by preferring equal temperament for such composers as François Couperin and J. S. Bach. Unlike Wesley Kuhnle, Dr. Barbour has not explored the sharp and flat tunings of meantone or worked out the tuning orders. The mathematics of the subject are extensively covered. London: Angus & Robertson.

BUKOFZER, MANFRED F., *Music in the Baroque Era from Monteverdi to Bach.* New York, W. W. Norton & Company, Inc., 1947. A useful background for the first half of the keyboard period. London: Hall.

COOKE, CHARLES, *Playing the Piano for Pleasure.* New York, Simon and Schuster, Inc., 1960. A good paperback self-teaching manual, if you wish to learn that way. London: Pollinger.

DART, THURSTON, *The Interpretation of Music.* London, Hutchinson & Co., 1954. I have chosen this as perhaps the best of a quantity of similar books about a subject in which one is always beginning and to which there can be no end.

DOLMETSCH, ARNOLD, *The Interpretation of the Music of the 17th and 18th Centuries Revealed by Contemporary Evidence.* London, Novello & Co. and Oxford University Press, reissue 1946. There is also an Appendix containing 22 illustrative pieces, separately published.

JAMES, PHILIP, *Early Keyboard Instruments from the Beginnings to the Year 1820.* London, The Holland Press, 1930. A handsome, scholarly, expensive book, well illustrated.

KUHNLE, WESLEY, *Tune It Yourself. Why?* Unpublished manuscript. The only thorough study of tuning for the musician or amateur who wishes to tune his instrument in the several historic temperaments. I list it here in the hope that it may soon be published.

Musical Instruments Through the Ages, Anthony Baines, ed. Harmondsworth, Middlesex, Penguin Books Ltd., 1961.

PARTCH, HARRY, *Genesis of a Music.* Madison, The University of Wisconsin Press, 1949. A thorough if idiosyncratic study of intonation by a composer who has put his knowledge to use by inventing and composing significant music for a 43-tone scale of just intonation. London: Hall.

Roger North on Music, John Wilson, ed. London, Novello & Co., 1959.

SACHS, CURT, *History of Musical Instruments.* New York, W. W. Norton & Company, Inc., 1940; London: Hall.

TOVEY, SIR DONALD FRANCIS, *Essays in Musical Analysis.* London, Oxford University Press, 1944. 7 vols. See especially the volume *Chamber Music.*

Musical Dictionaries:

APEL, WILLI, *Harvard Dictionary of Music.* Cambridge, Mass., Harvard University Press, 1944; London: Oxford University Press.

GROVE, GEORGE, *Dictionary of Music and Musicians,* 5th ed., Eric Blom, ed. London: Macmillan, 1955. 9 vols. Supplementary vol. 1961.

SCHOLES, PERCY A., *The Oxford Companion to Music,* 9th ed. London, Oxford University Press, 1955.

Tapes and Records:

KUHNLE, WESLEY, *Historical Survey of Keyboard Music,* recorded on tape with spoken text and many examples. Incomplete at the time the *History of Tuning* was commenced, the *Historical Survey* uses only meantone and equal temperament. The death of Mr. Kuhnle left it unfinished.

KUHNLE, WESLEY, *History of Tuning on Tape.* Spoken text and many examples, played on virginal, harpsichord, clavichord, and piano, of Pythagorean, tempered Pythagorean, just intonation, meantone, well-tempered, and equal temperament, expounded as temperaments and applied as tuning orders (methods of tuning). Mr. Kuhnle does not give the right and wrong of his examples but allows the listener to form his own conclusions on the evidence. All examples are played in a style of performance practice suitable to the best use of the particular tuning, masking its defects when possible, as would have been done by a skilled player of the period, and not aiming to show off its inadequacies. The examples of meantone explore both sharp and flat extensions of the meantone principle, demonstrating that keys and compositions heretofore believed to be unsuitable to meantone are in fact practical and intended for that tuning.

One could list individual phonograph records by hundreds and historical series by dozens. I shall mention only *The Columbia History of Music*, Vol. 1, edited by Percy Scholes, long out of pressing, for the examples of lute and viol consort playing by Arnold Dolmetsch and members of his family; and one record from the *Archive* series, issued by *Deutsche Grammophon*, which includes the *Duetto (Sonata) in E flat* for two pianos by J. S. Bach's last pupil, Johann Gottfried Müthel. This excellent performance on an original Stein and an original Walter piano of the period displays the very distinct clear texture of these instruments, with more overtone and less fundamental than a modern piano; the composition illustrates the carry-over of the elaborately embellished French clavecin style through the clavichord to the German piano.

INDEX

GEORGE ALLEN & UNWIN LTD
London: 40 Museum Street, WC1

Auckland: 24 Wyndham Street
Bombay: 15 Graham Road, Ballard Estate, Bombay 1
Bridgetown: P.O. Box 222
Buenos Aires: Escritorio 454-459, Florida 165
Calcutta: 17 Chittaranjan Avenue, Calcutta 13
Cape Town: 68 Shortmarket Street
Hong Kong: 44 Mody Road, Kowloon
Ibadan: P.O. Box 62
Karachi: Karachi Chambers, McLeod Road
Lahore: Nawa-I-Waqt Building, 4 Queens Road
Madras: Mohan Mansions, 38c Mount Road, Madras 6
Mexico: Villalongin 32-10, Piso, Mexico 5, D.F.
Nairobi: P.O. Box 4536
New Delhi: 13-14 Asaf Ali Road, New Delhi 1
Ontario: 81 Curlew Drive, Don Mills
Phillippines: 7 Waling-Waling Street, Roxas District, Quezon City
Sao Paulo: Caixa Postal 8675
Singapore: 36c Prinsep Street, Singapore 7
Sydney, N.S.W.: Bradbury House, 55 York Street
Tokyo: 10 Kanda-Ogawamachi, 3-Chome, Chiyoda-Ku

KARL GEIRINGER

MUSICAL INSTRUMENTS

Demy 8vo   *Second Edition (Fifth Impression)*   *35s net*

Covering a period of about 25,000 years, this work begins
with the whirring bones and clay drums of the Stone Age,
and then traces the whole development of European and
American musical instruments down to those of our own days.
It aims first to provide the student with the information he is
likely to require, but it is not intended for the student alone.
Its broad outlook will appeal to any reader interested in the
evolution of our cultural life. The author presents not only
facts, but explains, with the help of general history, the circumstances that have brought about the changes and developments described.

After an introduction dealing with acoustic principles, there
are seven historical chapters, each of which describes the
whole orchestral apparatus of the period under discussion.
The chapters get longer with the approach to modern times,
and the last, on the modern orchestra, contains the greatest
amount of detail. There are sixty-four monochrome plates and
two reproductions in full colour, and fourteen figures in the
text. Most of the plates are taken from contemporary originals
and represent the instruments in the players' hands, and not
merely as lifeless pieces of wood or brass.

'Very valuable book . . . a work of reference without parallel in
the English language. . . . Indeed, one is left with a doubt
which to admire more, the extent of Dr. Geiringer's learning or the sense of proportion which controls it.'

Times Literary Supplement

NORMAN CARRELL

BACH'S 'BRANDENBURG' CONCERTO

Demy 8vo   *22s net*

The book opens with a study of the historical scene and of the conditions under which Bach and his player colleagues lived, wrote and worked. It includes detailed descriptions of the instruments then in use and required by him in these compositions, which notes they could or could not play, and why certain passages in consequence took the shape or form they did.

The second part contains an analysis of the music; demonstrates how Bach built up whole movements from a single 3 or 4-note germ, and at the same time shows how the composer developed his own powers—how, for example, in addition to making any necessary changes to overcome technical deficiencies, he began to think about the musical suitability of passages given to certain instruments instead of just giving the same passage to any of the instruments he happened to have included in his concertante group.

J. W. N. SULLIVAN

BEETHOVEN: HIS SPIRITUAL DEVELOPMENT

Cr. 8vo   *Unwin Books*   *6s net*

This is not a technical discussion of Beethoven's music, nor is it a conventional biography depicting the sufferings and triumphs of genius. The facts of Beethoven's outward life are all here, the boy prodigy and his drunken father, the early cares and onset of deafness, the hopes of romantic love that were never realized, and the poverty and loneliness of the dying man. But more than these it is Beethoven's inner growth that interests Mr. Sullivan: how he developed from heroic defiance —'I will take Fate by the throat'— to a final victorious tranquillity from the strong turbulence of the symphonies to the transcendent vision of the last quartets. 'No man,' Mr. Sullivan points out, 'was more completely loyal to his own experience than Beethoven.'

GEORGE ALLEN AND UNWIN LTD